Asian Yearbook of International Economic Law

Volume 2022

The Asian Yearbook of International Economic Law (AYIEL) is dedicated to the rapidly developing legal field of International Economic Law (IEL) with a focus on Asia and the Pacific region. This region has been and still is one of the engines of world economy, and hosts a large number of economies of varying developmental levels, economic policies and legal jurisdictions. The AYIEL aims to publish top quality research outcomes in all areas of IEL, such as trade/WTO law, investment law, financial law, tax law, competition law, intellectual property law, dispute settlement, economic regulation and cooperation, regional economic integration, as well as other legal development of the Asian countries. While putting its focus in Asia, the AYIEL is not limited to IEL issues and developments in Asian countries. It consists of several major parts, including topical articles on the cutting-edge and profound issues of IEL, regional and national law relating to economic governance and integration, analysis of leading cases, book reviews and documentation. The editors of AYIEL are supported by an international Advisory Board consisting of world renowned scholars of IEL.

Manjiao Chi • Marc Bungenberg •
Andrea K. Bjorklund
Editors

Asian Yearbook of International Economic Law 2022

Springer

Editors
Manjiao Chi
University of International Business and Economics
Beijing, China

Marc Bungenberg
Saarland University
Saarbrücken, Saarland, Germany

Andrea K. Bjorklund
Faculty of Law
McGill University
Montreal, QC, Canada

ISSN 2662-7515 ISSN 2662-7523 (electronic)
Asian Yearbook of International Economic Law
ISBN 978-3-030-93477-4 ISBN 978-3-030-93475-0 (eBook)
https://doi.org/10.1007/978-3-030-93475-0

This Springer imprint is published by the registered company Springer Nature Switzerland AG
The registered company address is: Gewerbestrasse 11, 6330 Cham, Switzerland

Preface

The Asia-Pacific region has been and continues to be one of the engines of world economy. It hosts a large number of economies of varying developmental levels, economic policies, and legal jurisdictions. Given the complicated geopolitical situation and diverse cultural background in this region, and the fact that this region hosts some of the world's major economic powers, such as China, Japan, India, and Australia, developments in international economic law in Asia are likely to have a profound global impact. The *Asian Yearbook of International Economic Law* (AYIEL) is a timely initiative dedicated to the rapidly developing legal field of international economic law with a particular focus on Asia and the Pacific region.

The current volume is the very first volume of the AYIEL. In structure, it is composed of several sections. In addition to the "Theory and Trends", "Trade and Investment", and "Book Review" sections, it also contains a section of "Special Focus", which is dedicated exclusively to the issue of competition neutrality.

The section on "Theory and Trends" contains two articles. In her article "Asian Century and Post-pandemic Adjustments", *Mia Mikic* observes that while the Asian region is recovering from the pandemic and despite the trade decoupling between China and the USA, Asian economies may still benefit from economic globalization. In his article "Interesting Times: Soft Law in International Economic Governance", *Michael Hahn* argues that international economic governance has lost some of its reliability and predictability for several reasons, especially trade protectionism, and that soft law could play a helpful role in improving international economic governance.

The section on "Trade and Investment" contains four articles covering major Asian economies. In his article "The EU-China Comprehensive Agreement on Investment: Strategic Opportunity Meets Strategic Autonomy", *Henry Gao* argues that the key to understanding this historical agreement lies in the strategic and geopolitical considerations of the European Union (EU) and China, and reviews the development of the twin concepts of "strategic opportunity" in China and "strategic autonomy" in the EU, as well as what the confluence of these considerations means for the future of the agreement. In their article "Commonalities and

Differences in Investment Policies and Treaty Practices: A Comparative Study of China and Japan", *Shintaro Hamanaka* and *Manjiao Chi* discuss the respective foreign investment regulation system of the two leading Asian economies, and observe that while the two economies achieve economic development in very different external environments, their investment policies fundamentally share more commonalities than differences. In his article "Investor Obligations in India's New Bilateral Investment Treaties: Emergence of New Treaty Practice", *Prahbash Ranjan* highlights that India has developed a new Model BIT with the objective to strike a balance between investment protection and host state's right to regulate. While this BIT imposes various obligations on foreign investors, these obligations are negative in nature and often exist in the form of best-endeavour clauses; he suggests that India should consider imposing positive obligations on foreign investors in its treaty practice. In her article "Latest Developments of China's Foreign Investment Policy and Law", *Nanying Tao* outlines the latest developments in China's foreign investment governance, and discusses China's tendency to adopt the "new development philosophy" in international investment.

The "Special Focus" section explores the issue of competition neutrality. On 17 June 2020, the European Commission released a White Paper on levelling the playing field as regards foreign subsidies, aiming to address long-standing concerns across EU member states and industry that there may be a gap in both the international and European legal frameworks which makes the EU unable to effectively address distortions to the EU internal market caused by third-country subsidies. Shortly after the release of the White Paper, the Monopolies Commission of Germany organized a webinar on 21 October 2020, entitled "The reform proposals in the EU regarding state capitalism and foreign state subsidies". This section contains several papers from leading experts from various jurisdictions based on their presentations in the webinar.

In their article "From a White Paper to a Proposal for a Regulation on Foreign Subsidies: Filling a Regulatory Gap in Protecting the EU Internal Market", *Filip Krenek* and *Eddy De Smijter* introduce the making of the White Paper and the May 2021 proposal of a Regulation on foreign subsidies distorting the internal market as well as its political and economic contexts, and discuss the regulatory gap between the White Paper and the existing EU instruments that can be used to deal with foreign subsidies in various areas. In their article "Third-Country State Aid Regulation: The European Debate on Foreign Subsidies: Necessity and Possibilities of a Reform", *Jürgen Kühling*, *Thomas Weck*, and *Philipp Reinhold* compare the EU Commission's proposal with the partly divergent proposal by the German Monopolies Commission and address possible reactions of and long-term benefits for third-world countries such as China. In his article "Upgrading Subsidy Norms for the Digital Age: The EU White Paper's Contribution and Remaining Questions", *Jaemin Lee* points out that the subsidy rules in WTO law are insufficient to address various concerns, and the new subsidy rules proposed by the EU should be crafted to address these concerns. To achieve this goal, the EU should carefully deal with the compatibility of these rules with existing rules in WTO law and international investment agreements. In his article entitled "Levelling the Playing Field", *Achim*

Wambach argues that as China's social market economy is not compatible with EU competition policy and state aid control rules, the rising China is not merely a partner of the EU, but has also become "a systemic rival", and there is a need for the EU to take necessary measures towards fair competition in international markets. In his article "State Capitalism in ASEAN: State-Owned Enterprises Under the ASEAN Regional Competition Policy", *Alexandr Svetlicinii* argues that ASEAN member states adopt different approaches towards state-owned enterprises (SOEs) and state involvement in the operation of the markets, which creates challenges for the EU and other actors that attempt to build an international consensus on the issue of subsidies.

Last but not least, this volume also contains a book review section. In this section, *Weihuan Zhou* reviews Gregory Shaffer's latest book, entitled *Emerging Powers and the World Trading System: The Past and Future of International Economic Law* (Cambridge University Press, 2021).

The AYIEL is a fresh endeavour. We hope to make it a leading forum for academic exchanges in the field of international economic governance with a focus on Asia. This volume would not have been possible without the generous dedication of all the contributors, editor assistant Dr. Anja Trautmann, advisory board members, and readers. We look forward to receiving your feedback, submissions, and inquiries.

Beijing, China — Manjiao Chi
Saarbrücken, Saarland, Germany — Marc Bungenberg
Montreal, QC, Canada — Andrea K. Bjorklund

Contents

Part I
Theory and Trends

Asian Century and Post-Pandemic Adjustments

Mia Mikic

Contents

Abstract Asia had been readying itself to claim the twenty-first century as its own. Economic gravity was undoubtedly shifting from the "West" to Asia. However, the GFC has left a lasting mark on the global and regional economy by converting hyper-globalization into slowbalization with impacts on the growth of GVCs and FDI flows. After the GFC, the protectionist sentiment has settled in more comfortably. Furthermore, the forces behind low trade costs were losing their potency. The wavering public support to globalization in most advanced countries and some emerging economies gave rise to new forms of trade tensions involving the major trading economies (China and the United States) and the first and second tier of supplier economies. The onset of the pandemic in 2020 exposed the so-called "paradox of globalization." While making all deeply connected economies more vulnerable, globalization also makes them more resilient. It provides them with access to information, data, knowledge, technology, etc., for seeking networked solutions to the crises. In the context of GVC performance, apart from the initial hesitancy in early 2020, GVC quickly returned to operating at full capacity making a critical difference in fighting the pandemic. The main question for Asia a year and a half into the pandemic is how to recover from the crises stronger, respecting the principle of sustainable development and without losing sight of the Asian century aspirations.

M. Mikic (✉)
Asia-Pacific Research and Training Network on Trade (ARTNeT), United Nations ESCAP, Bangkok, Thailand

M. Chi et al. (eds.), *Asian Yearbook of International Economic Law 2022*,
Asian Yearbook of International Economic Law (2022) 2022: 3–10,
https://doi.org/10.1007/16517_2021_6, Published online: 19 December 2021

1 A Hyper-Globalization Ride

Asia had been readying itself to claim the twenty-first century as its own. Economic gravity was undoubtedly shifting from the "West" to Asia. Economy after economy on this continent has folded into the East Asian Miracle (World Bank, 1993). It started with Japan, followed by 'the little dragons' (Hong Kong, Republic of Korea, Singapore, and Taiwan), the tigers (Indonesia, Malaysia, Philippines, and Thailand), and finally 'a large dragon', China. And other economies, large (such as India) and smaller ones (Bangladesh, Sri Lanka, Viet Nam), were already with one foot in the door. There is little common to these economies apart from all of them more or less following what has become known as the East Asian development model—export-driven industrialization underpinned by the belief in the existence of benefits for participants in open markets for trade and investment. The Asian economies became a poster face for globalization and its benefits, mostly painted as the reduction of absolute poverty. Indeed, it is undeniable that Asia carried the world to its achievement of poverty reduction under the UN Millennium Development Goals.

Two decades into the twenty-first century, some, if not most Asian developing economies, might have some doubts about this development model. Unlike the countries in the European Union, North America, or more recently Africa, Asian countries never endeavored to establish a single trading block or an economic union. Despite this, one of the results of the Asian rise has been a steadily increasing volume and share of intra-regional trade and FDI flows in parallel to the growing fusion of their economies into the expanding global value chains (GVCs) and production networks. Before the Global Financial Crisis (GFC) of 2008–2009, the Asian Factory did not only join the European and North American production hubs but was tapped as becoming the world's factory. By that time, China already came on the global center stage, becoming a member of the World Trade Organization (WTO) in 2001 and quickly after a party of many regional and inter-regional free trade agreements (RTAs). It is an accepted view that it was due to China's sizable stimulus program that Asian economies had a relatively swift ride through the GFC.

2 The Beginnings of De-Coupling

However, the GFC has left a lasting mark on the global and regional economy by converting hyper-globalization into slowbalization with impacts on the growth of GVCs and FDI flows. Moreover, the "Great Trade Collapse"—"the steepest fall of world trade in recorded history" (Baldwin 2009), triggered some other changes of relevance for Asian trade and globalization in general. Let me briefly mention only a few.

One must start with the trade policy environment. After the GFC, the protectionist sentiment has settled in more comfortably. Mainstream political economy trade literature leads to expectations that governments would start using more protectionist measures when faced with the economic downturn. By inertia, it is assumed that these measures would be on the import side. Empirical literature may not be in full agreement on the overall number of protectionist measures (and their scope in terms of trade covered) put into place after the onset of the GFC. However, the evidence, which has been compiled through almost 30 reports meticulously prepared by the Global Trade Alert,[1] indicates that the policy environment impacting international business (business across borders) has become "murkier" (Evenett 2019). Both amount and structure of protectionist measures changed in favor of using more non-tariff measures and measures promoting exports while making the policy environment less transparent and increasingly uncertain, impacting the trade costs. At the same time, other elements in trade costs associated with economies of scale in transportation and information costs were not expected to go down much, if at all. All this made coordination and governance of GVCs costlier and signaled that perhaps there are not much more gains to be made in further expanding GVCs, particularly those complex, long chains crossing many borders.

These shifts towards more mercantilist trade and business policies did not happen in a vacuum. It appears that the public support in the West, especially the US, for globalization and free markets has weakened. In the US, the GFC and its aftermath exposed long-existing inequalities. They turned them into an acute social and economic concern giving rise to populist politics with long-term consequences for international relations and multilateralism. There is wavering, albeit gradual, trust of the US public in the free markets and globalization (Pew Research Center 2018, and other surveys),[2] even though Americans, in general, tend to worry more about domestic than global issues.

Given that the US has installed—as it is generally argued—the international trade (WTO) and financial (IMF) regimes, efficacies of these regimes require continuous US engagement. When it is lacking, coming to multilateral solutions is impossible. This outcome became drastically and alarmingly clear with the US administration in office during 2017–2020 with a preference for unilateral, arbitrary, and punitive policies over the coordinated, non-discriminatory and measures following internationally agreed rules.

At the same time, Asian developing economies, and especially China, were getting less convinced about the promise of globalization benefits. The rapid growth rates could not obscure mounting evidence of deep pockets of poverty, inequality,

[1]Global Trade Alert is an independent trade policy change monitor. See more at www.globaltradealert.org.

[2]"Publics in advanced and emerging economies alike generally agree that growing trade and business ties with other nations are good for their country, at least in theory. But far fewer are convinced that increased trade results in more jobs, higher wages or lower prices at home – all benefits frequently touted by economists and proponents of international trade." It is not unusual that public in principle sees trade as "good" for a country but not at a personal level (as not being able to link it to personal gains in terms of jobs, wages, prices, etc.). See more in Pew 2018 report https://www.pewresearch.org/global/2018/09/26/americans-like-many-in-other-advanced-economies-not-convinced-of-trades-benefits/.

and environmental degradation across the region. Furthermore, sandwiched between the West, increasing protectionism on goods trade and being reluctant about opening service sectors for emerging markets' providers, and the rise of China in almost every aspect made Asian economies weary of export dependence. They started to consider new paradigms with focus on domestic (or perhaps subregional) industrialization and self-reliance. China also began to rebalance its sources of growth towards domestic demand and through the elaborate Belt and Road Initiative (BRI). These were the first hints of decoupling.

Summarily, these changes in the international trade, investment, and business environment coupled with non-cooperative trade games between the US and China also joined by some other countries, triggered changes in GVCs participated by the Asian producers. As a result, some of these became less fragmented or less complex and entailing fewer different cross-border production stages (Anukoonwattaka and Mikic 2020). In addition, GVCs were becoming more regionalized with a growing domestic or regional value-added compared to the share of an extra-regional component. In short, in the aftermath of the GFC and in particular, with the ongoing and deepening trade tensions between two major powers, the United States and China, the GVCs involving Asian producers (especially China) have been getting shorter, less complex, and more domesticated even before the COVID-19 pandemic (Mikic 2021). If looking at the three major dimensions of cross-border flows, at the eve of the pandemic in late 2019, perhaps only trade in commercial services was moving upwards, while both merchandise trade and in particular FDI inflows were falling. However, in terms of economic growth, the global economy was considered to be healthy. We have started to accept that in many economies GDP can growth at higher rates than trade and FDI inflows, adding another de-coupling track (WTO 2020).

3 Despite the Pandemic, No Globalization Unravelling

The pandemic started in China and for a very moment it looked as both contagions—corona virus and supply chains—will stay in Asia (Mikic et al. 2020). Alas, that was a too optimistic view.

During the pandemic, GVCs have experienced additional vulnerabilities, facing both supply side and demand side risks lumped with the Great Lockdown (IMF 2020). Additional border controls and trade regulations have disrupted international transport networks, while disturbances in production and logistics have affected the supply of key inputs and goods. The lockdowns have also led to falling demand in most sectors, while the demand for medical supplies rose exponentially in all markets. In short, the policy reactions to the pandemic (lockdowns and closing borders, among others) contributed (or even triggered) the GVCs to be a transmitter of economic shocks across the borders. One channel of transmission was through demand as lower demand for final products in a given country meant reduced demand for inputs produced in other countries. Another channel of transmission was through supply channels where there was a lack of supply of parts and components produced and sold for forward assembly (see more details in Anukoowattaka and Mikic 2020).

The weak preparedness of public health to properly respond to the pandemic and a lack of explicit and clear multilateral and other-level provisions guiding trade policies in this time of crisis resulted in ad-hoc and uncoordinated regulations and restrictions regarding cross-border trade. In addition, both hard and soft infrastructure constraints limited capacity for adopting a contactless trade to adapt to the limits on human contacts imposed by the pandemic. The hurriedly imposed trade barriers (with some still in place in mid-2021) for the sake of pandemic containment quickly caused unintended (but luckily not long-lasting) consequences of a reduction in overall access to essential health supplies, food, and medicines through price distortions and product scarcity. As many of the products whose supply and prices were affected by the disrupted connectivity to overseas markets were seen as the "essential" goods, there was a backlash towards foreign supply, GVCs, and widespread calls for making these supply chains resilient through "bringing them home" or at least through near-shoring, localization and simplification (Bacchetta et al. 2021). Since these initial months of panic-driven border trade policy, the situation has 'normalized' so that by end of 2020 almost 60% of the new introduced measures were categorized as liberalizing, with a reminder restricting trade flows. However, on top of these direct border measures, many regulatory, procurement, FDI screening and other not-directly trade policy instruments have come into play mudding the water of trade environment. Trade logistics and transportation became one of the lead drivers of trade cost jump which has only gotten worse with the early signs of economic recovery in Asia.

According to June update of the WTO trade statistics (WTO 2020), Asia has been leading the trade recovery. Almost all regional economies were doing better than in the 1st quarter of 2019. Asian merchandise export volumes were up by 21% (year-on-year) while other regions recorded worse performances: Europe (+1.9%), South and Central America (−0.1%), North America (−2.2%), Africa (−4.6%), the Middle East (−8.4%), and the CIS (−13.9%). On the import side, all regions except Africa (−0.9%) and the Middle East (−2.7%) were in a plus range. WTO concluded that the trade recovery to date has been strongest in Asia and weakest in regions that export natural resources disproportionately.

The performance in FDI flows in 2020 leaves much to be desired with an average global fall of 35%, compared to 2019, with even deeper drop in the advanced economies (−58%), and a fall of greenfield FDI in developing countries by 42%. Nevertheless, among those dismal numbers, Asia does capture a growth of FDI inflow of 4% on average, with China gaining 6% larger inflows (UNCTAD 2021).

The World Bank also updated its Global Economic Prospects 2021 in June (World Bank 2021). While the recovery is very uneven across the world, the global economy appears to be on the post-pandemic mend. Here too Asia is in the lead with East Asia and Pacific set to grow 7.7% and South Asia 6.8% in 2021. This is of course including a catch-up swing to recover a big loss during the last year, but it is still much faster and stronger uptick than feared at the start of the pandemic.

4 Recovery and Adjustments Fit for Twenty-First Century

The challenge ahead for the region is not only how to recover from the shocks of 2020, but how to make sure it recovers stronger. There are many challenges ahead but those related to climate chance, social contract change, and technology change also open most opportunities.

Full recovery must refer to fully adopting the concept of sustainable development as the ecosystem within which a country (a society) designs its decisions about economic growth. For those familiar with the pandemic jargon, it is about "building back better" (BBB) or to borrow the most recent variant coined by G7 to "build back better world" (B3W). BBB means exiting a situation caused by a shock in such a way to build some additional resilience for better absorbing such a shock in future. However, the focus often remains, both in monitoring and in the design of policies, on a quantitative aspect of growth. In other words, a % change in growth of GDP, which also becomes a goal or the objective of the policies by doing that, we still focus on quantity, not quality of growth. We still put economic ahead or social and other dimensions. This is not likely to prepare us to respond to two most difficult challenges ahead—climate change and inequalities.

To change a societal objective and make a shift from simple economic growth to inclusive and environmentally responsible prosperity is not too simple as it requires better understanding of all stakeholders, policymakers included in what this change entails. Complementing and then later replacing the GDP growth as a metric of a national economy performance will be part of the process. Another part of the process will require designing relatively simple measures based on available, reliable and comparable data which can inform on the other dimensions of sustainability. Inequality, at all levels—income, wealth and access to opportunities—has been getting worse in many countries globally and in the Asian region. Once it is possible to measure progress more readily in reaching more inclusive growth, for example, it will also be possible to adopt fiscal measures more easily with more inclusive outcome such as a surcharge on personal income tax for the high earners, tax on excess profits or carbon tax. One must design a policy mix compatible with a pursuit of efficiency/GDP growth and resilience/collective well-being simultaneously.

Another element of BBB is linked to effective use of modern frontier technology, especially robotics and digital technology. The pandemic brought to the forefront the omnipotence of digital technology—for work, trade, payments, entertainment, health, and national security.

In fact, for many years before the pandemic lots of discussion took place on issues related to the "future of work", especially a large role of automation and robotics in the context of employment and production capabilities. Developing countries (especially in Asia) have been concerned about technological progress in their export destinations or competing economies possibly undermining labour cost arbitrage which has been a source of comparative advantage for many Asian economies.[3] Ever cheaper and easier to use technology has a potential to cause large shifts in how and where manufacturing is done, and this of course has implication for the Asian role of producer for the world. With technological progress, manufacturing GVCs will face an adverse effect—increasing production may not necessarily mean more jobs and in countries with so-called a demographic dividend that may create additional problems.

Furthermore, technology will be impacting what will be traded directly (i.e., goods across borders) or indirectly (for example, as designs to be printed using 3D printers in the destination market). The actual process of trading (logistics, payments etc) will be increasingly shifting to digital space which will require both hard and soft infrastructure adjustments.

Developing Asia of course suffers from rather wide digital divide (ESCAP 2021). Therefore one of the priorities of both public and private sector investment will have to be directed towards closing ghat gap.

In addition to the above important areas of adjustments, it is important for Asia and the rest of the world to find the way towards more cooperative interaction. At present the world geo-political arena appears to be only about strategic competition among the largest actors, notable the US and China for the dominance over the "opponent" and its spere of influence (to use the Cold Ware terminology).

This augmented objective of development (prosperity and social and environmental responsibility) requires a stable and predictable environment which is possible only when international relations among countries are following certain agreed upon rules often being set through different multilateral institutions. Moreover, these can be sustained only through regular international cooperation in seeking multilateral solutions.

While there are several important levels where there was a clear lack of international cooperation among world's governments directly and through various international organizations (IOs) and country groupings (for example G20, G7, African Union, etc). It is not sufficient for heads of international organizations to agree on cooperation. It is necessary that states themselves do so as they—being members of these IOs can then influence the work of IOs even further. The most recent example is the apparent agreement on the vaccine production and distribution among the key IOs (WHO, WTO, WIPO) but lacking a determined cooperation among key governments.

One thing is clear. The decades long process of globalization has produced a world that is very interdependent and thus extremely vulnerable. However, this vulnerability should be forcing all players to use advantages of interdependency—networked and synced technologies, easily shared information, data and knowledge, financial capacities—to name a few—to strengthen resilience for one and all.

[3]Empirical results of Kimura and Obashi (2021) show that the introduction of industrial robots seems to enhance network trade in East Asia, particularly with higher usage of cross-border service outsourcing. New technology is easier to use by smaller production units allowing more spread.

References

Anukoonwattaka W, Mikic M (2020) Beyond the COVID-19 pandemic: coping with the ‘new normal’ in supply chains. ESCAP Policy Brief, October 2020. https://www.unescap.org/sites/default/d8files/knowledge-products/Policy_brief_supply_chain.pdf

Bacchetta M, Bekkers E, Piermartini R, Rubinova S, Stolzenburg V, Xu A (2021) COVID-19 and global value chains a discussion of arguments on value chain organization and the role of the WTO, Staff Working Paper ERSD-2021-3. https://www.wto.org/english/res_e/reser_e/ersd202103_e.pdf

Baldwin R (2009) The great trade collapse: what caused it and what does it mean?. VoxEU.org 27 November 2009. https://voxeu.org/article/great-trade-collapse-what-caused-it-and-what-does-it-mean

ESCAP (2021) Beyond the pandemic: building back better from crises in Asia and the Pacific. https://www.unescap.org/sites/default/d8files/knowledge-products/Beyond%20the%20pandamic_Theme%20study.pdf

Evenett SJ (2019) Protectionism, state discrimination, and international business since the onset of the global financial crisis. J Int Bus Policy 2(1):9–36

IMF (2020) World Economic Outlook, April 2020. The Great Lockdown, Washington, D.C., https://www.imf.org/-/media/Files/Publications/WEO/2020/April/English/text.ashx

Kimura F, Obashi A (2021) New developments in international production networks: impacs of digital technologies. Asian Econ J Jun;35(2). https://doi.org/10.1111/asej.12240

Mikic M (2021) A few further thoughts on the topic of Re-organization of GVCs and deglobalization. TPRForum Blog. https://www.tprforum.org/blog-1

Mikic M, Yoo JH, Lobo RS, Roman P (2020) When China sneezes, Asia catches a cold, ESCAP blog of 14 February 2020. https://www.unescap.org/blog/when-china-sneezes-asia-catches-cold.

Pew Research Center (2018) Americans, Like Many in Other Advanced Economies, Not Convinced of Trade’s Benefits. 26 September 2018. https://www.pewresearch.org/global/wp-content/uploads/sites/2/2018/09/PG_2018.09.26_global-trade_FINALupdated.pdf

UNCTAD (2021) World Investment Report 2021: Investing in Sustainable Recovery, Geneva. https://unctad.org/webflyer/world-investment-report-2021

World Bank (1993) The East Asian miracle: economic growth and public policy. Oxford University Press, New York

World Bank (2021) Global Economic Prospects. June 2021. Washington, D.C., https://www.worldbank.org/en/news/press-release/2021/06/08/world-bank-global-economic-prospects-2021

World Trade Organization (2020) World Trade Statistical Review 2020. https://www.wto.org/english/res_e/statis_e/wts2020_e/wts20_toc_e.htm

Interesting Times: Soft Law in International Economic Governance

Michael Hahn

Contents

Abstract Soft law arrangements are increasingly preferred over international agreements in international economic relations. Despite its somewhat fluid nature, soft law's advantages—inter alia increased flexibility, pragmatism and less burdensome

---

This is the extended and annotated version of a presentation given on 31 January 2020 at VUW Faculty of Law (Old Parliament Building), Wellington, New Zealand. Many thanks to Professor Alberto Costi, the VUW Faculty of Law, the New Zealand Branch of the International Law Association and VUW's New Zealand Centre of International Economic Law for giving me that opportunity. The University of Waikato School of Law hosted me during Summer term 2020: many thanks to former Dean Wayne Rumbles, Dean Alpana Roy, and all my colleagues and friends at Te Piringa who always make my stays there so rewarding. Many thanks also to Yann Fauconnet, Ana Kressner and Linda Marti for their support regarding research and preparing the article for publication.

M. Hahn (✉)
Institute of European and International Economic Law and World Trade Institute, University of Bern, Bern, Switzerland
e-mail: michael.hahn@iew.unibe.ch

M. Chi et al. (eds.), *Asian Yearbook of International Economic Law 2022*,
Asian Yearbook of International Economic Law (2022) 2022: 11–44,
https://doi.org/10.1007/16517_2021_10, Published online: 30 April 2022

implementation by contracting parties—have given it an edge over judicialized legal commitments. The textbook example for a (so far) successful use of soft law are G-20/FSB standards that define the post-GFC international financial regulatory environment.

However, soft law's seemingly lighter touch can be treacherous, especially when used in bilateral relationships between unequal partners, such as the ones between global or regional hegemonic powers, on one hand, and small, possibly struggling partners, on the other hand. China's Belt and Road Initiative (BRI, also called OBOR) illustrates some of the downsides of soft law in that context.

Many of the reasons for the diminishing attractiveness of international agreements are to be found in peculiar domestic constitutional law situations. Some of the reasons, however, seem attributable to the well-intentioned ambition of international lawyers who may have to accept that a less than perfect international legal mechanism may be preferable to a non-existent or suspended legal mechanism.

In light of the many global issues that need fast and consensual solutions, such as climate change, the use of soft law will probably continue to increase.

1 Introduction

International economic governance has lost some of its reliability and predictability. There are many reasons for that, amongst them: Nations and non-state actors engage in international economic and financial relations in ways quite different from what would have been the reality on the ground in, say, 1994; China and India have reclaimed the position they occupied before an interruption that lasted almost two centuries; it has become challenging at best to capture the subjects of commercial transactions by the classic trilogy of goods, services, and IP rights; and the risks associated with trade as well as the objectives of international financial law have dramatically changed. So have the domestic and international rules, norms and customs that (in their aggregate form) may be described as "international economic governance". The multilateral trading system, with the World Trade Organization (WTO) at its centre, has largely failed to adapt; maybe because of that inability to reform, unilateral reactions to real, perceived or invented failures have diminished the system's stability. The rise of economic protectionism (and even nationalism), both in the countries taking back their rightful place, but also in Russia and notably in two Anglo-Saxon countries that celebrate a golden past that never quite existed, complicates things.

The inability, perhaps even refusal of the membership to adapt the WTO-rulebook to new developments—amongst others, the need for reconciling the State capitalism of certain Members with everybody else's interest in economic self-preservation (that used to be ensured by Trade Defence Instruments, but is not any longer) or addressing "new" phenomena (such as electronic commerce or nanotechnologies) where genuine uncertainty as to the appropriate regulatory environment exists—has led to ever increasing gaps between the law and the realities on the ground. The Appellate Body's efforts to close that gap one case at a time (and possibly a certain tone deafness with regard to certain diplomatic sensitivities) proved its undoing.[1] Its existence "in the real world"[2] ended (preliminarily) in 2019,[3] leaving those who would have been able to prevent that outcome to shed crocodile tears and engage in Dispute Settlement Understandings (DSU)-incompatible "appeals into the void".[4]

The diminishing regulatory power of rules and norms is not limited to economic governance. Rather, several great powers (and sometimes just stronger neighbours) seem to flaunt their international legal obligations more openly than was acceptable in the previous decades. Unfortunately, any somewhat comprehensive list of examples would include not just the usual suspects, but also actors whose attachment to international legal commitments used to be a foregone conclusion.

In this environment, where law seems to lose its regulatory force—in a manner of speaking: "is turning soft"—it seems counterintuitive that the conscientious softening of international legal obligations would provide an alternative or at least a second-best contribution to international (economic) governance. However, listening to certain voices, this is exactly what the good doctor would have recommended. In this view, for example, the WTO's dispute settlement mechanism (DSM) should leave more room for political evaluations. In tandem, Trump's US and Putin's Russia interpreted Article XXI GATT in an manner that was supposed to give Members the right to determine without any second-guessing that a measure they had taken was covered by Article XXI GATT and was thereby exempt from any review.[5] Similarly, by undoing the Appellate Body, and not even excluding "appeals into the void",[6] the US has considerably "softened" what used to be "hard law" and the closest thing in general international law to an effective quasi-judicial mecha-

[1] Johnson (2019). See also Lehne (2019), p. 104; Galbraith (2019), pp. 824–825; Howse (2020), p. 371; Altemöller (2021), pp. 139–140.

[2] *EC–Hormones*, WT/DS26/AB/R, para. 187.

[3] See for example Hedge (2019); farewell speech of Appellate Body member Hong Zhao: "Witnessing the attrition of Appellate Body members until the AB was unable to work was painful." https://www.wto.org/english/tratop_e/dispu_e/farwellspeechhzhao_e.htm.

[4] Hahn (2019), pp. 125–131.

[5] See for example Voon (2019), pp. 45–50; *United States–Certain Measures on Steel and Aluminium Products* (DS548) Opening Oral Statement by the European Union, 4 November 2019, https://trade.ec.europa.eu/doclib/docs/2019/november/tradoc_158427.pdf, pp. 14–26; *United States–Certain Measures on Steel and Aluminium products* (DS556), Opening Statement of The United States of America at the first substantive Meeting of the Panel, 12 November 2019, https://ustr.gov/sites/default/files/enforcement/WTO/US.Pnl.Mtg1.Open.Stmt.%28As%20Delivered%29.fin_2.pdf; *Russia–Measures Concerning Traffic in Transit*, Report of the Panel, WT/DS512/R, para. 7.4.

[6] Lester (2020).

nism for all disputes related to one of the most important international agreement, both because of its substance and its quasi-universal membership.

It seems that even the European Union (EU), on record as a staunch defender of the WTO system, now reserves the right to change (*ex post facto*) the rules of the game with a like-minded partner such as Canada. Under CETA, if investors receive more from the arbitrators than the contracting parties consider appropriate, the contracting parties have the power to custom-tailor the law to avoid *pro futuro* a similar conclusion by the arbitrators.[7]

The Court of Justice of the European Union (CJEU) goes as far as disallowing any internationally legally binding commitments if this may endanger, in the eyes of the judges, their role as guardians of the autonomy of the EU legal order.[8] Seen this way, "autonomy" is a close relative of the (lately popular) concept of "freedom from binding international legal obligations".

This paper is not aiming at exploring all or even a majority of the issues touched upon in the preceding remarks. Rather, enticed by the People's Republic of China's massive use of non-legally-binding Memoranda of Understanding (MoUs) with countries nudged to join the "Belt and Road" initiative, the use of "soft law" will receive a second look. This merits a closer inspection of the textbook success story of soft law in international economic governance, which is the post-Global Financial Crisis (GFC) financial architecture. It is built on the G-20-inspired activities of regulators, to some extent coordinated and administered by the Financial Stability Board (FSB). We will then turn to some of the current risks associated with the use of soft law in the context of Chairman Xi's grand project of Belt and Road Initiative (BRI[9]), before discussing whether, when and why the use of soft law may be advantageous from a governance perspective, and when it is really just a second best solution, benefitting either the strong in their relationships with the weaker or is a reflection of a not yet completed development process with a binding international agreement as prototypical conclusion.

[7] Article 8.31(3) of the Comprehensive Economic and Trade Agreement (CETA) between Canada, of the one part, and the European Union and its Member States, of the other part, OJ L 11, 14.1.2017, pp. 23–1079: "Where serious concerns arise as regards matters of interpretation that may affect investment, the Committee on Services and Investment may, pursuant to Article 8.44.3(a), recommend to the CETA Joint Committee the adoption of interpretations of this Agreement. An interpretation adopted by the CETA Joint Committee shall be binding on the Tribunal established under this Section. The CETA Joint Committee may decide that an interpretation shall have binding effect from a specific date."

[8] CJEU, Opinion 1/17, *CETA*, ECLI:EU:C:2019:341, paras. 107–108; see for that matter Hahn (2021), pp. 128–160; Riffel (2019), pp. 503–521; on how the EU deals with soft law, see Wessel (2021), pp. 72–92.

[9] Belt and Road Initiative, also known as One Belt, One Road (OBOR); Martinico (2020), pp. 140–142.

2 Soft Law: An Approximation

2.1 It Is What It Is...

Soft law is a choice of words that, at creation, would have been subject of criticism from any positivist lawyer.[10] The "softness" of "soft law" is not referring to the intensity of the legal obligation—if that was the case, UNESCO's Diversity Convention,[11] with its many best-endeavour clauses, or (parts) of the WTO's Antidumping Code[12] and its "desirable" lesser-duty rule would be labelled "soft law".

Rather, the "softness" that differentiates "soft law" from (international) "hard law" is its lack of being binding *as a matter of law*,[13] and thus, *per se* (on its own), not capable of triggering the (international) legal responsibility in case of disobedience or non-application. Thus, the term "soft law" means non-binding regulations or norms that are supposed to be adhered to by participating states—at first sight a less than helpful category.

But that latter concern appears "so 20th century" these days: "soft law" is now a term much in use.[14] This follows from the practice of states to create *politically binding* standards and rules that are *not* supposed to be *legally binding* which has increased dramatically in the last 30 years or so, not the least in the area of economic international governance, in particular the context of the post-GFC financial architecture.[15]

This having said, it is not a new insight that not being able to enforce a norm in a court of law (or, in the international realm, by an international dispute settlement mechanism or through the use of lawful countermeasures) *may*, in certain circumstances, be largely irrelevant for its capacity to shape, influence or even determine how individuals, state organs or nations behave.[16] In fact, norms that are not binding as a matter of law but influence individuals' or sovereigns' behaviour are at least as old as (what we call) the law. To take an example: the Westminster system is, as a matter of law, at its core a medieval affair (as illustrated by arcane but photogenic episodes such as the State Opening of Parliament[17]), but has been rendered fit for the

---

[10] See to that matter D'Aspremont (2008), pp. 1077–1087.

[11] Convention for the Protection and Promotion of the Diversity of Cultural Expressions, 20 October 2005, https://en.unesco.org/creativity/sites/creativity/files/passeport-convention2005-web2.pdf.

[12] Agreement on Implementation of Article VI of the General Agreement on Tariffs and Trade 1994, https://www.wto.org/english/docs_e/legal_e/19-adp_01_e.htm.

[13] Klabbers (2012), p. 226.

[14] See Thürer (2009) as well as Pauwelyn et al. (2012) and their different chapters for a general introduction; Brummer (2010) for a perspective on international finance law; Schaffer and Pollack (2010), pp. 706–799 for a perspective on international governance; Wessel (2021), pp. 72–92 for an EU perspective; general in context of the current Covid-19 pandemic: Eliantonio et al. (2021), p. 6.

[15] Lastra (2016), pp. 371–373; Muñoz (2019), pp. 247–260.

[16] Henkin (1979), pp. 21–22.

[17] UK Parliament, State Opening of Parliament, https://www.parliament.uk/about/how/occasions/stateopening/; see, e.g. https://www.youtube.com/watch?v=M7xeBtnUFEY.

purpose of a modern parliamentary democracy largely through changes of "conventions"[18]—i.e. unwritten and not legally binding understandings.[19] Thus, much of what has shaped not just the Westminster system of governance, but Western representative democracy overall[20] has seen the light of day not through changes of binding laws, but through norms, that albeit being strictly adhered to, are not law and not legally enforceable.

Similarly, in the private realm, certain non-legally-binding rules may be more powerful (and the consequences of their non-application much more consequential) than many legally binding rules. For example, some readers of this paper may, from time to time, and only by mistake, forget to pay on time and thereby act in violation of their contractual obligation; but they will never forget the anniversary of that special person, although any search for a corresponding legal obligation will prove unsuccessful. In international relations, extending *courtoisie* to foreign powers is as old as international relations, but only a small part of those customs and practices have developed, over time, first into customary law and later into treaty-based international obligations, such as diplomatic immunity.[21] "Not crossing the powerful neighbour" is also a good norm to follow; that is true for private citizens, office workers, and even states.

What is currently considered to be "soft law" in the international sphere is as heterogeneous as the few examples given in the preceding paragraphs for non-legally-binding practices, customs and norms. Their commonality is limited to two elements: they are on the one hand not legally binding and invocable in a court of law (in an environment where courts do exist) *but* on the other hand, they do shape behaviour,[22] as they are (prototypically) implemented, sometimes through law of the highest order, i.e. statutes, and not just executive branch rules and regulations.[23]

A good number of insightful papers by learned authors[24] have undertaken to develop categorizations and typologies of soft law. While this literature is supremely interesting, its attempts to categorize the reality on the ground seems to add only limited value for our purposes.[25] States and their agents, diplomats and decision-

[18] UK Parliament Glossary, https://www.parliament.uk/site-information/glossary/conventions/: "A convention is an unwritten understanding about how something in Parliament should be done which, although not legally enforceable, is almost universally observed. Occasionally a new convention is agreed in order to resolve a specific procedural issue that has arisen".

[19] See to that effect Bogdanor (2009), pp. 16–18.

[20] Including the protection of the political opposition as the legitimate government-in-waiting; Hockin (1971), pp. 50–68; Dimitrakopoulos (2008), pp. 319–341; cf. also Helms (2004), pp. 22–54.

[21] Diplomatic immunity is codified in the Vienna Convention on Diplomatic Relations 1962, https://legal.un.org/ilc/texts/instruments/english/conventions/9_1_1961.pdf.

[22] For example, in international finance law, see Brummer (2011), pp. 284–289.

[23] Pauwelyn (2012), pp. 145–147. See also Wang (2019), p. 225 for how China handles BRI before its national courts.

[24] For a general overview, see Pauwelyn (2012), pp. 125–161.

[25] Even though legal scholars have the tendency of putting things in little boxes all the time.

makers do what they deem useful, helpful, acceptable and relatable, not the least for the purposes of domestic consumption, not whether it meets the criteria of "soft law" developed in academic papers. The term has been coined by lawyers and social science academics,[26] and reflects the insight that certain forms of norm-setting by states and other subject of international law are intended to (and successfully do) shape states' behaviour and hence are too consequential to leave them in a category of (important) context and background for spotting newly emergent customary law or treaty law while at the same time not being a legal obligation in the technical sense.[27]

Thus, despite many efforts to develop criteria in order to sub-categorize soft law,[28] the essential criteria are limited to the two already mentioned above. *Negatively*, the norm established is not (possibly not yet) one of law, i.e. not binding as a matter of law, with all the consequences of violating a *legal* obligation, lacking in particular the right to trigger a dispute settlement mechanism or, in its absence, to take counter-measures (reprisals).[29] *Positively*, it must be determined that the pertinent norm is distinct from purely aspirational texts by its underlying quality as a behaviour-shaping norm. If the latter element is missing, it is not even "soft" law, but rather, simply "not law", such as (normally) non-binding resolutions, *communiqués* and the like. Of course, depending on the circumstances, all of these texts may morph into "soft law", if they are exceptionally destined or capable of shaping states behaviour in a systemic fashion, or even "classic" law if, e.g. a technically non-binding expression of political will constitutes the first expression of *opinio iuris,* one of the constituent elements of customary law. Another example would be a non-binding resolution or *communiqué* expressing solemnly that a heretofore controversially discussed concept is a well-established concept of regional customary law, thereby producing the very result it states as status quo.

Whether a text remains in the "non-law" category or rises to "soft" (or even "hard") law is to be determined in the usual ways of identifying the meaning (and status) of any text, not just any legal text: wording, context (including historical context and practice) and purpose.[30] Whether a G-7 or G-20 *communiqué* has no normative content whatsoever, despite the use of fancy words and aspirational language, or whether it establishes a new (albeit maybe not legally binding) rule, must be determined in much the same way as any other international legal material.[31]

[26] For a lengthy analysis and panorama, see Schaffer and Pollack (2010), pp. 706–799.

[27] To that matter, Klabbers (2012), p. 239.

[28] E.g. Pauwelyn (2012), pp. 131–141 suggesting four criteria: form, intent, effect and substance.

[29] See Article 22 (*Countermeasures in respect of an internationally wrongful act*) of the ILC's draft articles on Responsibility of States for Internationally Wrongful Acts (2001), General Assembly resolution 56/83 of 12 December 2001, Annex, and corrected by document A/56/49(Vol. I)/Corr.4, https://legal.un.org/ilc/texts/instruments/english/draft_articles/9_6_2001.pdf: "The wrongfulness of an act of a State not in conformity with an international obligation towards another State is precluded if and to the extent that the act constitutes a countermeasure taken against the latter State in accordance with chapter II of part three."

[30] See articles 31 and 32 VCLT.

[31] D'Aspremont (2008), p. 1082.

The working definition of soft law utilized for this paper is therefore much less ambitious than the categorizations that can be found in the literature. What matters is that the texts (soft law is without exception created on the basis of jointly drafted texts by a plurality of subjects of international law) establish norms in the broadest possible sense (encompassing, e.g. principles, rules, benchmarks or thresholds) that, pursuant to the norm in question, are expected to shape or influence state behaviour, despite lacking legally binding force. Such norms can be contained in language that expresses expectations, lays down best practices[32] that may or may not be the basis for peer or autonomous review. Both multilaterally and bilaterally established rules and standards[33] may meet the definition of soft law.

The use of the term "soft law" in cases where non-binding rules, norms or standards are *not* accompanied by sanctions (in the generic social science sense of the word, not in the sense of centralized reactions for internationally wrongful acts, such as measures under Chapter VII of the UN Charter[34]) would be inappropriate, as it would constitute an unhelpful camouflage rather than providing any insight. There is no point in using the term "law" without a social norm having some form of *heightened* impact. If that impact does not exist *de iure* (thus, no law proper), it needs to follow from the status of the text as a reflection of a strong political commitment (despite it not being legally binding) *and/or* from some form of (positive or negative) sanction. The nature of these sanctions may vary and may sometimes be difficult to discern: it could be mere reputational disadvantages or it could be the highly costly *de facto* exclusion from market access.[35] In any case, a monitoring process, be it a peer-review mechanism or a reporting system, would go a long way toward qualifying the norm as soft law, as such a set-up allows positive or negative feedback, and thus sanctions compliance. While a quantitative measurement may be difficult, the existence of a qualitatively measurable sanction would be constitutive for calling an inter-state-negotiated text "soft law" as opposed to, say, "interesting non-binding resolution". As always, "context is everything". If there is a well-established practice by private actors—such as credit ratings agencies or lenders—or soft-law-creators to

---

[32] But see for Switzerland: Swiss Federal Council, Consultation et participation du Parlement dans le domaine du droit souple ("soft law")—Rapport du Conseil féderal en réponse au postulat 18.4104, Commission de politique extérieure CE, 12 novembre 2018, 26 June 2019, https://www.newsd.admin.ch/newsd/message/attachments/57589.pdf, p. 6, which states in passing that best practices would not constitute soft law, as they do not tend to create international obligations. If the "best practice" is what the parties *commit* to (and even establish a monitoring system that attests compliance or non-compliance with that commitment), the former position cannot quite convince. For an English summary of the above-mentioned Swiss Federal Council's report, see Cicéron Bühler (2021).

[33] See e.g. OECD (2017). For an in-depth analysis of the legal nature and the impact of the OECD Transfer Pricing Guidelines, see Vega (2012). For an example within the EU, see European Supervisory Authorities (2014). For an analysis of the ESA Guidelines, see Schemmel (2016), pp. 455–504.

[34] Charter of the United Nations, 26 June 1945, https://www.un.org/en/about-us/un-charter/full-text.

[35] See, e.g. for international financial law, Brummer (2011), p. 305; for a general perspective on reputational sanctions in soft law, see, for example, Broude and Shereshevsky (2021), pp. 119–120.

put non-compliant actors in a commercially or otherwise disadvantageous position, this alone may suffice to put a document in the "soft law" basket.

Of course, having "no binding [legal] force"[36] does not exclude the possibility, that such texts may become reference point for specific legal obligations.[37] If, for example, an EU institution bases its practice on *opinions* and *recommendations*,[38] deviating from such non-binding-guideline-based practice may be a violation of non-discriminations obligations or other legal rules. In such case, the constant practice based on non-binding norms will be contrasted with the exceptional non-application.[39] In a similar fashion, a treaty establishing a legal obligation for the contracting parties to abide by "soft law"-norms renders what used to be non-binding (for tactical, procedural or aspirational reasons) into formal, hard law *inter partes*. The violation of the latter would entail the responsibility of the non-compliant state and the right of the infringed state to trigger a dispute settlement mechanism or resort to reprisals (countermeasures).[40] It goes without saying that any state practice, be it factual measures, documents, phone calls or, jointly with other, the passing of non-binding resolutions may or even must be used for the accurate interpretation of legal instruments proper, such as international treaties.[41]

2.2 Give Me One Good Reason …

Each and every time states opt for the creation of soft law rather than "hard law", there will be reasons. These reasons will vary wildly, but some features of soft law are almost always pertinent and contribute greatly to its attractiveness for state action relating to international governance, depending, of course, on one's perspective and one's role.

[36]As explicitly ordered for opinions and recommendations by Article 288 of the Treaty on the Functioning of the European Union (TFEU, consolidated version 26 October 2012), OJ C 326, 26.10.2012, pp. 47–390.

[37]Wessel (2021), p. 77.

[38]Pursuant to Article 288 TFEU.

[39]CJEU, C-322/88, *Grimaldi v Fonds des maladies professionnelles*, ECLI:EU:C:1989:646, para. 18: "national courts are bound to take recommendations into consideration in order to decide disputes submitted to them, in particular where they cast light on the interpretation of national measures adopted in order to implement them or where they are designed to supplement binding Community provisions". This case-law has been sparsely used since by the CJEU, but is still valid, see Korkea-aho (2018), p. 471.

[40]See also Wessel (2021), p. 75.

[41]D'Aspremont (2008), p. 1082.

2.2.1 Less Constitutional Limitations on Executive Action

Not being treaties for either the purpose of international law or domestic law,[42] the usual constitutional clauses for the involvement of parliaments in treaty-making do not apply to soft law instruments, at least *verbatim*. While it is clear that such consideration would not be without political disadvantages (and would be problematic as a matter of constitutional law), it cannot be excluded that the simplification of the procedure "at home" may have influenced some executive branch decision-makers to favour a lighter touch with regard to international norm setting.

In fact, the presumptive advantage on the "parliamentary front" is twofold. Firstly, in many Western jurisdictions, parliaments have a right to give some form of "advice and consent" *before a treaty is ratified* by the executive branch. Because of the constitutional reality in the United States, this means that when the presence of the US is desirable (and an executive agreement without parliamentary involvement is constitutionally impossible), the participants will be inclined to opt for the second-best solution, a soft-law document, as it is a foregone conclusion that the constitutionally required 2/3-majority in the Senate[43] will prove impossible to achieve in the current US political climate.[44] As soft law instruments are not treaties (neither pursuant to public international nor constitutional law), the right of any chamber of the US Congress (or any other parliament) to block the conclusion of an agreement is arguably not applicable to soft law texts; the downside, of course, is the diminishing reliability of international documents when governments change.[45]

Secondly, parliaments or parliamentary committees have increasingly a say *during negotiations*,[46] sometimes as a direct consequence of the rushed ratification

[42] Article II, Section 2, Clause 2 of the United States Constitution, https://www.law.cornell.edu/constitution/articleii#section2.

[43] Article II, § 2, cl. 2 U.S. Const.

[44] See e.g. Proceedings of the United States Senate in the impeachment trial of Donald John Trump, S. Doc 117-2, https://www.govinfo.gov/content/pkg/CDOC-117sdoc2/pdf/CDOC-117sdoc2-pt1.pdf.

[45] See Durney (2017), pp. 234–242. From a US perspective, the operational parts of the Paris Accord where not legally binding; see Sachs (2019), p. 867.

[46] Consultation of the relevant standing committees and/or approval by the latter of the negotiations mandate (and any amendments thereof). See e.g. Framework Agreement between the European Parliament and Commission, Annex III, OJ L 304, 20.11.2010, pp. 47–62: "In the case of international agreements the conclusion of which requires Parliament's consent, the Commission shall provide to Parliament during the negotiation process all relevant information that it also provides to the Council (or to the special committee appointed by the Council). This shall include draft amendments to adopted negotiating directives, draft negotiating texts, agreed articles, the agreed date for initialling the agreement and the text of the agreement to be initialled. The Commission shall also transmit to Parliament, as it does to the Council (or to the special committee appointed by the Council), any relevant documents received from third parties, subject to the originator's consent. The Commission shall keep the responsible parliamentary committee informed about developments in the negotiations *and, in particular, explain how Parliament's views have been taken into account.* (emphasis added)"; see also Urban (2021), paras. 1228–1285.

processes of the Marrakesh Agreements that was presented for (and received) parliamentary approval, despite the fact that the text of the Marrakesh Agreement had often not yet been translated into the language of the respective jurisdiction. Almost none of these mechanisms apply to the creation of soft-law-commitments.[47] As not all parliamentarians are equally appreciated by the experts of the executive branches, this may occasionally have been an incentive to not push for anything harder than soft law, thereby allowing the sister- and brotherhood of experts to work with less interference from legislators than would have been the case in a treaty negotiation format.

As a consequence, parliaments and parliamentary committees have seen their request for involvement regarding the creation of soft law being rejected, only to be told on other occasions expost facto that their country's soft law obligations required urgent parliamentary action, such as, e.g., new capital requirements for banks and other financial service providers.[48] In many countries, this has led to institutional pushbacks, with parliaments demanding stronger participation and/or consultation when it comes to the genesis of soft law.[49] While these discussions have been taking

[47] Although this would be possible in many jurisdictions, the executive branches tend to be rather restrictive with regard to inviting parliamentary participation in the context of soft-law-making. See for example the possibilities of the Swiss Federal Act on the Federal Assembly (SR 171.10), https://www.fedlex.admin.ch/eli/cc/2003/510/en, specifically Article 152, which allows executive branch to involve parliament also in the case of soft law: "1. The committees responsible for foreign policy and the Federal Council shall have regular contact with each other to exchange views. 2. The Federal Council shall inform the Presiding Colleges of the Councils and the committees responsible for foreign policy regularly, comprehensively and in good time of important foreign policy developments. The committees responsible for foreign policy shall also pass on this information to other committees involved in foreign policy related matters. 3. The Federal Council shall consult the committees responsible for foreign policy on important plans, … and on the guidelines and directives relating to mandates for important international negotiations before it decides on or amends the same. It shall inform these committees of the status of its plans and of the progress made in negotiations. … 4. In urgent cases, the Federal Council shall consult the presidents of the committees responsible for foreign policy. The presidents shall inform their committees without delay. 5. The committees responsible for foreign policy or other relevant committees may request that they be informed or consulted by the Federal Council." See also Article 5 of the Government and Administration Organisation Act (SR 172.010), https://www.fedlex.admin.ch/eli/cc/1997/2022_2022_2022/en: "The Federal Council shall regularly review the tasks of the Confederation and their implementation as well as the organisation of the Federal Administration. In doing so, it shall apply the criterion of necessity and assess whether the aims set out in the Constitution and the law have been achieved. It shall develop forward-looking solutions for action by the state." These possibilities remain largely unused; cf. Foreign Affairs Committee of the Swiss Senate (Conseil des États), Postulat 18.4104, Consultation et participation du Parlement dans le domaine du droit souple ("soft law"), 12 November 2018, https://www.parlament.ch/en/ratsbetrieb/suche-curia-vista/geschaeft?AffairId=20184104 (available in French). See also Langer (2020), pp. 244–246 and pp. 256–259.

[48] See Eliantonio and Ştefan (2021), pp. 159–175, with examples relating to the COVID-19 crisis.

[49] "The Commission will provide full information and documentation on its meetings with national experts within the framework of its work on the preparation and implementation of Union legislation, *including soft law* and delegated acts. If so requested by Parliament, the Commission may also invite Parliament's experts to attend those meetings (emphasis added)"; Framework

place, parliaments' efforts to bring soft law creation firmly under their control have had only limited success.

There are two further parameters of constitutional constraints that create an incentive to use soft law in some jurisdictions. Comparatively quick executive action by regulators demands, as a matter of domestic law in some jurisdictions, that the regulator starts the internal rulemaking process "with an open mind".[50] As these procedures may be the fastest way to move forward, any *legally binding* international standard would eliminate that type of executive law-making altogether—and thus constitute a deal-breaker when speed is of the essence. Lastly, one might want to add the wish to avoid judicial interference (not the least in the EU, with the ECJ's perceived tendency to protect by all means possible the autonomy of EU law)[51] as an aspect that may influence negotiators when considering the advantages of soft law.[52]

As understandable as these incentives may be, it should be underlined that "soft law" poses considerable challenges for parliaments and courts in domestic systems

Agreement on relations between the European Parliament and the European Commission, OJ L 304, 20.11.2010, p. 47–62. In Switzerland, although the operational management of foreign policy is carried out by the executive branch (the Federal Council), Article 166(2) of the Federal Constitution not only grants Parliament the right to "approve international treaties, with the exception of those that are concluded by the Federal Council under a statutory provision or an international treaty"; rather, pursuant to Article 166(1) Federal Constitution, the Federal Assembly more generally "shall participate in shaping foreign policy and supervise the maintenance of foreign relations", Federal Constitution of the Swiss Confederation of 18 April 1999 (Status as of 7 March 2021; SR 101), https://www.fedlex.admin.ch/eli/cc/1999/404/en. However, when soft law is adopted by the Federal Council, parliamentary participation rights have regularly not been fully honoured. In order to counteract this discrepancy, the Federal Council has formulated measures in a 2019 report to provide detailed information on soft law projects and to ensure timely involvement of Parliament. This is to be achieved through consultation, the transmission of working documents and reporting on relevant soft law projects, Swiss Federal Council, Consultation et participation du Parlement dans le domaine du droit souple ("soft law")—Rapport du Conseil fédéral en réponse au postulat 18.4104, Commission de politique extérieure CE, 12 novembre 2018, 26 June 2019, https://www.newsd.admin.ch/newsd/message/attachments/57589.pdf.

[50] For the US, see *i.a.* 5 U.S. Code § 553 (Rule making) of the Administrative Procedure Act, https://www.law.cornell.edu/uscode/text/5/553; see also Hickman and Thomson (2016), pp. 261–324.

[51] See CJEU, *Opinion 1/17 (CETA)*, ECLI:EU:C:2019:341 and *i.a.*, Contartese (2017), pp. 1627–1672; Hahn (2021), pp. 128–160; Koutrakos (2019), pp. 41–64; De Witte (2019), pp. 65–85; Nic Shuibhne (2019), pp. 9–40. See also the recent decision by the ECJ's Grand Chamber in Moldova/Komstroy (CJEU, C-741/19, *Moldova/Komstroy*, ECLI:EU:C:2021:655), where the Court concluded that, since an ECT tribunal is likely to interpret and apply EU law, the ECT cannot apply to intra-EU investment disputes (in line with the reasoning and outcome in *Achmea*, see CJEU, C-284/16, *Slowakische Republik/Achmea BV*, ECLI:EU:C:2018:158).

[52] Some Swiss observers have now proposed a purely political dispute settlement mechanism, with judicial elements in the enforcement phase, in order to avoid the dangers of having the ECJ project its views of the world to unwilling third parties (and largely reducing the foreign affairs powers of the EU institutions) earmarked by the founding treaties to be in charge of foreign relations. See Ambühl and Scherer (2021), paras. 28–34; Hahn (2021), pp. 128–160.

attached to the concept of separation of power, and impliedly for legal certainty and the rule of law.[53]

2.2.2 A Lighter Touch

"Soft law" instruments are supposed to influence states behaviour—or they would not be put in that category. However, the fact that the norms agreed upon are not technically binding and are only applied because of the *shared expectation* and a threat of at least reputational disadvantage in case of non-adherence allows to accept regulatory risks at creation which would have had to be eliminated, if the parties had opted for conclusion of an international treaty. Soft law would seem to be not only "soft" in the sense of not being legally binding, but also with a tendency to be more flexible with regard to the *degree* of implementation.[54] With regard to "hard law", the content of the norm will be determined, possibly by third-party-arbitrators, solely on the basis of the rules now enshrined in articles 31 and 32 VCLT; there will be lawful and illegal behaviour, with little room for grey areas. Regarding soft law, more often than not, nobody sits in judgment other than those present at creation, one of the main exceptions being the involvement of the IMF in the framework of the *Financial Sector Assessment Program*. But even then, the (non-judicial) assessors are aware of the examinees' difficulties, know the essence of what was agreed upon and are therefore capable of pragmatically twist and possibly even modify *de facto* the norm, if said encountered difficulties merit—in the eyes of those present at creation or at least from a pragmatic practitioner's perspective—that adaptation.[55] With a formal treaty instrument, that flexibility is not impossible, but the obstacles are theoretically and practically much more difficult to overcome. Legal advisers will inform decision-makers when an interpretation favoured by a partner would be beyond a tenable interpretation of an agreement. Allowing non-compliance with an international treaty is normally an important political precedent that does not bode well for its future relevance.

This built-in flexibility is particularly relevant in parts of the world, where the reluctance to enter into legally binding international agreements is greater than, say, in Western Europe.[56] But maybe more importantly, soft law obligations, despite their overall effectiveness and behaviour-inducing quality, tend to be a little bit less binding for the very important actors, who are inherently reluctant to give up their formidable (economic or other) weight in exchange for reciprocal assurances from much weaker and (individually, possibly even collectively) less relevant partners. Soft law will therefore be particularly appealing to this class of actors. It was a small

[53] For the EU, see Wessel (2021), p. 81.

[54] Brummer (2010), pp. 630–634.

[55] Brummer (2010), p. 633.

[56] Lately, this has been particularly the case with China in its implementation of the BRI, Wang (2019), pp. 41–43.

miracle that all three non-European permanent members of the Security Council had accepted the jurisdiction of the WTO-DSM. It lasted a quarter century and ended when a superpower, tired of receiving *equal* justice under the law, blocked the replacement of retiring Appellate Body members. During this period (which continues as of this writing), the same superpower and another permanent member of the Security Council claimed that whatever measure they took was beyond the jurisdiction of the WTO-DSM adjudicative organs, provided that they raised the defence of Article XXI GATT's essential security exception.[57]

3 The Success of Soft Law: The Post-GFC Global Financial Architecture

Exactly 1 month after the House that Lehman built had collapsed, on 15 October 2008, the G-8 proclaimed:

> changes to the regulatory and institutional regimes for the world's financial sectors are needed to remedy deficiencies exposed by the current crisis. We look forward to a leaders' meeting in the near future to adopt an agenda for reforms to meet the challenges of the 21st century.[58]

Another month later, at the "Summit on Financial Markets and the World Economy", the G-20 met at leaders' level for the first time to address the causes of the GFC. In an *Action Plan to Implement Principles for Reform,*[59] the Conference established five principles that were supposed to guide future endeavours: strengthening transparency and accountability; enhancing sound regulation; promoting integrity in financial markets; reinforcing international cooperation; reforming international financial institutions.[60] From the very beginning, it was understood that

[57] See e.g., *United States – Certain Measures on Steel and Aluminium Products*, Communication From The United States, https://docs.wto.org/dol2fe/Pages/FE_Search/FE_S_S009-DP.aspx?language=E&CatalogueIdList=249128,246598,246199,246202,246109,246110,246111,246115,246118,246147&CurrentCatalogueIdIndex=1&FullTextHash=&HasEnglishRecord=True&HasFrenchRecord=True&HasSpanishRecord=True: "The President determined that tariffs were necessary to adjust the imports of steel and aluminum articles that threaten to impair the national security of the United States. Issues of national security are political matters not susceptible to review or capable of resolution by WTO dispute settlement. Every Member of the WTO retains the authority to determine for itself those matters that it considers necessary to the protection of its essential security interests, as is reflected in the text of Article XXI of the GATT 1994."

[58] G8 Leaders Statement on the Global Economy, 15 October 2008, http://www.g8.utoronto.ca/summit/2008hokkaido/g8-finance-081015.htm.

[59] Declaration of the Summit on Financial Markets and the World Economy, Washington DC, 15 November 2008, http://www.g20.utoronto.ca/2008/2008declaration1115.html#plan.

[60] OECD, G20 Leaders' Declaration of the Summit on Financial Markets and the World Economy, Washington DC, 15 November 2008, https://www.oecd.org/g20/summits/washington-dc/declarationofthesummitonfinancialmarketsandtheworldeconomy.htm.

while these principles would be expected to be implemented *and* their implementation monitored, they would establish merely non-legally-binding standards. While the meta-regulatory agenda may be determined by heads of states and governments, it has been informed by the input and preparation of expert standard-setting bodies, both domestic and international. The G-20 is serviced the Financial Stability Board (FSB)—a direct descendant of the pre-existing G-7 Financial Stability Forum[61]—in which the most important domestic,[62] regional and international regulators and standard-setters for financial stability policies are represented,[63] with important financial and supervisory powers. The FSB aims to coordinate the development of regulatory, supervisory and other financial sector policies in order to further global financial stability[64] and is housed at and supported by the Basel-based Bank for International Settlement (BIS).[65]

Standards proposed by the FSB and endorsed by the G-20 have, by and large, been very well implemented,[66] often by the very actors that proposed them in the first place or even by legislative acts. In the latter case, non-binding international arrangements have thus been implemented in the most binding fashion possible under domestic law, a somewhat counterintuitive result.

It is important to highlight that the direct output of the G-20 and the FSB process has so far never been "hard" public *international* law obligations or legally binding *international* standards. Still, there is a (for lack of a better word: political) commitment to implement the agreed policies and standards, expressed by institutions with significant power to implement by whatever means necessary, including *"hard" domestic* law.[67] The only relevant actors not present are representatives of the respective parliaments, which explains the pushback in several countries.

---

[61] Ortino (2019), p. 195.

[62] Not just representatives of Finance Ministries but also the heads of central banks of the 20 members; certain important financial hubs in non-G20 states were added (*i.a.* Hong-Kong, Singapore, Spain and Switzerland); see https://www.fsb.org/wp-content/uploads/fsb-plenary-members.pdf.

[63] International Monetary Fund (IMF), World Bank, Bank for International Settlements (BIS), Organization for Economic Cooperation and Development (OECD), European Central Bank (ECB), ECB Banking Supervision European Commission, Basel Committee on Banking Supervision (BCBS), International Association of Insurance Supervisors (IAIS), International Organization of Securities Commissions (IOSCO), International Accounting Standards Board (IASB), Committee on Global Financial System (CGFS), Committee on Payments and Market Infrastructures (CPMI).

[64] Arner and Taylor (2009), pp. 497–500; for its predecessor's mandate, see Arner and Taylor (2009), pp. 489–491.

[65] Arner and Taylor (2009), p. 493.

[66] See both for pertinent successes and partial successes FSB reports on implementation: e.g. Implementation and Effects of the G20 Financial Regulatory Reforms, 2020 Annual Report, 13 November 2020, https://www.fsb.org/wp-content/uploads/P131120-1.pdf.

[67] Milano and Zugliani (2019), pp. 163–176.

3.1 The Rulebook: The Compendium of Standards

Reminiscent in substance and name of a "rule book", a term often used in the context of the Marrakesh Agreement, the FSB is publishing and regularly updating a "Compendium of Standards" which lists approximately 300 standards,[68] i.e. principles, practices, or guidelines to be followed in a given area. While Standards included in the *Compendium* are non-binding as a matter of law, the FSB has established four, rather vague criteria for inclusion:

> Standards included in the Compendium should:
>
> 1. be materially relevant for fostering sound financial systems *(relevant)*;
> 2. clearly set out guidelines on good practices in a form that can be implemented *(implementable)*;
> 3. have been issued by an internationally recognized body in the relevant area *(internationally recognised)*; and
> 4. have broad applicability across different jurisdictions *(widely applicable)*.[69]

The *Compendium* embraces a two-tier system. Whereas all published standards are "internationally accepted as important for sound, stable and well-functioning financial systems", the "key standards" are defined by their needing "priority implementation".[70] Also, the compendium contains both sectoral standards—addressing sectors of the economy and of institutional governance such as banking, securities and insurance industries, the corporate sector and how regulators are supposed to be positioned—and functional standards that address aspects of public and private governance.[71]

Given the FSB's *modus operandi* to not only develop policies aiming at spotted systemic risk, but also monitoring and peer-reviewing the adherence to the standards, the impact of the (non-legally binding) rule-making has been extraordinary. As the evaluation of whether these criteria are met is largely in the hands of the membership, implementation successes are second to none.[72] That is not to say that inclusion in the *Compendium* elevates FSB-/G-20-standards. In practice, what becomes part of the Compendium and what stays outside is rarely discussed by the membership and largely in the hands of international civil servants. However, its

[68] See Financial Stability Board, Browse the Compendium of Standards, https://www.fsb.org/work-of-the-fsb/about-the-compendium-of-standards/browse/.

[69] Financial Stability Board, The Compendium of Standards, https://www.fsb.org/work-of-the-fsb/about-the-compendium-of-standards/.

[70] Whereas the category "Other" contains standards that are "complementary in nature and cover particular functional areas"; Financial Stability Board, The Compendium of Standards, https://www.fsb.org/work-of-the-fsb/about-the-compendium-of-standards/.

[71] Including "accounting, disclosure and transparency, capital adequacy, regulation and supervision, information sharing, risk management, payment and settlement, business ethics, etc." Financial Stability Board, The Compendium of Standards, https://www.fsb.org/work-of-the-fsb/about-the-compendium-of-standards/.

[72] Brummer (2014), pp. 109–121.

very existence shows the real and perceived proximity between FSB-standards and legacy rules and norms.

3.2 *Monitoring Mechanisms as Key Feature*

Of course, not all soft law regimes are the same. In the context of (multilaterally agreed) international financial and economic soft law regulations—the focus of our discussion–, the specific control and reporting systems that standard-setters have implemented are a characteristic feature.[73] While obviously not determining whether the state acts are illegal or not, the mechanism renders public whether a participant is fully, partly or non-compliant with the (not-legally-binding) commitments it entered into.[74] The intensity of the review process is reminiscent of the competence of a supervising authority in a multi-layer governmental structure, although the reviewing authority will be, more often than not, a peer or a group of peers, who happens to be subject to a similar review. Arguably, the intensity of these control mechanisms has, on more than one occasion, exceeded the intensity associated with a complaint-based judicial DSM.

In contrast to a law-based compliance mechanism, the standards applied for assessment of financial soft law explicitly underscore the importance to take the particular situation of an assessed country into consideration.[75] While the baseline is clearly the agreed-upon norm, the margin of appreciation would seem to be much wider than what a court of law (not deciding *ex aequo et bono*) would have at its disposal.[76] Stakeholders may adapt their expectations of appropriate behaviour (and have done so in the past) after evaluations revealed a systemic disparity between reality on the ground and assumed state of affairs.[77] This sort of pragmatism would normally be associated with genuinely political mechanisms and may be one of the strongest incentives for avoiding a hard-law solution and a corresponding dispute settlement mechanism. The latter would lose any semblance of reputation and perception of even-handedness, if it was seen as too "pragmatic" and "country-specific". What is a virtue in one context, is a mission-endangering flaw in another one.

While the intensity of the assessment procedures attached to the standards that set up the current international financial architecture, surpasses that of other soft law

[73] See, for example, Bank for International Settlement, Core Principles for effective banking supervision, https://www.bis.org/basel_framework/chapter/BCP/01.htm, paras. 01.23–01.29 (Assessment of the Core Principles).

[74] See, for example, Implementation and Effects of the G20 Financial Regulatory Reforms, 2020 Annual Report, 13 November 2020, https://www.fsb.org/wp-content/uploads/P131120-1.pdf.

[75] Ortino (2019), p. 203.

[76] See Abbott and Snidal (2000), p. 440 and also Brummer (2015), pp. 96–97 and 253.

[77] Brummer (2010), p. 638.

regimes,[78] many of them do have some form of assessment or peer review that informs not only the participants but also the interested public at large on who was naughty and who was rather nice.[79] Of course, the approach of naming and shaming is not unheard-of in international law,[80] most notably in the area of environmental protection.[81] Regarding the latter, though, the combination of binding rules with flexible, non-judicial mechanisms seems to have relegated that international environmental law to a second-class status, manifest in the almost frantic and largely unsuccessful efforts to bring international environmental *contra legem* within the realm of the WTO Appellate Body' jurisdiction.[82] In contrast, soft law instruments' flexible, pragmatic but meticulous, review processes seem to have worked extremely well.

3.3 Why? Why Now?

There are thus plenty of good reasons for the success of soft law in the area of international financial law. One difference to trade law is that many of the government functions relating to financial stability are new to many, if not most actors. Whereas trade and tariffs date back to the beginning of the modern state—the right to collect taxes and transit duties is often present at the origin of what are today sovereign nations[83]—the task of regulating financial service providers or accounting firms may be relatively new to many states. However, the main reason was that the Global Financial Crisis made it obvious to all decision-makers that the risks associated with the highly desirable provision of cross border financial services and capital transfers could not be controlled by any single jurisdiction, even not by the home of Wall Street. With this background, international financial stability was again recognized as a global public good, worthwhile of joint efforts by the international community.

Because of the recognition of the importance of the matter, standards—reflecting best practices learned by the leaders in the field—genuinely help all actors, but in particular those who are new to the task.[84] "Helpfulness" is not a term typically associated with international legal obligations, which are more often than not perceived as a regulatory burden (on the regulated), whereas best-practices and

[78] Such as, in international environmental law, Wanner (2021), pp. 113–132.

[79] An important addressee and amplifier are credit ratings agencies (CRAs).

[80] Including in international finance law, see Brummer (2010), p. 641.

[81] See e.g. Hølleland et al. (2019), pp. 35–57.

[82] For the Shrimp/Turtle case *US - Shrimp*, see Howse (2002), pp. 491–522.

[83] One example concerning Switzerland were the rights granted by the Emperor to local actors to charge levies and taxes as *quid pro quo* for maintaining the St. Gotthard and other major Alpine passes.

[84] Gurrea-Martínez and Remolina (2019), p. 139.

standards benefit from being viewed as helpful guiding posts. In much the same manner, peer reviews inducing cooperation, as well as learning by receiving feedback in the assessment but also from assessing other partners (and learning from both their practices and mistakes) are less confrontational and tend to be perceived as adding value.

Ironically, the success of soft law has also much to do with its effectiveness, thus creating output legitimacy. Compliance is high, not the least because the consequences of non-compliance often surpass the undesirable consequences of breaking the law. As the number of "hard" obligations in the realm of the global international financial architecture is somewhat limited, the sanctions for non-compliance can occasionally be dramatic, including in particular the restriction or even elimination of market access.[85]

Another aspect which may be sometimes overlooked is the fact that the post-GFC financial architecture has not replaced the old infrastructure but has rather complemented it. Thus, the two flagship Bretton Woods institutions IMF and World Bank have internalized many aspects of post GFC-standard setting and implement it through their hard-law-based surveillance making support conditional on being compliant with soft-law standards.[86] Also, several free trade agreements (e.g. CETA, or the EU-Japan DCFTA)[87] explicitly refer to these standards, thereby providing a "classic" (and very significant) support to the new phenomenon of international economic governance that is soft law.

4 A Dark Side of Soft Law?

4.1 *The Missing Link: Reliability and Predictability*

The flexibility of soft law and the relative ease of "buying in" has a downside. While the remarks above have shown that the effectiveness of multilaterally agreed upon soft law is high and the implementation rate convincing, it would seem that strong actors (global or regional hegemons) may indeed obtain through the use of "soft" law the best of both worlds: the softness of soft law allows them, like everybody else, to accept uncertainties and engage in experiments in ways that would not be possible if a (binding) international agreement had been concluded. Nevertheless, commitments are normally honoured, thus creating an incentive for the hegemon, as for all other participants, to join and abide by the agreed-upon rules and norms. All the

[85] See Brummer (2010), pp. 638–639; Gurrea-Martínez and Remolina (2019), pp. 137–138.

[86] Brummer (2011), p. 280.

[87] Comprehensive Economic and Trade Agreement (CETA) between Canada, of the one part, and the European Union and its Member States, of the other part, OJ L 11, 14.1.2017, pp. 23–1079, Annex 13-C (Understanding on the dialogue on the regulation of the financial services sector); Agreement between the European Union and Japan for an Economic Partnership, OJ L 330, 27.12.2018, pp. 3–899, Annex 8-A No. 2.

while, it would be difficult to dispute that hegemons have an easier exit route open to them, if, on balance, an exit is what they find politically opportune.

This privileged status is, as a matter of fact, not fully absent with regard to binding agreements. Of course, the "security and predictability"[88] associated with legal rights and obligations is of interest for any contracting party, regardless of its weight. Great Powers shape more than smaller players the content of any multilateral rule that they adhere to (a consequence of their weight and influence on the international stage) and have a keen interest in the reliability of these instruments. But weaker states (and even the geopolitical non-entity EU)[89] have an even greater interest in that (real or perceived) reliability of any international agreement and of international law itself, as they have less alternatives when protecting their interests.[90] The former will be better prepared than the latter to stomach the undesirable consequences of non-compliance.

This having said, soft law may be quite hard, especially for the weaker and smaller partners of an inter-state relationship. That is particularly true in the absence of mechanisms to compensate somewhat for the power-differential that exists between major powers and the rest of the participants, a function implemented, e.g., by multilateral monitoring mechanisms typical for FSB-related soft law. In a way these mechanisms are a substitute (at the implementation stage) of the equalizing power of legal rights and obligations, as they also apply to the hegemons.[91] However, if the soft law relationship is bilateral, and not merely of purely aspirational character[92] (e.g. both sides commit to promote peace on Earth and cultural cooperation in the coming 5-year-period), the weaker partner may at some point sorely miss the greater precision and regulated reciprocity of a legal relationship. The Belt and Road Project may be a case in point.

---

[88] Panel Report, *US – Continued Zeroing* (2009), para. 7.182.

[89] The new Commission president, a former minister of defense of a Member state, wants to change that; see Communication from the Commission to the European Parliament, the Council, the European Economic and Social Committee and the Committee of the Regions, Trade Policy Review—An Open, Sustainable and Assertive Trade Policy, COM (2021) 66 final.

[90] Such as Switzerland, see Swiss Federal Council, Consultation et participation du Parlement dans le domaine du droit souple ("soft law")—Rapport du Conseil fédéral en réponse au postulat 18.4104, Commission de politique extérieure CE, 12 novembre 2018, 26 June 2019, https://www.newsd.admin.ch/newsd/message/attachments/57589.pdf, pp. 3–4; see also Wang (2019), p. 223.

[91] Key Attributes Assessment Methodology for the Insurance Sector, Methodology for Assessing the Implementation of the Key Attributes of Effective Resolution Regimes for Financial Institutions in the Insurance Sector, 25 August 2020, https://www.fsb.org/wp-content/uploads/P250820-1.pdf.

[92] Of the type often found in joint declarations on the occasion of state visits, when nothing relevant could be agreed upon.

4.2 *The Use of Soft Law in the Context of the Belt and Road Initiative*

Chairman Xi's initiative to re-establish China as the hub in a network of connectivity through the Belt and Road Initiative (BRI),[93] has attracted a lot of attention. Initially viewed as possibly lacking a clear business plan, it was later welcomed by most countries, including many Western partners—with the exception of the US which showed reluctance from the start of the project—only to now be viewed with increased suspicion not just in Western Europe but around the globe.[94] Here is not the place to discuss whether BRI is just a legitimate effort of China to exert influence, to counterbalance the still formidable influence of the US and help itself and some of its capacity-affluent industries by contributing to the development of connectivity with its Asian, African and European partners,[95] or rather, another manifestation of re-establishing Chinese dominance, certainly in the Asia Pacific, after 200 years of being relegated to the side-lines.

Rather, the goal is much more modest: how does one of the two "complete" superpowers of the twenty-first century—combining geopolitical, military, scientific and economic capabilities second to none—structure its international relations in the context of the BRI, which is clearly (at least: also) an exercise in international economic relations and thus international economic governance.

4.2.1 Speak Softly ...

The network of by now more than 200 foundational documents on which the land-based Road and the maritime Belt is built[96] is characterized by the almost exclusive use of explicitly non-binding Memorandums of Understanding (MoUs), which would seem to be textbook examples of bilateral soft law: non-binding technically, but in light of the importance of the project for China and its supreme leader Xi personally, benefitting from strong credibility due to the pressure to abide by the agreed upon obligations.[97] This is reinforced by the fact that the majority of the Central Asian, South Asian and African states participating are in desperate need of money and struggle with their internal governance. The European states participating in substance (and not only politely symbolically)—including Montenegro,[98]

---

[93] Chaisse and Matsushita (2018), pp. 163–186.

[94] Baloch (2021); Higgins (2021); Venkateswaran (2020).

[95] See for example Bitas (2017), pp. 146–147; for a Chinese perspective, see Ryan (2016), p. 230 and Ming (2016), pp. 316–317.

[96] Wang (2021), p. 282.

[97] Wang (2019), p. 42.

[98] For an insight into the China—Montenegro relations and their impact on Montenegrin economy see Kovačević (2021). See also Hurley et al. (2018) and Vladimirov and Rolland (2021).

Serbia,[99] Greece, Italy[100] or Hungary—face, more often than not, significant budgetary and political challenges.

But in contrast to EU and US practice that tends to aim at reducing complexity in treaty-making and prefers few deviations from a given model agreements, China is prepared to administrate a very heterogeneous cluster of texts.[101] Somewhat counterintuitively for a government emphasizing "harmony" and the absence of dissent, the Chinese leadership seems to prioritize participation of as many partners as possible over homogeneity with regard to the foundational documents of the BRI.[102] There appears to be no minimum threshold for taking part, and, as a consequence, the MoUs known to the public show a significant degree of divergence.[103] However, limiting oneself to this soft-law, entry-level layer of governance that are the MoUs, would not seem appropriate in light of the fact that the BRI partnership is based on a hybrid structure.

4.2.2 . . . and Carry a Big Stick

Whereas the fundament of the BRI relationship may be soft law, the operational regime built on it is very much shaped by hard law.[104] Both the agreements related to infrastructure-building and the associated lending arrangements fall squarely into the latter category.[105] While closer inspection of the (legal) texts was initially all but impossible, informed insights of the legal structure of China-financed infrastructure measures have become possible lately.[106]

The available material shows that, in a nutshell, China[107] does not put its money where its mouth is. Instead of being a champion of the developing world and those in

[99] For an insight into the China—Serbia relations see e.g. Vladimirov and Rolland (2021); Le Corre (2018), p. 36.

[100] Interesting analysis as to the MoU with Italy in Martinico (2020), pp. 131–144.

[101] Wang (2019), p. 41; Wang (2021), pp. 284–285.

[102] Wang (2019), p. 34.

[103] Wang (2021) pp. 283–288.

[104] This is not to say that soft law does not have very impactful implications or "substantial effects" on hard law instruments; it will very often send "political signal to domestic actors", Wang (2021), p. 287. E.g. it seems to have been instrumental for granting preferential treatment to Chinese companies in several countries, including Montenegro or Serbia, where they appear to be partially exempted from national competition, public procurement and/or customs laws. Vladimirov and Rolland (2021), pp. 8–9 list projects in Serbia awarded directly to Chinese companies in avoidance of public tender procedures. Cf. Montenegrin Law on Highway Bar-Boljare (Official Gazette of Montenegro, Nr. 052/14 from 16 December 2014), that regulates the highway construction project Bar-Boljare, awarded to China Road and Bridge Corporation and financed by EXIM Bank of China, and exempts those involved from certain labour, tax and customs regulations. See Higgins (2021).

[105] Wang (2019), p. 43.

[106] See Gelpern et al. (2021).

[107] Including its state agencies and any private corporation engaged in BRI activities abroad, as the latter will not be in a position to not follow the wishes of the political centre.

dire straits, it is an aggressive lender.[108] While none of the conditions that have become public are unheard of, the combined and joint use of one-sided contract clauses renders the overall construct particularly burdensome for the debtors. The results are almost comically one-sided, fully mirroring the power differential between the partners—"win-win" here clearly means securing two wins for one of the two sides. That impression follows from the accumulation of the rates charged, other provisions establishing the dependency of individual contracts from the overall relation with China,[109] and, in addition, creating conditionality with contractual relationships entered into with other lenders and partners.[110]

Under these circumstances, it may be of little surprise that considerable work has been invested into shielding the conditions of these agreements but also the amount of debt from the populations of the countries concerned, the public at large[111] and, most disconcertingly, from other sovereign lenders. It seems that treaty clauses exist, pursuant to which the debtor is prohibited from informing its other lenders, even when debt-restructuring measures (including those dreaded "haircuts" where lenders agree to forgive a certain percentage of their debt) are being negotiated in order to prevent state bankruptcies.[112] This would insulate China and its lenders from

[108] Gelpern et al. (2021); see also Riesberg (2019), pp. 43–47; but see also Jones and Hameiri (2020).

[109] Some loan agreements list the termination of diplomatic relations between China and the borrowing country among other events of default, enabling the lender to demand immediate repayment in such an event. See e.g. the Facility Agreement between China Development Bank and the Government of the Republic of Ecuador, https://www.documentcloud.org/documents/20488262-ecu_2016_523, Article 18.13.2, p. 50, and the Facility Agreement between China Development Bank and National Bank of Costa Rica from 17 November 2008, https://www.documentcloud.org/documents/20488121-cri_2008_424, Article 21.14, p. 24.

[110] Unsurprisingly, this has led to sustained criticism by the US government (calling it a "debt-trap"); however, and more worryingly, several involved BRI states have complained about this situation in the context of ASEAN, see Erie (2021), p. 61. For a debt sustainability analysis by the World Bank, see Bandiera and Tsiropoulos (2020); see also Hurley et al. (2018), p. 112.

[111] So have e.g. many documents that are related to the construction and the loan agreements concerning the highway Bar – Boljare in Montenegro (awarded to China Road and Bridge Corporation and financed by EXIM Bank) been declared secret, MANS (2020).

[112] Clauses that exclude "Chinese" debt from the debts of other creditors such as Paris club, can, inter alia, be found in the Preferential Buyer Credit Loan Agreement between the EXIM Bank of China and the Government of Montenegro from 30 October 2014, https://www.documentcloud.org/documents/20488741-mne_2014_432, Article 6.10, p. 12; in the Government Concessional Loan Agreement between the EXIM Bank of China and the Government of the Kyrgyz Republic from 15 June 2015, https://www.documentcloud.org/documents/20488738-kgz_2015_427, Article 6.13, p. 13; or in the Term Facility Agreement between China Development Bank and the Republic of Argentina, https://www.documentcloud.org/documents/20484893-arg_2019_471, Article 19.5, p. 48. Far-reaching confidentiality clauses can be e.g. found in the Government Concessional Loan Agreement between the EXIM Bank of China and the Government of Uganda from 16 January 2019, https://www.documentcloud.org/documents/20488887-uga_2019_486, Article 8.7, p. 17; in the Preferential Buyer Credit Loan Agreement on Jujuy Photovoltaic Power Plant Project between the EXIM Bank of China and the Government of Argentina, https://www.documentcloud.org/documents/20484888-arg_2017_417, Article 8.7, p. 19, and in the Preferential Buyer's Credit Loan

collective efforts to restructure debt, undertaken to avoid the debtor's bankruptcy.[113]

Unavoidably, such contractual provisions would seem to strengthen the Chinese lenders hands in more ways than one: if the plan works, the generosity and solidarity of other countries institutional lenders (directed to a country in distress) will fill the coffers of a superpower. However, if the plan does not work due to the reluctance of other lenders to undertake the necessary restructuring in light of China's holding out, the latter has de facto a veto power over the future of a country on the verge of bankruptcy.[114]

Whether by design or by coincidence, the so far successful "soft-law", flexible custom-tailored effort to attract participants to the BRI has become, for those partners who need help for infrastructure measures, the first step to a ladder that leads to an "unequal treaty" scenario that is rightly so despised by the former victims of Western colonialism.

5 Lessons to Be Learned

5.1 The Goal: Reciprocal and Mutually Advantageous Arrangements

When Brazil, Chile, China, Cuba, India, Lebanon, Myanmar, Pakistan, Syria, South Africa, Sri Lanka, Zimbabwe—and also some Western countries—expressed, in the preamble of the GATT, that they wanted to achieve a better future by entering into reciprocal and mutually advantageous arrangements, this heterogeneous group of countries laid down a mission-statement, a *leitmotiv* for their future cooperation: their GATT-based (international) relations should be structured in ways that would be beneficial to all sides involved. The negotiators and drafters present at creation of the GATT[115] were neither naïve nor oblivious to the reality that a majority of signatories was poor, had suffered enormously during the war (and that included the victorious western European countries) and that the US benefitted from an undisputed hegemonic position. As the GATT was supposed to be a part of the post-war world order, it was also clear that the potential benefits were not limited to transactional gains. Rather, participating in an agreement establishing potentially the new economic world order had a value in itself.

Agreement on the New Centennial Water Source-Kaliwa Dam Project between the EXIM Bank of China and Metropolitan Waterworks and Sewerage System (Philippines) from 20 November 2018, https://www.documentcloud.org/documents/20488747-phl_2018_422, Article 8.9, pp. 21–22. See also Gelpern et al. (2021), pp. 22–25; and Acker et al. (2020).

[113] See Barney and Souksakoun (2021), pp. 102–105 for the case in Laos, and Roby (2020), p. 242 for Latin America. In general, see also Alden (2020); Rajah et al. (2019); Lin and Sharma (2021); Parks (2019); see also Yue and Nedopil Wang (2020).

[114] This seems to have happened in the context of Sri Lanka's grant of a 99-year lease on its ports to China after defaulting on its loans. See for that matter Balding (2018).

[115] Acheson (1969), passim.

It is also no coincidence that the preamble speaks of "arrangements", not of "rights and obligations". Many features of the old GATT were diplomatic and "soft".[116] As late as 1972, the ECJ emphasized that aspect in *International Fruit*,[117] to arrive at the (then surprising) conclusion that the GATT could not be invoked by private actors.[118] However, the softness of GATT's diplomatic tool-box gave way to a more legalistic (and ultimately case-law-based) system of regime governance: this manifested itself in the establishment of the Legal Affairs Division[119] and ultimately in the establishment of a *Standing Appellate Body* in the framework of the Marrakesh Agreement. Lawyers and economists alike were convinced that the hard-law-rules-based reliability and predictability for all partners, big and small, developing and developed would prove beneficial. While it is obvious that soft law needs the actual consensus of all parties involved, the on-going demise of the WTO shows that public international law—inherently less direct in its grip of the subjects of the legal order than domestic law—needs more than a general and unspecific consensus about ultimate goals, such as "preserving the multilateral trading system". Rather, it seems that a more specific and granular commitment is required when the inherently contentious issue of transnational economic interchange is at stake.

This recognition of an almost old-fashioned sense of trust as the base of a working relationship is very much alive in the post-GFC financial regulations, as career civil servants develop the standards that they sent to their political masters who sign off on them. It is also present in many of the most recent "Deep Trade Agreements"—the participants in these projects either fully share values as well as political and economic philosophies (EU, USMCA) or at least a genuine common intent to promote trade in the region, and a determination to leave their vast political differences aside (CPTPP, AfCFTA, RCEP) in that context.

A similar level of trust did exist between GATT parties; in the near-universal WTO it has faded away. Even the most obvious and per se universally acceptable (and as such uncontroversial) development of WTO law could not be passed in the last quarter century, as it was linked with the most outrageously controversial issues. The slow train-wreck of the WTO's development into an organisation in which only the administrative arm (the Secretariat) with its teams of highly competent international civil servants is in working shape, whereas the legislative (negotiating) function and the dispute settlement function are in varying stages of disarray, illustrates the undesirable consequences of the lack of the political will to make the system work for all participants, newcomers and founding partners alike.

---

[116] Irwin et al. (2008), pp. 177–188.

[117] CJEU, Joined Cases 21 to 24/72, *International Fruits*, ECLI:EU:C:1972:115.

[118] Waelbroeck (1974), pp. 615–616; Cottier (2009), pp. 307–326. See also CJEU, C-280/93, *Germany v. Council (Banana market)*, ECLI:EU:C:1994:367.

[119] WTO, LAD at 30 – The 30th anniversary of the legal affairs division, s.d., https://www.wto.org/english/tratop_e/dispu_e/lad30bday_e.htm.

5.2 *Misplaced Confidence in the Disciplining Force of Law*

The confidence that existed with regard to the notion of law and the sophisticated quasi-judicial dispute settlement mechanism may have, counterintuitively and against all intentions, contributed to that demise. If that analysis is correct, the question arises what features of WTO law and possibly public international (economic) law have to change to re-establish fitness for purpose—or to acknowledge it is time to bode farewell to a World Trade Organization with genuinely universal mission statement and rather accept that maybe the truly universal disciplines must be limited whereas the granular details are reserved to closer relationships, be they based on location or on shared values and culture.

5.2.1 A Coalition of the Unwilling?

With the benefit of hindsight, it seems that the confidence in the disciplining power of GATT/WTO "legal rights and obligations" contributed significantly to their preparedness to open their club of largely market-based, western democracies to former non-members: absolute monarchies (such as Saudi Arabia) and communist and authoritarian superpowers (such as China and Russia). The received wisdom was that the protocols of accessions (with their WTO*plus* obligations for newcomers) and the highly effective dispute settlement mechanism would ensure—for the purposes of WTO law—that the new Members would fall in line.

That expectation turned out to be only partially true: whereas, e.g. China has significantly changed some of its laws and practices to conform with its WTO obligations (Article XVI(4) WTO-A) and has an impressive track-record as to the implementation of adopted Appellate Body reports, other superpowers were openly dismissive of WTO law since the moment of their accession.

At the same time, certain Chinese practices that are difficult to reconcile with its WTO-obligations continued and sometimes even became pronounced over time. That is particularly true with regard to its defensive and offensive support measures for SOEs and its approach to technology "transfer".[120] While some of the complaints by the North Atlantic powers and Japan should be discounted as tactical exaggerations, one cannot help but recognize the plausibility of some of the complaints that US, Japan and the EU have voiced.[121] Similarly, China's economic model that

[120] See European Commission, White Paper on levelling the playing field as regards foreign subsidies, 17 June 2020, COM(2020) 253 final; Commission Staff Working Document, Impact Assessment Accompanying the Proposal for a Regulation of the European Parliament and of the Council on foreign subsidies distorting the internal market, 5 May 2021, SWD(2021) 99 final. For a glimpse into the internal (controversial) EU discussion, see Evenett et al. (2020), pp. 413–422; Beck and Ruessmann (2020), pp. 423–434; Crochet and Hedge (2020), pp. 841–863; Editorial Comment, Common Market Law Review (2020), pp. 1365–1385.

[121] Joint Statement of the Trilateral Meeting of the Trade Ministers of Japan, the United States and the European Union, 14 January 2020, https://trade.ec.europa.eu/doclib/docs/2020/january/

brings together a radical market structure, on the one hand, and a political system where the Party, and since 2018 its leader, are always right, on the other hand, has proven to be a challenge with regard to full WTO compatibility. By applying standards that may be useful for capturing state involvement in transparent Western Member States[122] but will typically fail in a system where command and control is ubiquitously exercised through omnipresent party cells and every branch of a government's *raison d'être* is to advance the party's wishes, the WTO apparatus did not deliver on the original expectation that the WTO legal system would eventually ensure compatibility of all new Members policies with the letter and spirit of the GATT/WTO system.

5.2.2 Over-Judicialization and its Price

Thus, while on the one hand the law has underdelivered, it may have overdelivered in other areas. 70% of all appeals submitted to the Appellate Body had some success. That means that not only hundreds of government officials had not quite understood what the Appellate Body considered to be the law. It also meant that the Panels and most importantly, the *Legal Affairs Division* that supports these panels and prepares their work had not quite understood the law and its interpretation. One explanation for this unique situation is that the Appellate Body, like a cruel ruler, had always wanted to have the last word, an untenable hypothesis, considering the outstanding personalities and lawyers that made up the Appellate Body. Another possibility is that the Appellate Body had developed a case-law of such complexity (no doubt in order to ensure just the right outcome) that it had become unintelligible but to a very select subgroup of addressees. In the latter case, it may have gone too far: the rules of the game need to be understood by the players, not just their coaches.

Also, the very idea of a court-like procedure, established firmly by the WTO-Dispute Settlement Understanding in 1994, was that *equal justice* before the law was beneficial for the weak and the strong alike. The special interests of the very strong were recognized and being taken care of as a function of the negotiating process, during which the biggest player could not only legally but also *de facto* block any unwanted legal development, whereas even a wealthy but small player such as Switzerland or New Zealand would not have quite the same bargaining

tradoc_158567.pdf; see also Chinese state capitalism: A challenge for the European market economy, Chapter IV of the Biennial Report XXIII of the Monopolies Commission ("Competition 2020") pursuant to Section 44 (1) sentence 1 of the Act Against Restraints on Competition, https://www.monopolkommission.de/images/HG23/Main_Report_XXIII_Chinese_state_capitalism.pdf; as well as Joint Communication to the European Parliament, the European Council and the Council, EU-China—A strategic outlook, JOIN/2019/5 final.

[122] See *United States – Countervailing Duty Measures on Certain Products from China*, Report of the Appellate Body, WT/DS437/AB/R.

power.[123] But once agreed upon, the rules of the game were to be the same for the entire membership, and hence an equalizing element. But it is that equal treatment that was found to be offensive to some, be it because a hegemon wanted special treatment, or because the Appellate Body falsely viewed very dissimilar practices as falling into the same legal category.

Thus, there is no doubt that the attractiveness of hard legal rules and judicial scrutiny seems to have diminished. Legal rules do not *mix and match* well with political trends such as the increased popularity of authoritarian approaches to both domestic and international governance, the increased short-termism of negotiators that cannot dare to report to capital anything less than a "win" based on results of quantitative modelling, or the emergence of new players that have successfully acquired the capacity to block, but are far from getting their partners to agreeing to reforms.

Then there are the judicial actors: not only did the Appellate Body allow nearly 70% of appellants to claim (some form) of victory; maybe more importantly, its distancing (in the tradition of leading Western courts[124]) from any attempt to explore what the state parties through their *negotiators* had intended, relying instead on its not always easy to understand interpretation of a legal text treated as a quasi-constitutional document, claiming to adhere slavishly to the VCLT, triggered slow-burning resentment. While the Appellate Body's brutal culling by a twice-impeached one-term US President is certainly not indicative of its perception in the membership, signs of irritation over the (proudly) legalistic approach to interpreting commercial agreements (as well as the explicit disregard for the negotiating history) had manifested itself much earlier.[125]

Domestically, certain courts have significantly reduced the power of the political organs in charge for foreign (economic) relations to pursue rules-based negotiating outcomes in the name of constitutionally "purity". The ECJ's "autonomy" jurisprudence has become a projection of domestic constitutional concepts on foreign relations, a dangerous development that weakens the Commission, the Council and by now even the Parliament,[126] and leads foreign powers to propose diplomatic dispute settlements without treaty-based adjudicative organs to avoid the wrath of the Luxembourg court.[127] Also, an increasing number of states, including states which had pushed BITs and ISDS down the throats of the rest of the world, became

---

[123] Whereas the participation of small non-sophisticated players was often reduced to just watching from a distance.

[124] *Marbury v. Madison*, 5 U.S. 137, Feb. 1803, https://supreme.justia.com/cases/federal/us/5/137/; CJEU, 26/62, *Van Gend en Loos,* ECLI:EU:C:1963:1.

[125] Cartland et al. (2012), pp. 991–1014 with many examples; for a US perspective, see Statement by Warren Maruyama, General Council, Office of the United States Trade Representative, Senate Finance Committee, 22 May 2008, https://www.finance.senate.gov/imo/media/doc/052208wmtest.pdf, p. 4; see also Pauwelyn and Pelc (2019), pp. 28 and 32–36. For a political analysis at the end of the Trump Administration, see Hillman (2020).

[126] See Hahn (2021), pp. 128–160.

[127] Ambühl and Scherer (2021), paras. 29–32.

disenchanted with the rule of international law the moment they found *themselves* restricted in their adaptation to new circumstances.

Lastly, it seems that by now a majority of developing topics—from climate change to AI, from migration to medical supply—are today discussed from the vantage point of geopolitics and security interests. That is bad news for rules-based international relations. Security interests (vital interests) and *necessity* are code for "we obey the rules, as long as we deem them advantageous for our immediate interests". In a day and age where the very existence of global public goods—such as a trading system that allows economic interchange, global financial stability that avoids a financial break-down or a climate stabilization that avoids the end of the world–, this tactical approach to maximize immediate interest runs against the strategic interest to preserve certain of these global goods which, by definition, cannot be produced even by the mightiest of the mighty actors alone.

The reliability and stability of international relations is such a public good. International relations based on agreed upon rules applicable to all, with very limited exceptions should therefore be in the strategic interest of every state, unless one considers it possible to perfectly shape the world according to one's political priorities. Given recent evidence to the contrary, such an idea is utterly debunked. For the remainder of the twenty-first century the focus will lie on preserving some form of orderly and norm-based order to address the many global challenges, most importantly global warming, followed closely (and inter-relatedly) by sustainable economic development. If that order can only be achieved through "soft-law", so be it. The alternative may be the law of the jungle, and a repeat performance of follies committed a century ago. There should be no mistaking, though: once a political consensus weakens, and genuine disputes arise between states on whether a promise is kept or whether the promised consideration is being paid or not, only a proper legal infrastructure provides the reliability and certainty that is associated with "hard" law. While said reliability and certainty is limited—the WTO gives evidence of that limitation—it has the strength to *temporarily* bridge phases of uncertainty, during which parties may abide by their obligation, if only to not break the law and incur the ensuing political cost, thereby creating time and opportunity to develop substantive solutions.

Rules and norms regulating state behaviour will remain fundamental for peaceful cooperation and economic well-being for the planet's population. If that is achieved by instruments that fall outside the realm of hard law, we lawyers may disappointedly see a second-best solution only. But a solution it is, despite the inherent advantage legal rules and ultimately judicial systems have proven to provide.

References

Abbott KW, Snidal D (2000) Hard and soft law in international governance. Int Organ 54(3):421–156

Acheson D (1969) Present at the creation. W.W. Norton & Company, New York

Acker K, Brautigam D, Huang Y (2020) Debt relief with Chinese characteristics. Johns Hopkins University, School of Advanced International Studies, China Africa Research Initiative Working Paper No. 2020/39, June 2020, https://papers.ssrn.com/sol3/papers.cfm?abstract_id=3745021

Alden C (2020) Understanding debt and diplomacy: China, 'debt traps' and development in the global South. SENACYT–FID–18–034 Working paper 01/2020, http://eprints.lse.ac.uk/110974/1/WorkingPaper01_FIN_04indd.pdf

Altemöller F (2021) WTO appellate body without legitimacy?: the criticism of the dispute settlement system and the response of the WTO member states. Global Trade Cust J 16(4):139–148

Ambühl M, Scherer D (2021) Schweiz-EU: wie weiter?. Jusletter 2 August 2021

Arner DW, Taylor MW (2009) The global financial crisis and the financial stability board: hardening the soft law of international financial regulation? Univ New South Wales Law J 32: 488–513

Balding C (2018) Why democracies are turning against Belt and Road: Corruption, debt, and backlash. Foreign Affairs, 24 October 2018, https://www.foreignaffairs.com/articles/china/2018-10-24/why-democracies-are-turning-against-belt-and-road

Baloch SM (2021) Protests in Pakistan erupt against China's belt and road plan. Demonstrations shut down Gwadar, where Chinese are blamed for lack of water and electricity and threat to local fishing. The Guardian, 1 September 2021, https://www.theguardian.com/environment/2021/aug/20/water-protests-in-pakistan-erupt-against-chinas-belt-and-road-plan

Bandiera L, Tsiropoulos V (2020) A framework to assess debt sustainability under the belt and road initiative. J Dev Econ 146:102495

Barney K, Souksakoun K (2021) Credit crunch: Chinese infrastructure lending and Lao sovereign debt. Asia Pac Policy Stud 8(1):94–113

Beck J, Ruessmann L (2020) Enforcement of EU TDI measures: addressing the challenges of the 21st century. Global Trade Cust J 15(9):423–434

Bitas BC (2017) ASEAN. In: Wang G, Lee AYL, Leung PMF (eds) Essentials of the laws of the belt and road countries. Zhejiang University Press, Hangzhou, pp 132–171

Bogdanor V (2009) The new British constitution. Oxford University Press, Oxford

Broude T, Shereshevsky Y (2021) Explaining the practical purchase of soft law. In: Cohen HG, Meyer T (eds) International law as behaviour. Cambridge University Press, Cambridge, pp 98–127

Brummer C (2010) Why soft law dominates international finance – and not trade. J Int Econ Law 13(3):623–643

Brummer C (2011) How international financial law works (and how it doesn't). Georgetown Law J 99(2):257–328

Brummer C (2014) Minilateralism: how trade alliances, soft law, and financial engineering are redefining economic statecraft. Cambridge University Press, Cambridge

Brummer C (2015) Soft law and the global financial system: rule making in the 21st century. Cambridge University Press, Cambridge

Cartland M, Depayre G, Woznowski J (2012) Is something going wrong in the WTO dispute settlement?. J World Trade 46(5):979–1015

Chaisse J, Matsushita M (2018) China's "belt and road" initiative: mapping the world normative and strategic implications. J World Trade 52(1):163–186

Cicéron Bühler C (2021) Soft Law: How to Improve Its Democratic Legitimacy While Ensuring Effective Governmental Action in Foreign Affairs, 2 September 2021, https://opiniojuris.org/2021/09/02/soft-law-how-to-improve-its-democratic-legitimacy-while-ensuring-effective-governmental-action-in-foreign-affairs/

Contartese C (2017) The autonomy of the EU legal order in the ECJ's external relations case law: from the "essential" to the "specific" characteristics of the union and back again. Common Mark Law Rev 54(6):1627–1672

Cottier T (2009) International trade law: the impact of justiciability and separations of powers in EC law. Eur Const Law Rev 5(2):307–326

Crochet V, Hedge V (2020) China's 'going global' policy: transnational production subsidies under the WTO SCM agreement. J Int Econ Law 23(4):841–863
D'Aspremont J (2008) Softness in international law: a self-serving quest for new legal materials. Eur J Int Law 19(5):1075–1093
De Witte B (2019) The relative autonomy of the European Union's fundamental rights regime. Nordic J Int Law 88(1):65–85
Dimitrakopoulos DG (2008) Norms, strategies and political change: explaining the establishment of the convention on the future of Europe. Eur J Int Rel 14(2):319–341
Durney J (2017) Defining the Paris agreement. Carbon Clim Law Rev 11(3):234–242
Editorial Comment (2020) Protecting the EU's internal market in times of pandemic and growing trade disputes: some reflections about the challenges posed by foreign subsidies. Common Mark Law Rev 57(5):1365–1385
Eliantonio M, Ştefan O (2021) The elusive legitimacy of EU soft law: an analysis of consultation and participation in the process of adopting COVID-19 soft law in the EU. Eur J Risk Regul 12(1):159–175
Eliantonio M, Korkea-aho E, Vaughan S (2021) EJRR special issue editorial: COVID-19 and soft law: is soft law pandemic-proof?. Eur J Risk Regul 12(1):1–6
Erie MS (2021) Chinese law and development. Harv Int Law J 61(1):51–116
European Supervisory Authorities (2014) Joint Guidelines on the convergence of supervisory practices relating to the consistency of supervisory coordination arrangements for financial conglomerates, JC/GL/2014/01
Evenett SJ, Dion Sud J, Vermulst E (2020) The European Union's new move against China: countervailing Chinese outward foreign direct investment. Global Trade Cust J 15(9):413–422
Galbraith J (2019) United States continues to block new appellate body members for the World Trade Organization, risking the collapse of the appellate process. Am J Int Law 113(4):822–831
Gelpern A, Horn S, Morris S, Parks B, Trebesch C (2021) How China lends: A rare look into 100 debt contracts with foreign governments. CGD Working Paper 573, 31 March 2021, https://www.cgdev.org/publication/how-china-lends-rare-look-into-100-debt-contracts-foreign-governments
Gurrea-Martínez A, Remolina N (2019) The dark side of implementing Basel capital requirements: theory, evidence, and policy. J Int Econ Law 22(1):125–152
Hahn M (2019) From whom the bell tolls: the WTO's third decade. In: Elsig M, Hahn M, Spilker G (eds) The shifting landscape of global trade governance world trade forum. Cambridge University Press, Cambridge, pp 121–155
Hahn M (2021) Never get high on your own supply– 'autonomy of the EU legal order' and effective treaty- based dispute settlement mechanisms. In: Hahn M, Van der Loo G (eds) Law and practice of the common commercial policy. The first 10 years after the treaty of Lisbon. Brill, Leiden, pp 128–160
Hedge V (2019) As WTO's dispute settlement body dies a dysfunctional death, what comes next?. The Wire, 11 December 2019, https://thewire.in/trade/wto-dispute-settlement-body-defunct
Helms L (2004) Five ways of institutionalizing political opposition: lessons from the advanced democracies. Gov Oppos 39(1):22–54
Henkin L (1979) How nations behave: law and foreign policy, 2nd edn. Council on Foreign Relations, New York
Hickman K, Thomson M (2016) Open minds and harmless errors: judicial review of post-promulgation notice and comment. Cornell Law Rev 101(2):261–324
Higgins A (2021) A pricey drive down Montenegro's highway 'from nowhere to nowhere'. The New York Times, 14 August 2021, https://www.nytimes.com/2021/08/14/world/europe/montenegro-highway-china.html
Hillman J (2020) A Reset of the World Trade Organization's Appellate Body, 14 January 2020, https://www.cfr.org/report/reset-world-trade-organizations-appellate-body
Hockin TA (1971) The roles of the loyal opposition in Britain's house of commons: three historical paradigms. Parliam Aff 25(1):50–68

Hølleland H, Hamman E, Phelps J (2019) Naming, shaming and fire alarms: the compilation, development and use of the list of world heritage in danger. Transnl Environ Law 8(1):35–57
Howse R (2002) The appellate body rulings in the shrimp/turtle Aase: new legal baseline for the trade and environment debate. Columbia J Environ Law 27(2):491–522
Howse R (2020) Making the WTO (not so) great again. J Int Econ Law 23(2):371–389
Hurley J, Morris S, Portelance G (2018) Examining the debt implications of the belt and road initiative from a policy perspective. CGD Policy Paper 121, March 2018, https://www.cgdev.org/sites/default/files/examining-debt-implications-belt-and-road-initiative-policy-perspective.pdf
Irwin D, Mavroidis P, Skyes A (2008) The genesis of the GATT. Cambridge University Press, New York
Johnson K (2019) How Trump may finally kill the WTO. Foreign Policy, 9 December 2019, https://foreignpolicy.com/2019/12/09/trump-may-kill-wto-finally-appellate-body-world-trade-organization/
Jones L, Hameiri S (2020) Debunking the myth of 'debt-trap diplomacy': how recipient countries shape China's Belt and Road Initiative. Chatham House Research Paper, 19 August 2020, https://www.chathamhouse.org/2020/08/debunking-myth-debt-trap-diplomacy
Klabbers J (2012) International courts and informal international law. In: Pauwelyn J, Wessel R, Wouters J (eds) Informal international lawmaking. Oxford University Press, Oxford, pp 219–240
Korkea-aho E (2018) National courts and European soft law: is Grimaldi still good law?. Yearb Eur Law 37(1):470–495
Koutrakos P (2019) The autonomy of EU law and international investment arbitration. Nordic J Int Law 88(1):41–64
Kovačević M (2021) Vulnerabilities to Chinese influence in Montenegro. Center for International Private Enterprise, January 2021, https://en.cdtmn.org/wp-content/uploads/2021/02/Vulnerabilities-to-Chinese-influence-in-Montenegro-final.pdf
Langer L (2020) Implications of soft law regimes for small states: the experience of Switzerland and Liechtenstein. Swiss Rev Int Eur Law 30(3):235–264
Lastra RM (2016) The coming age of international monetary and financial law after the global financial crisis. J Int Econ Law 19(2):371–373
Le Corre P (2018) China's rise as a geoeconomic Influencer: Four European case studies, November 2018, Asia Focus #93. Institut de Relations Internationales et Stratégiques, https://www.iris-france.org/wp-content/uploads/2018/11/Asia-Focus-93.pdf
Lehne J (2019) Crisis at the WTO: is the blocking of appointments to the WTO appellate body by the United States legally justified?. Carl Grossmann Verlag, Berlin
Lester S (2020) Guest post: update from 'the void': questions for the new Interim Appeal Agreement (IAAA). International Economic Law and Policy Blog, 30 January 2020, https://ielp.worldtradelaw.net/2020/01/guest-post-update-from-the-void-questions-for-the-new-interim-appeal-agreement-iaaa.html
Lin X, Sharma S (2021) Does China engage in debt-trap diplomacy?. IPS Working Paper Series No. 1, January 2021, https://commons.ln.edu.hk/cgi/viewcontent.cgi?article=1000&context=ipswp
MANS (2020) Put bez kraja. Četvrti izvještaj o izgradnji autoputa Bar – Boljare [Endless Road, Fourth Highway Bar – Boljare Construction Report], September 2020, http://www.mans.co.me/wp-content/uploads/2020/10/Cetvrti-izjvjestaj-o-izgradnji-autoputa-PUT-BEZ-KRAJA.pdf
Martinico G (2020) Comparative law reflections on the use of soft law in the belt and road initiative. In: Martinico G, Wu X (eds) A legal analysis of the belt and road initiative: towards a new silk road?. Palgrave Macmillan, Cham, pp 131–144
Milano E, Zugliani N (2019) Capturing commitment in informal, soft law instruments: a case study on the Basel committee. J Int Econ Law 22(2):163–176

Ming L (2016) “One belt and one road” and international law: a Chinese perspective. In: Wang G, Li W, Liang MF (eds) International law perspectives on the belt and road initiative. Zhejiang University Press, Hangzhou, pp 307–317

Muñoz JGP (2019) Governance of the global financial system: the legitimacy of the BCBS 10 years after the 2008 crisis. J Int Econ Law 22(2):247–260

Nic Shuibhne N (2019) What is the autonomy of EU law, and why does that matter?. Nordic J Int Law 88(1):9–40

OECD (2017) OECD Transfer Pricing Guidelines for Multinational Enterprises and Tax Administrations 2017. OECD Publishing, Paris, https://doi.org/10.1787/tpg-2017-en

Ortino M (2019) The governance of global banking in the face of complexity. J Int Econ Law 22(2):177–204

Parks B (2019) Chinese Leadership and the Future of BRI: What Key Decisions Lie Ahead?. CGD Note, July 2019, https://www.cgdev.org/sites/default/files/chinese-leadership-and-future-bri-what-key-decisions-lie-ahead.pdf

Pauwelyn J (2012) Is it international law or not, and does it even matter?. In: Pauwelyn J, Wessel R, Jan Wouters J (eds) Informal international lawmaking. Oxford University Press, Oxford, pp 125–161

Pauwelyn J, Pelc K (2019) Who Writes the Rulings of the World Trade Organization? A Critical Assessment of the Role of the Secretariat in WTO Dispute Settlement, 6 October 2019, https://papers.ssrn.com/sol3/papers.cfm?abstract_id=3458872

Pauwelyn J, Wessel R, Wouters J (2012) Informal international lawmaking. Oxford University Press, Oxford

Rajah R, Dayant A, Pryke J (2019) Ocean of debt? Belt and road and debt diplomacy in the Pacific. Lowy Institute Research Paper, 30 October 2019, https://think-asia.org/bitstream/handle/11540/11389/debt-diplomacy-Pacific_WEB.pdf

Riesberg P (2019) The give-and-take of BRI in Africa, New Perspectives in Foreign Policy Issue 17, https://www.csis.org/give-and-take-bri-africa

Riffel P (2019) The CETA opinion of the European Court of Justice and its implications – not that selfish after all. J Int Econ Law 22(3):503–521

Roby V (2020) China’s growing influence in Latin America. Am J Econ Sociol 79(1):233–244

Ryan C (2016) Economics, geo-politics, culture and environment. In: Wang G, Li W, Liang MF (eds) Intenational law perspectives on the belt and road initiative. Zhejiang University Press, Hangzhou, pp 219–230

Sachs NM (2019) The Paris agreement in the 2020s: breakdown or breakup. Ecol Law Quart 46(3):865–910

Schaffer GC, Pollack MA (2010) Hard vs. soft law: alternatives, complements, and antagonists in international governance. Minn Law Rev 94(3):706–799

Schemmel J (2016) The ESA guidelines: soft law and subjectivity in the European financial market – capturing the administrative influence. Indiana J Global Stud 23(2):455–504

Thürer D (2009) Soft law. In: Max Planck Institute for Comparative Public Law and International Law, Max Planck Encyclopaedia of Public International Law [MPEPIL], last updated March 2009, https://opil.ouplaw.com/view/10.1093/law:epil/9780199231690/law-9780199231690-e1469?prd=EPIL

Urban M (2021) Les accords interinstitutionnels, vecteurs de parlamentarisation des relations extérieures, Étude des accords interinstitutionnels et de leur usage dans le cadre de la procédure de négotiation et de conclusion des accords internationaux. Dossier de droit européen No. 34, Schulthess, Geneva/Zurich/Basel

Vega A (2012) International governance through soft law: The case of the OECD transfer pricing guidelines. TranState Working Papers, No. 163, University of Bremen, Collaborative Research Center 597 - Transformations of the State, https://www.econstor.eu/bitstream/10419/59530/1/717832643.pdf

Venkateswaran L (2020) China's Belt and Road Initiative: Implications in Africa. Observer Research Foundation Issue Brief No. 395, https://www.orfonline.org/research/chinas-belt-and-road-initiative-implications-in-africa/

Vladimirov M, Rolland C (2021) The Chinese economic footprint in Central and Eastern Europe: Impact on energy transition and climate. Center for Study of Democracy, Policy Brief No. 97, January 2021, https://csd.bg/fileadmin/user_upload/publications_library/files/2021_01/BRIEF_97_ENG_WEB.pdf

Voon T (2019) The security exception in the WTO law: entering a new era. Am J Int Law 113:45–50

Waelbroeck M (1974) Effect of GATT within the legal order of the EEC. J World Trade 8(6):614–623

Wang H (2021) The belt and road initiative agreements: characteristics, rationale, and challenges. World Trade Rev 20(3):282–305

Wang J (2019) China's governance approach to the belt and road initiative (BRI): relations, partnership, and law. Global Trade Cust J 14(5):222–228 (referred to as Wang J (2019))

Wanner MST (2021) The effectiveness of soft law in international environmental regimes: participation and compliance in the Hyogo framework for action. Int Environ Agreements 21(2):113–132

Wessel RA (2021) Normative transformations in EU external relations: the phenomenon of 'soft' international agreements. West Eur Polit 44(1):72–92

Yue M, Nedopil Wang C (2020) Brief: Public debt in Belt and Road Initiative (BRI): How Covid-19 has accelerated an ongoing problem of China's lending. Green BRI Center, International Institute of Green Finance, December 2020, https://green-bri.org/wp-content/uploads/2020/12/2020_China_Debt_Belt_and_Road_BRI-1.pdf

Part II
Trade and Investment

The EU-China Comprehensive Agreement on Investment: Strategic Opportunity Meets Strategic Autonomy

Henry Gao

Contents

Abstract This article provides a critical analysis of the EU-China Comprehensive Agreement on Investment, which has been regarded as one of the most important international agreements concluded by both sides in recent years. The paper starts with a critical summary of the Agreement, which reveals that the Agreement failed to add much in terms of substance. What, then, explains the rationale for the Agreement? This article argues that the key to understand the Agreement lies not in the narrow commercial interests, but more in the broad strategic and geopolitical considerations of both the EU and China. The article concludes with a review of the development of the twin concepts of "strategic opportunity" in China and "strategic autonomy" in the EU, as well as what the confluence of these considerations would mean for the future of the Agreement.

H. Gao (✉)
Singapore Management University, Singapore, Singapore

M. Chi et al. (eds.), *Asian Yearbook of International Economic Law 2022*,
Asian Yearbook of International Economic Law (2022) 2022: 47–70,
https://doi.org/10.1007/16517_2021_1, Published online: 21 December 2021

On 30 December 2020, the EU and China finally concluded in principle[1] the EU-China Comprehensive Agreement on Investment (CAI) after a marathon negotiation spanning seven years and 35 rounds. Highly praised by both sides, the Agreement was hailed as "the most ambitious agreement that China has ever concluded with a third country" by the EU,[2] and a "high-level" agreement that matches "international high-level economic and trade rules" by China.[3] But does the rhetoric really match the reality? If not, what are the reasons for the negotiation and conclusion of the Agreement? What will be the prospect for the ratification of the Agreement? This paper answers these important questions with a thorough and critical analysis of the text of the CAI, along with an in-depth review of the behind-the-scenes strategic considerations which shaped the CAI, as well as how the future holds for the Agreement.

1 A Critical Summary of the CAI

The CAI includes a total of six sections, which can be further divided into two groups:

The first are the substantive provisions, which includes Section I on objectives and general definitions, Section II on investment liberalization, Section III on regulatory framework, and Section IV on investment and sustainable development.

The second are the procedural and institutional provisions, which includes Section V on dispute settlement and Section VI on institutional and final provisions. These sections are analysed in detail below.

1.1 Objectives and General Definitions

According to Article 1, the main objective of the Agreement is to "lay down the necessary arrangements for the liberalisation of investment". This means that the Agreement is different from the normal Bilateral Investment Treaties (BITs), which have traditionally focused on investment protection, with investment liberalization included only as a more recent development after free trade agreements such as the North American Free Trade Agreement (NAFTA) started to incorporate investment in its scope. Having investment liberalization as the main objective also explains the

[1]For EU's announcement, see EU and China Reach Agreement in Principle on Investment, IP/20/2541 of 30 December 2020; for China's announcement, see 中欧领导人共同宣布如期完成中欧投资协定谈判-新华网, 30 December 2020, http://www.xinhuanet.com/world/2020-12/30/c_1126929012.htm.

[2]Key Elements of the EU-China Comprehensive Agreement, IP/20/2542 of 30 December 2020.

[3]商务部条法司负责人就如期完成中欧投资协定谈判答记者问, 31 December 2020, http://www.mofcom.gov.cn/article/news/202012/20201203027541.shtml.

CAI's lack of common BIT provisions on substantive rights for investors, such as expropriation and compensation, fair and equitable treatment, and minimum standard of treatment. Instead of trying to restrict the regulatory power of the government to protect the rights of investors, the second paragraph of the article on objectives explicitly reaffirms the Parties have "right to regulate within their territories to achieve legitimate policy objectives, such as the protection of public health, social services, public education, safety, the environment, including the fight against climate change, public morals, social security or consumer protection, privacy and data protection or the promotion and protection of cultural diversity."

For the EU, such explicit affirmation of the regulatory power reflects, on the one hand, the ever-expansive regulatory regime in the EU, and on the other hand, the need to assuage the fears by the EU member states on the possible encroachment of their domestic regulatory framework by the CAI. From the perspective of China, such carefully-crafted clause is also necessary, especially in view of the hard lessons China has learned in the twin WTO cases of *China–Raw Materials* and *China–Rare Earth*, where due to of the lack of explicit reference to the general exception clause of the GATT, China was denied the right to justify its export restrictions under GATT Article XX. Thus, it is better to spell out these exceptions upfront, even though the preamble does reaffirm the Parties' "respective rights and obligations under the WTO Agreement". As I mentioned in another article, such an approach is also reflected in China's negotiating proposal in other forums, such as the e-commerce Joint State Initiative negotiation in the WTO.[4]

The focus on investment liberalization also means that the agreement will not qualify as a free trade agreement in goods or services. Under the existing WTO framework, these two types of free trade agreement can potentially be justified under the GATT and GATS respectively, so long as they satisfy the necessary requirements therein, i.e., Article XXIV of the General Agreement on Tariffs and Trade (GATT), or Article V of the General Agreement on Trade in Services (GATS). While the WTO also has another Agreement on Trade-Related Investment Measures (TRIMS), TRIMS does not provide exceptions for an agreement that focuses solely on investment liberalization. This might raise some interesting legal issues, as I will discuss below in Part IV.

The other part of Section I is on "general definitions", or definitions of general terms which are used frequently in the agreement. Such terms include for example, "enterprise", "measure", "operations", "investor of a Party" or "non-Party", "natural person". Many of these definitions follow closely those of the WTO Agreements or other free trade agreements and BITs. For example, the definitions on "measures by Members" and "services" follow the definitions under Article I.3 of the GATS verbatim, while the only difference between the CAI definition on 'activities performed in the exercise of governmental authority' and GATS definition on "a service supplied in the exercise of governmental authority" is the replacement of "service" with "activities".

[4] Gao (2021a).

At the same time, there are also some definitions which are not really general, but specific to a sector or type of activity. The former includes definitions on 'aircraft repair and maintenance services', 'selling and marketing of air transport services', 'computer reservation system (CRS) services' and 'ground handling services", which are specific to the sector of air transport services and auxiliary air services. The second is the definition on 'commercial considerations', which only applies to "covered entities" (which is how the CAI defines State Owned Enterprises as explained below) under Article 3bis of Section II.

1.2 Investment Liberalisation

Section II is the heart of the Agreement and sets out in detail the investment liberalization commitments. It starts by noting that the Section applies to "measures or treatment adopted or maintained by a Party affecting the establishment of an enterprise or the operation of a covered enterprise by an investor of the other Party in its territory", which essentially means measures affecting investment. Following the tradition of the GATS, it also excludes governmental activities, government procurement, and air transport services and auxiliary air services other than: aircraft repair and maintenance services; the selling and marketing of air transport services; computer reservation systems (CRS) services; and ground handling services. Audio-visual services are also excluded, probably due to the reservations from certain EU member states such as France.

Most of the other provisions in the Section can be divided into two broad categories:

First are the market access commitments, which are scheduled pursuant to Article 2. The list of types of market access restrictions under Article 2 closely follows that of Article XVI of GATS, except that it does not include the last type of restriction, i.e., "limitations on the participation of foreign capital in terms of maximum percentage limit on foreign shareholding or the total value of individual or aggregate foreign investment". Instead, such limitations are scheduled under the national treatment restrictions as mentioned below, as they also constitute national treatment discriminations by their very nature. The specific limitations are scheduled in Annex III of the Agreement, i.e., the schedule of specific commitments and limitations on market access. It also follows the example of services schedule under the GATS in two ways: first in the adoption of a positive listing approach, which means that only services sectors explicitly listed in the schedule are subject to liberalization commitments; second in the adoption of the GATS scheduling format, which includes a horizontal section of limitations or commitments which apply to all sectors, as well as sector specific commitments which are organized according to sectors and sub-sectors with detailed commitments or restrictions. The only difference is that, unlike the GATS schedules which include three columns of commitments on market access, national treatment and additional commitments respectively, the CAI schedules only include the column on market access after the column of sectors and sub-sectors.

Second are the commitments on domestic regulation. More specifically, these includes commitments relating to Article 4 (National Treatment), Article 5 (Most-Favored-Nation Treatment), Article 3 (Performance Requirements), and Article 6 (Senior Management and Boards of Directors). With respect to these obligations, the Agreement adopts the negative listing approach instead of the positive listening approach on market access commitments. This means that, unless a restriction has been scheduled, these obligations are presumed to apply. More specifically, two types of restrictions can be scheduled according to Article 7: existing non-conforming measures scheduled in Annex I, which the Parties can continue to maintain but may not make it more restrictive; and reservations scheduled in Annex II, which allows the Parties to retain the flexibility to adopt new restrictions in the future.

It is not surprising to see in the Agreement these provisions and commitments on market access and domestic regulations, as they have been quite common in the investment chapters of free trade agreements. But in addition to these, the Agreement has also broken new grounds by including two new articles on State-Owned Enterprises (SOEs) and regulatory principles.

Until very recently, provisions on SOEs have been very rare in trade[5] and investment agreements.[6] This only changed in the last decade with the US Model BIT in 2012 and the negotiations on TPP, TTIP, USMCA and China-US BIT. In addition to the global trend, the inclusion of SOE regulation in the CAI also reflects the EU's long-standing concerns over the market distorting effects of the anti-competitive behaviours of SOEs at all levels. At the EU level, the Commission issued a Staff Working Document "On significant distortions in the economy of the People's Republic of China for the purposes of trade defence investigations" in December 2017,[7] which devoted 25 pages to the problem of Chinese SOEs. At the international level, the EU also issued a trilateral statement with the US and Japan on the side-lines of the 11th WTO Ministerial Conference held in Buenos Aries in the same month to address the "critical concern" of "unfair competitive conditions caused by ... state owned enterprises".[8] SOE also featured prominently in the EU's new trade strategy document unveiled in Feb 2021, which calls for new rules on "competitive neutrality" in view of market distortions created by SOEs[9] and is

[5] Kong (2017).

[6] Wang and Gallagher (2016).

[7] European Commission, On significant distortions in the economy of the People's Republic of China for the purposes of trade defence investigations, SWD(2017) 483 final/2.

[8] See https://ustr.gov/about-us/policy-offices/press-office/press-releases/2017/december/joint-statement-united-states.

[9] European Commission, Annex on Reforming the WTO: Towards a Sustainable and Effective Multilateral Trading System, February 2021, https://trade.ec.europa.eu/doclib/docs/2021/february/tradoc_159439.pdf, pp. 9–10.

likely to lead to a proposal for new plurilateral negotiations on the issue in the WTO.[10]

Interestingly, the term "State-Owned Enterprises" or "SOE" never formally appears in the CAI. Instead, it is referred to in the Agreement as "covered entity", a seemingly innocuous expression probably chosen carefully to avoid the controversies surrounding SOEs. Moreover, by using "covered entity", the CAI is also able to expand the coverage from just those owned by the government (either through majority share or majority voting rights), to those where the government has the power to control either the board or the decisions of the enterprises or "the power to legally direct the actions or otherwise exercise an equivalent level of control in accordance with its laws and regulations". This is consistent with the WTO jurisprudence on "public body" in the context of subsidy regulation, where the Appellate Body emphasized the need to "demonstrate that the government exercises meaningful control over the conduct of [an] entity" and promoted a functional approach on whether the enterprise "possesses, exercises or is vested with governmental authority".[11] The last two parts of the definition on "covered entities" also cover cases of monopoly and duopoly, where ownership by the state is not required. With such broad definition, the CAI covers most situations where the competitive environment is undermined due to government ownership or control, or monopolistic power of the enterprise.

The article then listed two obligations for covered entities. The first is the obligation to act in accordance with commercial considerations and provide non-discriminatory treatment in their purchases or sales of goods or services. The EU regards this as a significant achievement and calls the CAI "the first agreement to deliver on obligations for the behavior of state-owned enterprises". But as discussed below, this is nothing new and simply repeats what was already in China's WTO accession package. The other is the transparency obligation, which grants the right to a Party to request the other Party to "supply information about the operations of [a covered] entity related to the carrying out of the provisions of [the Article on SOEs]". This includes information on ownership and the voting structure, special shares and voting rights, organisational and management structures, annual revenue or total assets, exemptions, immunities and equivalent measures, and government authorities responsible for exercising the ownership function and regulatory power. The list of information seems quite comprehensive and could provide a useful means to nudge China to police the behaviours of SOEs according to CAI requirements. Making the information request a government-to-government exercise also removes the fear of retaliation which might prevent EU firms from venting their complaints to China. It would be interesting to observe whether this provision would work in practice.

The Article on Regulatory principles requires regulatory authorities to be impartial, non-discriminatory and independent in exercising the regulatory function.

[10] See Inside US Trade, Weyand proposes WTO plurilateral on 'competitive neutrality' led by EU, U.S., 10 March 2021.

[11] Appellate Body Report, *United States–Definitive Anti-Dumping and Countervailing Duties on Certain Products from China*, WT/DS379/AB/R (adopted 25 March 2011). paras. 317–318.

Again here the concern seems to be uneven administration of regulatory measures, given that many SOEs in China enjoy cosy relationships with their regulators built from both historical ties and sharing of a common pool of personnel, especially at the most senior level. This is most obvious in the telecommunications sector, where Shang Bing, the former CEO of China Unicom, was promoted to be Vice Minister of the Ministry of Industry and Information Technology, before being appointed as the Board Chairman of China Mobile.[12] Indeed, this also explains the similarity between this Article and Section 5 of the WTO Reference Paper on Telecommunications, which lays down the regulatory principles for the telecommunication sector.[13]

1.3 Regulatory Framework

This section spells out detailed obligations on the regulatory principles, which are further divided in three sub-sections covering domestic regulation, transparency and financial services sector respectively. They largely build on corresponding provisions in the GATS, with the sub-section on domestic regulation focusing mainly on licencing and qualification requirements and procedures as in Article VI of the GATS; the sub-section on transparency combining the obligations on publication, contact point and provision of information under GATS Article III, and those on administrative proceedings, review and appeal under GATS Article VI; and the sub-section on financial services copying the Annex on Financial Services.

Of course, there are also some innovations in drafting, with the Article on transparency of subsidies being the most interesting. Building from the rules in the WTO Agreement on Subsidies and Countervailing Measures, the Article breaks new ground by expanding the scope of coverage from trade in goods to services, a feat yet to be achieved in the WTO despite the built-in mandate to negotiate rules on services subsidies in GATS Article XV. In addition, the Article also includes a provision on transparency of subsidies, which applies to the following sectors: business services, communication services, construction and related engineering services, distribution services, environmental services, financial services, health related services (privately funded), tourism and travel related services, and transport services. According to the Article, information on services in these sectors shall be published no later than two years after the CAI enters into force. The Article further provides opportunities for government-to-government consultations on subsidies with negative effects on its investment interests, but falls short of subjecting such disputes to the full-blown state to state dispute settlement system under the Agreement.

---

[12] 工信部副部长尚冰任中国移动董事长奚国华不再担任, 24 August 2015, http://district.ce.cn/newarea/sddy/201508/24/t20150824_6303817.shtml.

[13] For a detailed analysis on the Reference Paper, see Gao (2008).

1.4 Investment and Sustainable Development

Provisions on sustainable development has been a key feature in EU's recent trade agreements, which often cover issues on environment protection, human rights, labor rights and corporate social responsibility.[14] However, such clauses have been missing from the latest investment protection agreements concluded by the EU, probably because the EU also signed free trade agreements with these countries and thus there was no need to put these issues in the investment protection agreements.[15] The CAI, however, is different, as it would be very difficult, at least in the short to medium term, for the EU to conclude a free trade agreement with China due to political reasons. Thus, the CAI breaks with the tradition of the investment protection agreements and includes a section on sustainable development divided into 3 sub-sections:

The first sub-section sets out the context and objectives of the section, with provisions on the overarching principles on sustainable development as found in the relevant international documents, corporate social responsibility, public participation, and sustainability impact review.

The next two sub-sections cover environment and labour rights respectively and follow similar pattern. They both start by recognizing the Parties' right to regulate, before listing more detailed obligations on the levels of protection: not too lax to attract investment, but at the same time, not too harsh so as to "constitute a disguised restriction of investment or an unjustified discrimination between investors and investments of the Parties". In particular, the Agreement specifies that the Parties shall not, "through a sustained or recurring course of action or inaction, fail to effectively enforce its [environmental/labour] laws, as an encouragement for investment". The two sub-sections also call for dialogue and cooperation on investment-related environmental and labour issues between the Parties, and require each Party to effectively implement the multilateral environmental and labour agreements it has ratified. In addition to the passive obligations noted above, the Parties also agree to promote investments favouring green growth and decent work.

In addition to environmental protection and labour rights in general, the Agreement also singled out one key issue in each area. The one for environment is climate change, to which both the EU and China have been politically committed. The one for labour is forced labour, which includes the obligations in ILO Conventions No 29 and 105, two instruments China explicitly committed to make "continued and sustained efforts on its own initiative to pursue ratification". This is significant especially in view of the recent controversy on China's alleged forced labour practices in Xinjiang.

Probably due to the sensitivity of the issue to China, the Section on sustainable development is not subject to the normal dispute settlement system of the CAI.

[14] European Commission, Sustainable Development, https://ec.europa.eu/trade/policy/policy-making/sustainable-development/.

[15] See the EU's recent investment protection agreements with Singapore and Vietnam.

Instead, it has its own dispute settlement system. The process starts with bilateral consultations between the Parties, and may proceed to a Panel of Experts if the dispute is not satisfactory resolved within 4 months. The Panel process largely models after that of the WTO, except without the official adoption and implementation processes. Instead, the Panel report is only supposed to provide a basis for the Parties to work out ways to address the dispute. One striking feature of the dispute settlement process in Section IV is the provisions on transparency of the proceedings. For example, the Agreement requires the Parties to make the Panel hearing open to the public, and make publicly available the request for consultation and Panel establishment, the submissions and statements of the Parties, the Panel report, and the final agreed solution between the Parties. In addition, an article specifically provides for the right for natural and legal persons from a Party to participate as *amicus curiae* in panel proceedings. Once implemented, this would provide unprecedented access for non-governmental organizations on environmental and labour issues from the EU to participate in dispute settlement proceedings involving China. Coupled with the wide range of public-participation rights, the transparency of such proceedings are likely to create strong pressure on China, which sometimes can be even more powerful than binding dispute settlement procedures.

1.5 Dispute Settlement

The Section on dispute settlement adds "teeth" to the obligations contained in the CAI by providing "an effective and efficient mechanism" for resolving disputes, albeit with two caveats: First, as the Agreement yet to include provisions on investor protection, the scope of the dispute settlement mechanism is limited to those within the current Agreement, i.e., on investment liberalization commitments and regulatory principles. Second, the dispute settlement mechanism in the Agreement is only state to state, and does not include investor state dispute settlement mechanism, which is typically found in BITs. Of course, this does not mean that the Parties do not wish to include these issues. Instead, according to Article 3 of Section VI, the Parties agree to continue their negotiations to include "state of the art provisions" on both issues, which they strive to conclude within 2 years of the signing of the CAI.

The dispute settlement mechanism follows closely that of the WTO, and includes confidential bilateral consultation, arbitration by a three-person panel, interim report and final report, determination of reasonable period of time for implementation, compliance review, and retaliation in the form of suspension of concessions and other obligations. It also provides for the possibility of resolving the dispute through mediation and mutually agreed solution, as well as suspension, resumption and termination of panel proceedings. There are also a few innovations compared to WTO rules. For example, the Article on applicable law and rules of interpretation explicitly state that customary rules on interpretation of public international law include those codified in the Vienna Convention of the Law of Treaties. Another example is the Article on transparency, which explicitly makes panel hearings open to the public and grants right to natural and legal persons to submit *amicus* briefs to the panel. Given the controversy these issues have raised in the WTO dispute settlement system, such clarifications are quite welcome. The Section also contains two Annexes, with the one on rules of procedure for state-to-state dispute settlement fully developed, while the one on code of conduct for panellists and mediators still under discussion at the time of writing of this paper.

1.6 Institutional and Final Provisions

This Section is composed of two sub-sections. The first sub-section sets out the institutional framework, which includes an investment committee at the level of Vice President of the European Commission and Vice Premier of China; a Working Group on Investment at the level of EU Director General on Trade and Vice Minister of China's Ministry of Commerce (MOFCOM); and a Working Group on Sustainable Development at senior officials' level. The second sub-section includes final provisions which address various miscellaneous issues, such as the amendment and termination of the Agreement, general exceptions and security exceptions, provisions on payments and transfers on current accounts and capital movements, and safeguard and balance of payment measures. One Article requires the Parties to "have a regular dialogue with non-state stakeholders in a balanced representation of economic, environmental and social interests",[16] which is designed to provide access to government by business firms, NGOs and civil society groups.

Before the conclusion of the CAI, many EU Member States have already concluded many BITs with China, which often includes clauses on investor protection and investment state dispute system absent in the CAI. Thus, the CAI explicitly states that these agreements will remain in place and "not superseded or terminated by this Agreement".[17] Moreover, the same Article also states that the CAI shall "be an integral part of the overall bilateral relations as governed by the Trade and Economic Cooperation Agreement or a future Framework Agreement", which implies that the EU and China are expecting the negotiation of a broader trade agreement in the future.[18] The last part of the Article states that "nothing in this Agreement requires them to act in a manner inconsistent with their obligations under the WTO Agreement", which means that the Parties need to comply with the WTO rules at the same time.[19] Of particular relevance here would be the Most Favored Nation (MFN) principle. While normally free trade agreements can be justified pursuant to GATT Article XXIV or GATS Article V, the exception is not available here as the CAI agreement, with its limited scope, would not be able to satisfy the

[16] EU-China Comprehensive Agreement on Investment (CAI), sub-section 2, Article 1.

[17] EU-China Comprehensive Agreement on Investment (CAI), sub-section 2, Article 15.

[18] EU-China Comprehensive Agreement on Investment (CAI), sub-section 2, Article 15.

[19] EU-China Comprehensive Agreement on Investment (CAI), sub-section 2, Article 15.

substantial trade coverage requirements under the two clauses. More specifically, it covers mainly trade in services, and mainly in one mode of supply: Mode 3 on commercial presence, with some commitments on Mode 4: movement of natural persons. This would make it hard to be justified under the GATS, as Article V explicitly states that such agreements "should not provide for the a priori exclusion of any mode of supply".[20] In practice, this means that most if not all of the market access commitments under the Agreement must be granted to other WTO Members.

2 An Assessment of the Market Access and Rules Commitments

To prove its point that the CAI is "the most ambitious agreement that China has ever concluded with a third country", the EU kept emphasising in its summary on the key elements of the CAI that "China has not made such far-reaching market access commitments with any other partner" (in the manufacturing sector) and "China has not previously committed openness to foreign investment" (in research and development in biological resources). Yet, closer examination reveals that such assertions are at best dubious as many of the concessions are neither "unprecedented"[21] nor "not previously committed". Instead, as the examples below illustrate, many of these commitments are either already available as part of China's own autonomous liberalization, or have already been committed by China in other agreements.

2.1 China's Autonomous Liberalization

Under China's commitments in Annex I: Entry 6—Manufacture of Transportation Equipment to the CAI, China agrees to lift two existing restrictions on foreign investments in the automobile manufacturing sector contained in the Special Administrative Measures for Market Access of Foreign Investment (Negative List) (2019 Edition): limiting foreign investment to no more than 50% shares; and restricting each foreign investor to no more than two joint ventures in passenger cars within the territory of China. According to the entry, both restrictions would be removed "after 2022".

However, both restrictions have already been scheduled for removal in the Special Administrative Measures for Market Access of Foreign Investment (Negative List) (2020 Edition),[22] which was issued in June 2020, or six months before the

[20] GATS, footnote 1 to Article V.

[21] EU and China Reach Agreement in Principle on Investment, IP/20/2541 of 30 December 2020.

[22] 中华人民共和国国家发展和改革委员会，中华人民共和国商务部，"外商投资准入特别管理措施 (负面清单)(2020年版), http://www.gov.cn/gongbao/content/2020/content_5532623.htm.

CAI was concluded. Moreover, according to the Negative List (2020 Edition), both restrictions were supposed to be removed "in 2022", which could take effect up to a year before the CAI obligations kick in. In fact, such commitments were already noted two years earlier in the 2018 edition of the Negative List.[23]

The same entry in China's commitments in Annex I also notes that "the measures listed in this entry does not apply to investments by foreign investors in the manufacture of new energy automobiles and special purpose automobiles". Again, however, this is nothing new, as both sectors have already been liberalized in the 2018 edition of the Negative List.

Similarly, China's commitments in Annex I: Entry 12—Telecommunication Services to the CAI allows EU investor investing in internet data center service (including content delivery network service), subject to an equity cap of 50%. Again, however, the same commitment was already made by China in the Hainan Free Trade Port Special Administrative Measures for Market Access of Foreign Investment for Negative List (2020 Edition), which was issued a day after the conclusion of the CAI negotiation.[24] While the CAI commitments are arguably broader than the commitments under the Hainan negative list as the latter does not allow such services to be provided to Chinese territories other than the Hainan free trade port, it would not be hard for firms wishing to avail of such services to move their data centres to Hainan. Moreover, despite restrictions on paper, entrepreneurial firms like Amazon have been reportedly providing cloud services in China through creative legal arrangements since 2013.[25]

2.2 *Pre-existing Commitments in Other Agreements*

At the same time, many other commitments in the CAI were already committed in other agreements. For example, under Annex III: Schedule of specific commitments and limitations on market access, China commits to remove all restrictions on insurance and insurance-related services including life insurance, non-life insurance, reinsurance and services auxiliary to insurance. However, such commitment has already been made by China in its Phase One Agreement with the US, which states that China shall remove "the foreign equity cap in the life, pension, and health insurance sectors and allow wholly U.S.-owned insurance companies to participate in these sectors" as well as "any business scope limitations, discriminatory

[23] 中华人民共和国国家发展和改革委员会，中华人民共和国商务部，"发展改革委商务部令2018年第18号外商投资准入特别管理措施(负面清单)(2020年版)，http://www.mofcom.gov.cn/article/b/f/201806/20180602760432.shtml.

[24] 海南自由贸易港外商投资准入特别管理措施(负面清单)(2020年版)，http://www.gov.cn/zhengce/zhengceku/2021-01/01/content_5576049.htm.

[25] Amazon Teams With Companies In China For Cloud Service, The Wall Street Journal of 18 December 2013, https://online.wsj.com/article/SB10001424052702304866904579266272134981780.html?st=fcjg25g1xedbxjv&reflink=desktopwebshare_permalink.

regulatory processes and requirements, and overly burdensome licensing and operating requirements for all insurance sectors (including insurance intermediation)" by 1 April 2020, or 9 months before the conclusion of the CAI.[26]

Moreover, in some parts, EU insurance companies actually got a worse deal compared to US firms. Under CAI's Annex I Entry 31—Insurance, EU agrees that China will be able to maintain the requirement that the aggregate shareholding percentage of domestic insurance companies in an insurance asset management company shall be no less than 75%, and such restrictions will only be lifted by China "within three years from the date of entry into force of this Agreement". In contrast, under the Phase One Agreement, China explicitly affirmed that "there are no restrictions on the ability of U.S.-owned insurance companies established in China to wholly own insurance asset management companies in China". As the Phase One Agreement was signed in January 2020 and the CAI is unlikely to come into effect before 2022 (see discussions on the ratification process below), this means that EU firms lag behind their American counterparts for at least 5 years in the ability to establish wholly-owned insurance asset management companies in China.

Another widely-publicized concession is disciplines on the behaviour of Chinese SOEs, where the CAI requires SOEs to "act in accordance with commercial considerations in their purchases or sales of goods or services" and accord to EU investors "treatment no less favourable" than they accord to Chinese investors.[27] Again this does not add much to China's commitment in its 20-year-old WTO Accession Working Party Report, which already requires China to "ensure that all state-owned and state-invested enterprises would make purchases and sales based solely on commercial considerations, e.g., price, quality, marketability and availability, and that the enterprises of other WTO Members would have an adequate opportunity to compete for sales to and purchases from these enterprises on non-discriminatory terms and conditions."[28] Moreover, the scope of the covered activities is further reduced by a footnote in the CAI section, which explicitly notes that the obligations on non-discriminatory treatment and commercial considerations "does not apply to situations of trade in goods and to supply of services other than through establishment of an enterprise and operation of a covered investment".[29] In other words, these two obligations only apply to sale or purchase transactions between Chinese SOEs and EU firms investing in China, but not to EU firms with no commercial presence in China.

As to disciplines on SOEs, the only thing new seems to be an expansive definition adopted by the CAI, which includes, in addition to firms where the government

[26] United States Trade Representative, Economic and Trade Agreement Between the Government of the United States of America and the Government of the People's Republic of China, https://ustr.gov/countries-regions/china-mongolia-taiwan/peoples-republic-china/phase-one-trade-agreement/text, Article 4.6: Insurance Services.

[27] EU-China Comprehensive Agreement on Investment (CAI), Article 3bis, Covered Entities.

[28] WTO, Report of the Working Party on the Accession of China, Ministerial Conference, Fourth Session, Doha, 9-13 November 2001, WT/MIN(01)/3, 10 November 2001, para. 46.

[29] EU-China Comprehensive Agreement on Investment (CAI), section II, fn. 8 to Article 3bis.

controls more than 50% ownership or voting rights, also those where the government has the power to appoint a majority of the board, control the decisions of the enterprise, legally direct the actions or otherwise exercise an equivalent level of control. However, even on this issue, one may well argue that, with the recent development of the jurisprudence on "public body" by the Appellate Body in *US – Countervailing Measures (China) (Article 21.5 – China)*,[30] such an expansive definition might no longer be necessary.

3 The Strategic Dimension

As we can see from the discussions in the preceding section, China's commitments on market access and regulatory issues are not as ambitious as the EU has broadcasted. Moreover, as most of China's concessions in the CAI schedules are made in the services sector, they would have to be made available to all other WTO Members on an MFN basis even if any concession is entirely new. This is because the Agreement, by covering mainly mode 3—commercial presence, cannot be justified as a services FTA under Article V of the GATS.

On the other hand, the EU's commitments are even more limited compared to China. This is confirmed by the news release by the Commission upon the publication of the market access commitments under the CAI, which noted that "[a]ny restrictions the EU or its Member States may have in place remain unaffected, as well as the policy space needed, for example, to enable the autonomous measures."[31]

So why then, did the EU and China still chose to forge ahead with the CAI despite the lack of major substantive benefits? In my view, the deal on the CAI must be understood in the broader context of geopolitical strategy, which permeates the whole life cycle of the CAI from the inception and negotiation, to its conclusion and ratification.

3.1 Inception

When people look back at international economic relations in the early twenty-first Century, 2013 has to be a watershed year. The year before, China overtook the US as

[30] Appellate Body Report, *United States – Countervailing Duty Measures on Certain Products from China*, Recourse to Article 21.5 of the DSU by China, WT/DS437/AB/RW and Add.1, adopted 15 August 2019.

[31] Commission publishes market access offers of the EU-China investment agreement, 12 March 2021, https://trade.ec.europa.eu/doclib/press/index.cfm?id=2253.

the world's biggest trading nation in goods.[32] In response, the US stepped up its efforts at "organizing trade relations with countries other than China so that China starts feeling more pressure about meeting basic international standards"[33] on two fronts. First, in the Asia Pacific region, the US continued to push to expand the membership of the TPP. In April 2013, the US finally brought into the TPP Japan, the world's third largest economy and the second largest economy among TPP members then.[34] Second, the US also reached out to the EU across the Atlantic, which led to the launch of the Transatlantic Trade and Investment Partnership (TTIP) negotiations in June 2013.[35]

China responded with its own initiatives. In July 2013, China agreed to drop its blanket restrictions on investment to relaunch the negotiations on the BIT with the US, which has not been making much progress despite being launched in 2008.[36] In September and October 2013, President Xi also announced the land-based Silk Road Economic Belt, which links China with Europe through Central and Western Asia, and the sea-based twenty-first Century Maritime Silk Road, which connects China with Southeast Asian countries, Africa, and Europe. Later combined as the Belt and Road Initiative (BRI), they would become a key pillar of China's foreign economic policy. In November 2013, China and the EU also announced at the EU-China Summit the launch negotiations for "an ambitious investment agreement", which later morphed into the CAI.[37] Together with the RCEP which was launched in November 2012, the BRI and CAI became key components in China's strategic toolbox against the US.

3.2 Negotiation

In January 2014, the first round of EU-China investment agreement was held. The initial progress was rather slow, and it took 2 years before the two sides reached

[32]China Overtakes US to Become Biggest Trading Nation, South China Morning Post of 12 February 2013, https://www.scmp.com/news/article/1148330/china-overtakes-us-become-biggest-trading-nation.

[33]Southeast Asian Nations Announce Trade Bloc to Rival U.S. Effort, New York Times of 21 November 2012.

[34]Statement by Acting U.S. Trade Representative Demetrios Marantis Regarding Japan and the Trans-Pacific Partnership, April 2013, https://ustr.gov/about-us/policy-offices/press-office/speeches/transcripts/2013/april/dep-nsa-froman-amb-marantis-cc-tpp.

[35]Remarks by President Obama, U.K. Prime Minister Cameron, European Commission President Barroso, and European Council President Van Rompuy on the Transatlantic Trade and Investment Partnership, 17 June 2013, https://obamawhitehouse.archives.gov/the-press-office/2013/06/17/remarks-president-obama-uk-prime-minister-cameron-european-commission-pr.

[36]U.S., China Agree to Restart Investment Treaty Talks, Reuters on 12 July 2013.

[37]Statement by President Barroso at the press conference of the EU-China Summit, SPEECH/13/959 of 21 November 2013.

agreement on the scope of the negotiations.[38] For the next two years the negotiations made some progress, but the pace was still rather slow. The negotiation could have languished like the ill-fated US-China BIT negotiation, but Trump's trade war brought a sense of urgency to both the EU and China.

On 22 March 2018, President Trump signed a Presidential Memorandum[39] directing the USTR to raise tariffs against Chinese products pursuant to the USTR's Section 301 Report into China's Acts, Policies, and Practices Related to Technology Transfer, Intellectual Property, and Innovation, which was issued on the same day.[40] The EU was not spared either, as the US announced additional duties on steel and aluminium imports from the EU in the same month, which finally took effect in June 2018,[41] one month before the imposition of 25% tariffs on Chinese products.

United against a common enemy, the EU and China accelerated the negotiations on their investment agreement, which resulted in the exchange of market access offers during the 20th EU-China Summit held in July 2018.[42] As the trade war raged on, the negotiations on the investment agreement also intensified. The 21st EU-China Summit in April 2019 set 2020 as the deadline for "the conclusion of an ambitious EU-China Comprehensive Investment Agreement",[43] which sent the talks into a frenzy. Starting from June 2020, 15 rounds of negotiations were held in a short span of one and half years. This more than doubles the pace of the negotiations in the preceding years, which only averaged four rounds a year.

3.3 Conclusion

As the agreement was nearing completion, geopolitical forces started to emerge again. Upon winning the US Presidential election, Joe Biden announced on 25 November 2020 that "America is back – we're at the head of the table

[38]EU and China agree on scope of the future investment deal, 15 January 2016, https://trade.ec.europa.eu/doclib/press/index.cfm?id=1435.

[39]Presidential Memorandum on the Actions by the United States Related to the Section 301 Investigation, 22 March 2018, https://www.whitehouse.gov/presidential-actions/presidential-memorandum-actions-united-states-related-section-301-investigation/.

[40]USTR, Findings of the Investigation into China's Acts, Policies, and Practices Related to Technology Transfer, Intellectual Property, and Innovation Under Section 301 of the Trade Act of 1974, 22 March 2018, https://ustr.gov/sites/default/files/Section%20301%20FINAL.PDF. For a detailed history of the trade war, see Gao (2021b).

[41]European Commission reacts to the US restrictions on steel and aluminium affecting the EU, IP/18/4006 of 31 May 2018.

[42]EU-China leaders' meeting: EU must do more to tackle legal breaches by Chinese companies in Europe, say civil society organisations, Bankwatch Network of 14 September 2020.

[43]Joint Statement of the 21st EU-China Summit, 10 April 2019, https://eeas.europa.eu/delegations/china_en/60836/Joint%20statement%20of%20the%2021st%20EU-China%20summit.

again".[44] The comment sparked anxiety in the EU as many Europeans interpreted this to imply a return to "the status quo ante of Brussels expected to play second-fiddle to Washington".[45] As if to make the message even more explicit, on 23 December 2020, Biden's pick for national security adviser Jake Sullivan retweeted[46] a Reuter's story[47] dated 18 December on the imminent conclusion of the EU-China investment deal with the comment that the new administration would "welcome early consultations with our European partners on our common concerns about China's economic practices".[48]

The EU, however, had different calculations. First, the EU was not the first to enter a bilateral deal with China. It was simply following the footsteps of the US, which signed the bilateral Phase One deal with China at the beginning of 2020. The EU is concerned that the purchase commitments under the Phase One deal would be fulfilled at the expense of EU exporters.[49] This is why EU trade commissioner Valdis Dombrovskis regarded the CAI as simply "levelling up" with the US which secured market access and level playing field commitments from China in the Phase One deal.[50] Second, the Phase One deal also taught the EU important lessons about China's negotiating style. With more than 100 sentences containing "China shall", and only 5 sentences containing "the United States shall" (including two sentences with "China and the United States shall"), the Phase One deal proves that China's resistance to one-sided deals may be overcome under certain circumstances. This is also demonstrated in the CAI, not only by the uneven concessions between the two sides, but also by the reports that China's request to access the EU's nuclear energy market[51] and insertion of a Huawei clause[52] were both rejected by the EU while the EU's demands on commitments on forced labour was accepted by China at the last minute.[53] Third, the EU was worried that, had it wait until the new Biden

[44]Biden's 'America is back' is good news for Germany, CNBC of 25 November 2020.

[45]EU-China Deal May Give Biden's Team More Options, Asia Times of 31 December 2020, https://asiatimes.com/2020/12/eu-china-deal-may-give-bidens-team-more-options/.

[46]See https://twitter.com/jakejsullivan/status/1341180109118726144?s=20.

[47]China, EU aim for investment pact by year-end, Germany says, Reuter of 18 December 2020.

[48]Biden Team Voices Concern over EU-China Investment Deal, Financial Times of 22 December 2020.

[49]EU trade commissioner Phil Hogan criticises US-China phase one trade deal, claims it is unlikely to boost competitiveness or jobs, South China Morning Post of 17 January 2020, https://www.scmp.com/news/world/europe/article/3046460/eu-review-us-china-deal-any-wto-challenge-says-trade-commissioner.

[50]EU and China Agree New Investment Treaty, Financial Times of 30 December 2020.

[51]Chinese demands on nuclear power investment complicate EU talks—WiWo, Reuters of 23 December 2020.

[52]China tried to punish European states for Huawei bans by adding eleventh-hour rule to EU investment deal, South China Morning Post of 8 January 2021, https://www.scmp.com/economy/china-economy/article/3116896/china-tried-punish-european-states-huawei-bans-adding.

[53]China's Last-Minute Pledge on Forced Labor Saved Investment Accord, EU Envoy Says, Caixin of 20 January 2021.

administration assumed office, it might not be able to conclude the deal with China. Instead, concluding the deal with China independently is regarded as a major step in achieving the EU's "strategic autonomy".[54] Moreover, the EU insisted that such autonomous action should not hinder the cross-Atlantic cooperation, just as the Phase One deal wouldn't.[55]

On the other hand, for China, signing a deal before the new Biden administration came into office also has at least three advantages. First, it prevents the new administration from being able to sabotage the deal, as they did not have official channels of communication with the EU before assuming office. Second, it also signals to the new Biden administration that China always has the option of turning to the EU, should the relationship with the US deteriorate further. Indeed, at least by judging from Biden's harsh comments against China on the campaign trail, it would be naïve for China to assume that the new administration would play nice with China. This is especially true when the reckoning under the Phase One deal is taken into account, as China was quite far behind in meeting the purchase targets under the agreement, meeting only less than 60% of the specified targets as of January 2021.[56] Third, a deal with the EU also helps to bolster China's international reputation, which has suffered major setbacks in 2020 due to the COVID-19 pandemic and China's aggressive style of diplomacy.[57]

Thus, on 30 December 2020, the EU and China concluded in principle the negotiations for the CAI, despite the complaints from the US.[58]

3.4 *Ratification*

So far, all the stars seem to have aligned perfectly to guide the CAI from inception to conclusion. However, the successful conclusion of the CAI might well mark the end of luck for the CAI. As per EU internal procedure, the text of the agreement shall first go through the necessary legal and technical review, before it is approved by the European Council and translated into all official languages.[59] Then it will be referred

---

[54] Europe wants 'strategic autonomy'—it just has to decide what that means, Politico of 15 October 2020, https://www.politico.eu/article/europe-trade-wants-strategic-autonomy-decide-what-means/.

[55] EU and China Agree New Investment Treaty, Financial Times of 30 December 2020.

[56] US-China Phase One Tracker: China's Purchases of US Goods, PIIE of 25 May 2021, https://www.piie.com/research/piie-charts/us-china-phase-one-tracker-chinas-purchases-us-goods.

[57] Unfavourable Views of China Reach Historic Highs in Many Countries, Pew Research Center of 6 October 2020, https://www.pewresearch.org/global/2020/10/06/unfavorable-views-of-china-reach-historic-highs-in-many-countries/.

[58] EU and China Reach Agreement in Principle on Investment, 30 December 2020, https://trade.ec.europa.eu/doclib/press/index.cfm?id=2233.

[59] Will the EU-China Investment Agreement Survive Parliament's Scrutiny?, The Diplomat of 27 January 2021, https://thediplomat.com/2021/01/will-the-eu-china-investment-agreement-survive-parliaments-scrutiny/.

to the European Parliament, which will decide with a majority vote within a year.[60] Unfortunately, the European Parliament is not really known for being friendly towards China. Instead, it has for years been criticising China over allegations ranging from human rights violations to economic aggression.[61] This is not really surprising because, as representatives of the people, the Members of the European Parliament regard as their main task voicing the concerns of their constituencies, rather than clinching major trade and investment deals like the Commission. Such an approach is clearly reflected in the in its December 2020 "Resolution on forced labor and the situation of the Uyghurs in the Xinjiang Uyghur Autonomous Region".[62] To make it worse, on 22 March 2021, China imposed sanctions on ten EU individuals, which included five Members of the European Parliament.[63] In protest, the European Parliament cancelled a meeting to review the CAI and the Chairman of the Parliament's Trade Committee reportedly said that "[t]here has to be a solution of these sanctions before we come back to ordinary business on this".[64]

Thus, before China lifts its sanctions on the five parliamentarians, the CAI will not even enter the ratification process. Even if this hurdle is cleared, the aftertaste of such a foul play would probably cast a shadow over the minds of many Members of the European Parliament. Trying to persuade 700+ parliamentarians will prove to be a much harder task than the dozens of officials in DG-trade, especially as these parliamentarians see their roles as much broader than the narrow confines of trade and investment interests.

4 Conclusion: Strategic Opportunity Meets Strategic Autonomy

In his report at the 16th National Congress of the China Communist Party (CCP) held in November 2002, then Chinese President and Party General Secretary Jiang Zemin presciently announced that "the first two decades of the 21st Century will be an important window of strategic opportunity that China must firmly grasp to make great achievements".[65] Such "strategic opportunity" was the result of China's accession to the WTO, but it did not really come quite effortlessly at that time.

[60] Ibid.

[61] Ibid.

[62] Texts Adopted on 17 December 2020, https://www.europarl.europa.eu/doceo/document/TA-9-2020-0375_EN.html.

[63] China hits back at EU with sanctions on 10 people, four entities over Xinjiang, Reuters of 22 March 2021.

[64] EU-China Deal Grinds into Reverse After Tit-for-Tat Sanctions, Reuters of 23 March 2021.

[65] 江泽民同志在党的十六大上所作报告全文，全面建设小康社会，开创中国特色社会主义事业新局面, 2002-11-18, https://www.fmprc.gov.cn/web/ziliao_674904/zyjh_674906/t10855.shtml.

When President George W. Bush came into office in January 2001, he vowed to be "tough and firm" on China and labelled China as a "strategic competitor".[66] In April of that year, the bilateral relationship reached new low when a US Navy spy plane collided with a Chinese fighter jet.[67] However, 9/11 created a unique opportunity that China quickly seized to turn the table in its favour. At 8:45 AM on 11 September 2001, an American Airlines plane was highjacked by terrorists and crashed into the north tower of the World Trade Centre Building in New York City.[68] Less than 20 minutes later, another plane crashed into the south tower.[69] At 9.30 AM, President Bush addressed the country and called this a "national tragedy" caused by "an apparent terrorist attack on our country".[70] Due to the time difference, it was night time in Beijing when the attacks happened. Upon watching the news on the attacks, President Jiang immediately called a meeting of the Politburo Standing Committee. At 1.47 AM Beijing time, or just 5 h after the first attack, President Jiang called President Bush to condemn the attacks and send condolences to American people.[71] On 18 October 2001, President Bush visited Shanghai in his first overseas trip since 9/11, where he met President Jiang and agreed that the US and China should develop "a constructive and cooperative relationship".[72] Such warm relationship in turn cleared the way for China's WTO accession at the WTO Ministerial Conference held in Doha, Qatar, the following month.

Ten days after meeting President Bush, President Jiang gave a speech to the Chinese military, in which he used Sino-US relationship as the example that China should actively "create advantageous strategic situation at the international level".[73] When he met the drafting group for the 16th Party Congress Report in January 2002, President Jiang first used the expression "the first two decades of the 21st Century will be an important window of strategic opportunity that China must firmly grasp to make great achievements", which was latterly duly copied into the Report.

Leveraging on the "window of strategic opportunity" brought by the WTO accession, China was able to grow its trade and economy exponentially and emerged the largest trader and second largest economy in the world. However, as the second

[66] Baum (2001), p. 192.

[67] U.S. Plane in China after it collidies with Chinese Jet, New York Times of 2 April 2001.

[68] National Transportation Safety Board, Flight Path Study—American Airlines Flight 11, 19 February 2002, https://nsarchive2.gwu.edu//NSAEBB/NSAEBB196/doc01.pdf.

[69] National Transportation Safety Board, Flight Path Study—United Airlines Flight 175, 19 February 2002, http://www.gwu.edu/~nsarchiv/NSAEBB/NSAEBB196/doc03.pdf.

[70] Remarks by the President After Two Planes Crash Into World Trade Center, 11 September 2001, https://georgewbush-whitehouse.archives.gov/news/releases/2001/09/20010911.html.

[71] 吴建民, 中国对"9·11事件"的快速反应,《中外书摘》2008年 第06期, https://www.xiaoshuo.online/zhongwaiwz/zwsz2008/zwsz20080614-1.html.

[72] President George W. Bush and President Jiang Zemin, U.S., China Stand Against Terrorism, Remarks During Press Availability, 19 October 2001, https://2001-2009.state.gov/s/ct/rls/rm/2001/5461.htm.

[73] 营造有利战略态势，增强国家战略能力，二○○一年十月三十一日，江泽民文选，第三卷，352–353.

decade was drawing to a close, it seems that the window of opportunity was closing fast as evidenced by the refusal by the major Western countries to recognize China's market economy status, and the subsequent trade war launched by the US against China. Reflecting on the issue in his Report at the 19th Party Congress in 2017, President Xi made the political judgment that "while there are deep and complex changes both domestically and internationally, China's development is still in an important window of strategic opportunity".[74] The 5th Plenum of the 19th Party Congress held in October 2020 repeated this by stating that "for now and the period afterwards, China's development is still in an important window of strategic opportunity, but there are new developments and changes in both the opportunities and challenges".[75] The same language was also copied into the CCP Central Committee's Recommendations on Making the 14th Five-year Plan and the 2035 Vision which was adopted on the same day, which recommends that China shall "actively seek change" and try to "promote international cooperation by taking advantage of China's huge market".[76]

On the other hand, the EU was also moving towards its own "strategic autonomy". The concept started as an idea of the French, when they published their 1994 white paper on defence.[77] Gradually, however, it was accepted by all of the big three EU member states: Germany, France and Italy.[78] The concept was adopted by the EU in 2016 when it unveiled its Global Strategy, which was supposed to "nurtures the ambition of strategic autonomy" for the EU.[79] With Trump's election as US president and Brexit, the concept started to take off among the governments of EU member states.[80] While there was some ambiguity on the exact content of the concept, the bigger EU member states typically perceive it as referring to decision-making autonomy.[81] This is recently confirmed by the new trade strategy paper issued in February 2001, where the EU further refined it as a concept of "open strategic autonomy" which emphasises "the EU's ability to make its own choices

---

[74] 决胜全面建成小康社会，夺取新时代中国特色社会主义伟大胜利-在中国共产党第十九次全国代表大会上的报告，(2017年10月18日)，http://www.gov.cn/zhuanti/2017-10/27/content_5234876.htm.

[75] 中国共产党第十九届中央委员会第五次全体会议公报，(2020年10月29日中国共产党第十九届中央委员会第五次全体会议通过)，http://www.12371.cn/2020/10/29/ARTI1603964233795881.shtml.

[76] 中共中央关于制定国民经济和社会发展第十四个五年规划和二○三五年远景目标的建议，(2020年10月29日中国共产党第十九届中央委员会第五次全体会议通过)，http://www.12371.cn/2020/11/03/ARTI1604398127413120.shtml.

[77] Livre Blanc Sur La défense Et La sécurité Nationale, http://www.livreblancdefenseetsecurite.gouv.fr/pdf/le-livre-blanc-sur-la-defense-1994.pdf.

[78] Franke and Varma (2019), p. 6.

[79] Shared Vision, Common Action: A Stronger Europe. A Global Strategy for the European Union's Foreign And Security Policy, https://eeas.europa.eu/archives/docs/top_stories/pdf/eugs_review_web.pdf.

[80] Franke and Varma (2019), p. 7.

[81] Franke and Varma (2019), pp. 10–11.

and shape the world around it through leadership and engagement, reflecting its strategic interests and values”.[82]

Against such background, we can see that the CAI is what you get when China’s “strategic opportunity” meets with EU’s “strategic autonomy”. This seems to be the official views of both the EU and China as well. For example, the EU’s new trade strategy paper explicitly recognizes the CAI as part of the efforts of “open strategic autonomy” with “a combination of active engagement, both at bilateral and multilateral level, and of parallel development and implementation of autonomous instruments necessary to protect the EU’s essential interests and values—in full compliance with its international commitments”.[83] When President Xi Jinping talked to German Chancellor Merkel on 7 April 2021, he emphasized that “China-Europe relations are facing new development opportunities and various challenges. The key is to firmly grasp the general direction and main tone of the development of China-Europe relations from a strategic height, have mutual respect and dispel distractions. China’s development is an opportunity for the EU, and we hope that the EU will make a correct judgment independently and truly achieve strategic autonomy.”[84] The same message was also repeated at the virtual summit between Xi and Merkel and French President Emmanuel Macron held later that month.[85]

In conclusion, it was the conflation of strategic considerations that gave birth to the CAI, but this, paradoxically, also means that the CAI comes with unique birth defects. When the geopolitical forces shift, as we have seen over the past few months, the fate of this major investment deal might also be cast in doubt, especially as it is now entering the most political part of the process—ratification by the European Parliament. To make the ratification happen, the Parties should be trying to insulate it from geopolitical tensions, rather than further entangling it in geopolitical and strategic considerations.

References

Baum R (2001) From ‘strategic partners’ to ‘strategic competitors’: George W. Bush and the politics of U.S. China policy. J East Asian Stud 1(2):191–220

Franke U, Varma T (2019) Independence Play: Europe’s Pursuit of Strategic Autonomy. European Council on Foreign Relations, July 2019., https://ecfr.eu/wp-content/uploads/Independence-play-Europes-pursuit-of-strategic-autonomy.pdf

[82]European Commission, Trade Policy Review—An Open, Sustainable and Assertive Trade Policy, COM(2021) 66 final of 18 February 2021, p. 4.

[83]European Commission, Trade Policy Review—An Open, Sustainable and Assertive Trade Policy, COM(2021) 66 final of 18 February 2021, p. 9.

[84]习近平同德国总理默克尔通电话，http://www.xinhuanet.com/politics/leaders/2021-04/07/c_1127304170.htm.

[85]习近平同法国德国领导人举行视频峰会，http://www.xinhuanet.com/politics/leaders/2021-04/16/c_1127339605.htm.

Gao H (2008) Reference Paper on basic telecommunications. In: Wolfrum R, Stoll PT, Feinäugle C (eds) Max Planck commentaries on world trade law, WTO – trade in services, vol 6. Martinus Nijhoff, Leiden/Boston, pp 718–747

Gao H (2021a) Across the Great Wall: E-commerce joint statement initiative negotiation and China. In: Peng S, Lin C-F, Streinz T (eds) Artificial intelligence and international economic law: disruption, regulation, and reconfiguration. Cambridge University Press, Cambridge, pp 295–318

Gao H (2021b) WTO reform and China: defining or defiling the multilateral trading system? Harv Int Law J. 1–39.

Kong Q (2017) Emerging rules in international investment instruments and China's reform of state-owned enterprises. Chinese J Global Gov 3(1):57–82

Wang L, Gallagher N (2016) Introduction to the special focus issue on state-owned enterprises. ICSID Rev 31(1):1–4

Commonalities and Differences in Investment Policies and Treaty Practices: A Comparative Study of China and Japan

Shintaro Hamanaka and Manjiao Chi

Contents

Abstract This paper examines commonalities and difference between China and Japan with regard to investment policy and treaty practices. Despite that the two countries achieve economic development in very different external environment, their investment policies fundamentally share more commonalities than differences. Both used investment policy as a core component of industrial policies and regarded

---

Special thanks are due to Ms. Huanjia Yao, LLM Candidate of UIBE Law, for her helpful research assistance.

S. Hamanaka
Institute of Developing Economies, Japan External Trade Organization (IDE-JETRO), Tokyo, Japan
e-mail: Shintaro_Hamanaka@ide.go.jp

M. Chi (✉)
Center for International Economic Law and Policy (CIELP), University of International Business and Economics (UIBE), Beijing, China
e-mail: chimanjiao@uibe.edu.cn

M. Chi et al. (eds.), *Asian Yearbook of International Economic Law 2022*,
Asian Yearbook of International Economic Law (2022) 2022: 71–88,
https://doi.org/10.1007/16517_2021_2, Published online: 9 December 2021

investment critically important as a source of technology, in addition to capital. For both China and Japan, the fundamental goal was to build-up their own national industries for self-reliance, and maintenance of policy space for industrial polices was critically important. However, although Japan was able to rely on the World Bank loans as the source of capital, while securing technology transfer between foreign and domestic private sectors arranged by the Japanese government, China had a greater need for inward investment for development, and has signed a large number of IIAs that may restrict policy space.

1 Introduction

Many scholars and policy makers would agree that one of the most critical factors that determine the future course of regional cooperation and integration in Asia is the relation between China and Japan. Just like the relation between Germany and France has been the cornerstone of European cooperation and integration, whether the two gigantic economies in Asia can cooperate in a constructive and substantial manner has huge implications to regional cooperation in Asia. The rising China would be able to lead regional cooperation in Asia even without the participation of Japan, but other countries may feel more comfortable and more positively engage in regional cooperation, when the two countries share co-leadership to a degree. Strong China-Japan partnership can be said to be the prerequisite for the Asian solidarity.

There is no doubt that geo-political rivalry exists between China and Japan, however. This certainly makes the tension between the two countries high in areas that have relatively large security implications such as cooperation in outer space. However, this does not necessarily mean that all types of economic cooperation involving the two becomes impossible. Whether the two countries can actually deepen cooperation largely depends on issue areas. There might be a relatively large room for cooperation in, for example, environmental issues where the both parties are likely to be better-off. But at the same time, just like the case of finance, there is an issue area where cooperation becomes very difficult despite potentials; China recently established Asian Infrastructure Investment Bank (AIIB), but Japan decided not to join.[1]

What about "trade" cooperation? While trade cooperation in the past mainly deals with trade liberalization, recent trade negotiations cover extra-trade issues such as investment, services and intellectual property. In other words, recent trade negotiation has shifted its focus from tariff reduction to so-called "rule-making".[2] So, one of the essential questions that we should consider is whether China and Japan can agree upon international rules applicable to commerce in Asia and beyond. While

[1]Hamanaka (2016).

[2]Hamanaka (2019).

Regional Comprehensive Economics Partnership (RCEP) was signed by the fifteen regional countries including both China and Japan in December 2020, this should be regarded as a first important step into deeper integration in Asia, rather than the goal of long-lasting negotiations. This is because many important rule-related issues are still pending under RCEP, subject to future negotiations. For example, in the field of investment, whether or not to introduce investor-state dispute (ISDS) in RCEP is a future built-in agenda, which should be re-negotiated within 2 years after the enforcement of RCEP. So as the application of dispute settlement provisions to e-commerce chapter, to be discussed in 2 year time.

Among various rule-making issues covered by recent trade agreements, this section look into investment in details. Despite the rapid increase in international investment flows and number of investment treaties in the world as well as in Asia, investment rule-making and investment treaty practices are under-studied.[3] We believe investment deserves close analysis given its critical role in developing national economies. While trade comes and goes, investment stays. Therefore, policymakers should strike delicate balances on several fronts, including the balance between public and private fixed capital formation, and that between domestic and foreign investment accumulations. How to deal with foreign investment and technologies attached to it is the most critical economic and developmental policies for many developing countries. It is not an exaggeration if one argues that nations' "philosophical" differences regarding the economic and social development are best showcased in investment policies and investment treaty practices.

One may think that China and Japan have employed totally different approaches to investment governance. This may well be true because China has been a developing country that has relied on inward investment conducted by multi-nationals while Japan has been a developed country that has heavily invested overseas. And in fact, during RCEP negotiations, Japan insisted upon the inclusion of the ISDS clause while China was against to it. However, going beyond specific positions regarding particular investment clauses, whether and to what degree the two countries share the developmental philosophy is a critical but poorly explored question so far. To be more specific, between the two countries one may find more common grounds than differences regarding the role of public policies and market mechanisms upon achieving the best-mix of the foreign and domestic capitals for the national development. In fact, it seems the two countries more or less shared the same ultimate goal: developing Japan in the 1960s and developing China in the 1980s clearly envisioned that they should eventually catch up other developed countries by building-up a full set of own industries by employing various types of industrial policies.

This chapter is structured as follows. The next section reviews investment policies and investment treaty practices of China. Then we will conduct comparable analysis for Japan. Section 4 will first point out important commonalities between China and Japan in terms of investment policies and investment treaty practices.

[3] Chaisse and Hamanaka (2014).

Then, we will discuss two important differences between the two countries with some explanations why such differences exist. The bottom line is that there are more commonalities between the two if we analyze investment from development philosophical perspectives. The final section concludes.

2 China's Investment Policy and Treaty Practices

2.1 Review of China's Investment Policy

China has adopted a nationalistic investment policy over the past years. China's policies have a clear stress of serving the national economic development, and have undergone substantive changes over the past decades, with the development of China's situation. For almost three decades since the establishment of the PRC, China had been isolated by the international community and adopted a closed-door policy. During this period, bout inbound and outbound investments were minimal. This situation has changed since the end of the 1970s, when China started economic form and adopted an open-door policy. There emerged a pressing need for China to change its policies and enact laws to attract foreign investment to help boost its national economy.

Since China's opening up to the 1990s, a number of national laws have been adopted aiming at facilitating and attracting foreign direct investment to China. Three milestone laws have been made during this period, namely the Law of the People's Republic of China on Sino-Foreign Equity Joint Ventures (1979), the Law of the People's Republic of China on Foreign Invested Enterprises (1986), and the Law of the People's Republic of China on Sino-Foreign Contractual Joint Ventures (1988). These three laws are often called as "the three foreign investment laws of China", which has provided the legal framework for China's foreign investment governance for over three decades. China has also adopted many regulations and rules for the purpose of implementing these laws. The main purpose of these laws was to create a friendly legal environment to help attract foreign investment to China. As a result, a number of joint ventures have been set up in China, especially in developed regions. According, China has already become a major destination of foreign investment at the global level since the latter half of the 1990s. The three laws have recently been invalidated since the adoption of the Foreign Investment Law in 2020.

The accession to the World Trade Organization (WTO) in 2001 marks a milestone of the development of China's investment law. In order to comply with its WTO obligations, China took efforts to abolish and amend a large number of national laws and regulations, many of which are concerned with FDI governance.[4]

[4]See China's State Council Information Office, White Paper: China and the World Trade Organization, http://www.china.org.cn/chinese/2018-07/12/content_56233567.htm. See also Protocol on

Particularly, China has abolished the relevant laws and rules on performance requirement, local contents and foreign exchange balance, which are incompliant with the TRIPS agreement.[5] Since its WTO accession, China has gradually become the second biggest destination of foreign investment in the world, next only to the United States.[6]

When China and the U.S. resumed negotiations of a bilateral investment treaty (BIT) in 2008, market access was a major issue on the negotiation agenda. The two countries agreed to negotiate the BIT on the basis of 'negative list', i.e. granting national treatment to foreign investment in pre-establishment stage while subject to a 'negative list'. This approach is a substantial deviation of China's traditional approval system with regard to market access of foreign investment, and symbols a bold step towards opening up of its domestic market. To prepare for the negotiation and possible conclusion of this historical BIT, China has established a number of pilot free trade zones (FTZs) since 2013. A main purpose of the FTZs is for foreign investment regulation on basis of the 'negative list' issued by the FTZs. Since 2016, China has adopted a national 'negative list', meaning that the 'negative list' approach has been nationally implemented. According to some statistics, this approach has helped China in attracting more foreign investment.[7]

It should also be noted that, with its economic growth, China's outbound investment has also increased. In this regard, two major developments should be mentioned, namely, the 'Going Abroad Strategy' (GAS) and the Belt and Road Initiative (BRI). The GAS was adopted in the latter half of the 1990s, aiming primarily at encouraging Chinese enterprise, especially state-owned enterprises to invest abroad.[8] More recently, starting from 2013, China has implemented the Belt and Road Initiative (BRI). While the BRI is not a formal international arrangement, it mainly aims at promoting China's overseas influence in global economic governance, with promoting outbound investment as a key aspect. The implementation of the BRI has caused broad concerns on various grounds, but it seems undisputed that the BRI has played a major role in shaping China's outbound investment governance regime. In this sense, the BRI could also be deemed as a foreign investment policy.

Finally, it should be noted that China's investment policies have never been static. Rather, they are in constant change. Especially, in recent few years, given that the markets and investment policies in the U.S. and Europe have undergone profound changes, and that China's economic development has slowed down, China's

---

the Accession of the People's Republic of China, https://docs.wto.org/dol2fe/Pages/SS/directdoc.aspx?filename=q:/WT/L/432.pdf&Open=True.

[5] Chenggang (2019).

[6] UNCTAD (2021).

[7] See Ministry of Commerce of the People's Republic of China, 2019 Report on Foreign Investment in China, http://images.mofcom.gov.cn/wzs/202008/20200819101923422.pdf (original in Chinese).

[8] China Council for the Promotion of International Trade, An Analysis of The Formation and Supporting Policy System of the Going Abroad Strategy, http://oldwww.ccpit.org/Contents/Channel_1276/2007/0327/30814/content_30814.htm (original in Chinese).

investment policies are likely to be further changed to be fit for the changing political and economic situations both abroad and at home.

2.2 *Review of China's Investment Treaty Practices*

China's BIT-making efforts started since its economic reform and opening up in late 1970s. To a large extent, China's BIT-making has been profoundly influenced by the development of its investment policies. Up to the present, China has concluded over 130 BITs. These BITs could be roughly categorized into three generations.

BITs concluded during the 1980s and the latter half of the 1990s are often deemed as China's first generation BITs. The major purpose of concluding BITs is to help create an investment-friendly environment in order, so that China could be deemed as a destination attractive to foreign investment. Most of China's early BITs are concluded with developed countries that were China's major investment exporting countries, especially European countries. Indeed, China's first BIT was concluded with Sweden in 1981. Almost half of China's existing BITs are first generation BITs. These BITs often do not include national treatment clause and are only equipped with a narrowly designed ISDS clause, only allowing "disputes relating to the amount of compensation for expropriation" to be submitted to international arbitration. Many of these BITs have expired and renegotiated. Some of these BITs, especially those with European countries have been renegotiated. However, few of these renegotiated BITs have been updated to second generation BITs. Interestingly, almost all investment arbitration cases involving China or Chinese investors rely on first-generation BITs.

Since the adoption of the GAS and with the increase of China's outbound investment, China's BIT-making strategy has also changed. BITs concluded since this point of time to around 2010 are generally known as the second generation BITs. Many of these BITs are concluded with Asia and American countries. A distinct feature of such BITs is that protection of Chinese overseas investment and investors has become a priority of China's BITs, in addition to protection of foreign investment in China. Accordingly, national treatment clause and broadly construed ISDS clauses have become frequently seen in these BITs. Especially the ISDS clauses of these BITs generally allow any dispute relating to an investment to be submitted to international arbitration, which has caused heated debate among Chinese scholars. Interestingly, however, the number of ISDS arbitrations based on the second (and third) generation BITs is smaller than that of the first generation.[9]

The third generation BITs of China are limited in number, which were concluded since the 2010s. While these BITs do not have substantive difference with the second

[9]In some cases, investors can only rely on 1st generation BITs as they are the only BITs. In a few cases, such as in case where a Korean investor sued China, investors chose to invoke first generation BIT, as it seems these BITs have clear ISDS clauses are simpler than 2nd and 3rd generation BITs.

generation BITs with regard to ISDS and national treatment clauses, they try to be more 'balanced' with regard to the protection of foreign investment and the public interest of states.[10] While the third generation BITs largely adopted the model of the second generation BITs, a major feature of these BITs lies in their incorporation of 'social clauses' and exception clauses. The purpose of these clauses is to grant host states more policy freedom in taking regulatory measures for public interest purposes. A typical example of such BITs is the China-Canada BIT concluded in 2012.

It is worth mentioning that China and the European Union (EU) have agreed in principle a comprehensive agreement on investment (CAI) in December 2020, after seven years of intense negotiations. While at the writing time, the EU has decided to suspend the efforts leading to the possible ratification of the CAI as a response to China's sanctions on some EU citizens and entities,[11] the CAI is deemed as a high-level and unusual investment agreement China has ever concluded. Notably, the CAI include provisions and sections on certain highly contentious issues that have been rarely addressed in China's existing IIAs, such as market access to certain service industries, sustainable development and domestic regulation of investment.[12] If ratified, the CAI could be a milestone investment agreement for China and implies a new generation of Chinese IIA.

Two extra aspects should be noted. First, China's efforts of negotiating a BIT with the U.S. failed. Yet, it is of interest to note that this BIT could have been the first Chinese BIT that deals with the sensitive and important issue of market access of foreign investment. Currently China and the EU are negotiating an investment agreement, which is also likely to incorporate market access commitments. If the agreement is concluded, it is likely to have profound impacts on China's foreign investment governance. Second, aside from BIT-making, it should also be noted that most of the free trade agreements (FTAs) of China also contain an investment chapter, which are different forms. These chapters could play a similar role of a BIT. Since the 2010s, China's BIT-making pace has been slowed down, while efforts for FTA-making has been intensified.

3 Japan's Investment Policy and Treaty Practices

3.1 Review of Japan's Investment Policy

The two laws that had guided investment policies of postwar Japan, namely the Foreign Exchange and Foreign Trade Control Law (Foreign Exchange Law) and the

[10] See Berger (2013).

[11] Euronews of 19 May 2021, EU Suspends Efforts to Ratify Controversial Investment Deal with China, https://www.euronews.com/2021/05/04/eu-suspends-efforts-to-ratify-controversial-investment-deal-with-china.

[12] See Berger and Chi (2021).

Foreign Capital Law came into force in 1949 and 1950 respectively. Aiming at the secured balance of payment environment favorable to the economic reconstruction, the Foreign Exchange Law regulated international trade and international investment outflow. Meanwhile, investment inflow was covered by the Foreign Capital Law. Under this law, investment inflow was generally not allowed. Only investment conducted by foreign firms with useful technologies, which was expected to have good impact on the external balance and economic development of Japan was admitted and protected, with the joint venture requirement (the Japanese side should hold the majority share), with good examples being RCA (Radio Cooperation of America), IBM[13], GE, and Philips, among others. Alternatively, commercial presence that does not remit the profit to the home country can be established outside the Foreign Capital Law (so-called "yen-based companies"). While the General Headquarters (GHQ) expected that capital and investment restrictions imposed basing on the two laws would be relaxed as the Japanese economy recovers, in reality, the Japanese government continued to use them as a policy tool until the 1980s.

While Japan restricted capital inflows, it did not face a serious shortage of foreign reserves. This is partly because whenever the Japanese economy rapidly expanded and its imports sharply increased, the central bank increased the interest rate to slow down the economy to maintain the minimum level of foreign reserves. Another critical reason was that Japan was able to rely on the loan from the World Bank. Huge infrastructure projects such as *Shinkansen* (bullet trains) and electricity power plants were financed by the World Bank with a relatively low interest rate.[14] This is one of the reasons why there was no need for Japan to attract FDI by signing BITs with European countries or the United State.

The Japanese economy rapidly grew in the 1960s. In 1961, the Ikeda Administration launched the plan to double the national income of Japan within 10 years, which was actually achieved ahead of the plan. In 1964, when Tokyo hosted the Olympic Games, Japan became the member of Organisation for Economic Co-operation and Development (OECD). Because OECD requests its members not to impose restrictions on capital and investment flows, the fellow OECD members, the US in particular, put pressures on Japan to deregulate capital and investment restrictions. Meanwhile, the Japanese economy fully recovered by the mid-1960s. Japan established the Asian Development Bank (ADB), Japan-sponsored multilateral development bank, in 1966, and became the second largest economy in the world, overtaking West Germany in 1968.

Thanks to the economic recovery and pressures from OECD, Japan started to relax restrictions on investment flows after the late 1960s. First, restrictions on

[13]Because IBM Japan, fully owned by IBM World Trade Cooperation, was established in 1949, before the launch of the Foreign Capital Law, it was unable to remit the profit to the US. There were negotiations between the mid 1950s and early 1960s to incorporate IBM Japan under the Foreign Capital Law and to determine the details of technology transfer between IBM and other Japanese electronics companies.

[14]The list of Japanese infrastructure projects financed by the World Bank loan can be found at: https://www.worldbank.org/en/country/japan/brief/world-banks-loans-to-japan.

inward investment was gradually relaxed. In 1967, foreign ownership below 50% was allowed in the 33 sectors, while full foreign ownership was allowed in 17 sectors. In 1969, foreign ownership below 50% was allowed in the 160 sectors, while full foreign ownership was allowed in 44 sectors. In 1970, foreign ownership below 50% was allowed in the 33 sectors, while full foreign ownership was allowed in 17 sectors. In 1971, the negative list approach was introduced for the sectors that have foreign ownership restriction below 50%. In 1973, inward investment into Japan was fully liberalized with the exception of five sectors (agriculture, mining, oil, leather and retail sectors[15]). The Foreign Capital Law was eventually abolished in 1980. Second, restrictions on outward investment was also relaxed. The government started to liberalize outward investment in 1969 and in principle, outward investment was fully liberalized in 1972. Meanwhile, the Foreign Exchange Law was revised in 1979. Under the revised law, no permission was required for outward investment from Japan; prior notification suffices.

However, this did not mean that there was no barrier on inward investment. Japanese bureaucrats made desperate effort to continue to oversee national economic development.[16] As widely pointed out, there were structural barriers on investment flows, which are particularly persistent in Japan. Those structural barriers include: cross-holdings of stock held by group companies called *keiretsu* relationship, weak enforcement of antimonopoly law, unique and complex distribution system, among others.[17] Arguably, the Japanese government took advantage of those structural barriers to avoid the surge in inward investment and to protect Japanese industries. For example, Large Retail Store Law, under which a prospective owner of a large retail store must obtain approval from a council for the area in which the store to be located, was only abolished in 2000.

During the majority of postwar Japanese history, Japanese policymakers regarded export and outward investment as critical for the development of the Japanese economy, and little emphasis was placed on inward investment. It was only in 2003 when the government set the target of inward investment flow. In 2011, the Program for Promoting Japan as an Asian Business Center and Direct Investment into Japan was approved. In 2013, the Cabinet approved the Action Plan of the Growth Strategy, in which the target of inward investment was set at 3.5 trillion yen by 2020. The Japan External Trade Organization (JETRO) published the first volume of JETRO Investment Japan Report in 2015. Interestingly enough, the promotion of inward investment seems to be in line with the promotion of inbound travelers.[18] Only after recognizing that its economy started to shrink, Japan started to rely on external human and financial resources.

Japan's outward investment increased after the Plaza Accord in 1985. Since then, outward investment is constantly higher than its inward investment and the gap

[15]The retail sector was fully liberalized in 1975.

[16]Pempel (1998).

[17]Lawrence (1993).

[18]In 2003, the Japan Tourism Action Plan was approved by the inter-ministry meeting.

between the two has been growing. Outward investment marked particularly a sharp increase in the last decade. In contrast, inward investment flow into Japan has been stagnant. While there was an increasing trend before 2008, such collapsed during the global financial crisis. Only after 2015, inward investment started to mark a steady growth.

3.2 *Review of Japan's Investment Treaty Practices*

Until the end of the 1990s, Japan signed only 8 BITs (first generation BITs).[19] This is surprisingly a small number, given that there were already 1941 BITs worldwide by 1999. The majority of the then BIT partners of Japan were small economies with relatively insignificant economic implications to Japan, with a notable exception of China. During this period, no Southeast Asian countries, which were already an important investment destination for Japanese MNCs, signed BIT with Japan. It was usually the partner side that requested the signing of BIT with Japan, with an expectation that such would bring Japanese investment into their domestic markets. BITs signed by Japan during this period covered both pre-establishment and post-establishment MFN. However, with regard to NT, only post-establishment is covered. ISDS is also covered by the first generation BITs. Among them, Japan-China BIT (1988) is exceptional because even the scope of post-establishment NT is limited[20] and the scope of ISDS is significantly narrow.[21] Because Japan did not have the Model BIT, it was flexible enough to tailor the treaty receptive to partners' needs. In general, the prohibition of performance requirement is not covered by the first generation BITs or the scope of prohibited measures is very limited.

One of reasons why Japan was not keen to sign BITs in the 1990s was that Japan prioritized multilateral approach to international investment governance over bilateralism.[22] There were two multilateral fora where investment was discussed. First, at the OECD ministerial meeting in 1995, the launch of negotiation for Multilateral Agreement on Investment (MAI) was agreed. The MAI was expected to cover not only post-establishment but also pre-establishment. Once signed, non-OECD members were also expected to join MAI. Japan was a strong proponent of MAI at both policy and industry levels. However, in December 1998, the decision was made to terminate the negotiations for MAI. Second, at the first WTO ministerial meeting in Singapore in December 1996, ministers agreed to establish working group on trade and investment. The concerned parties agreed at the working group that not

[19] Those Japanese BITs include: Egypt (1977), Sri Lanka (1982), China (1988), Turkey (1992), Hong Kong (1997), Pakistan (1998), Bangladesh (1998) and Russia (1998).

[20] Policies inconsistent with NT can be introduced, provided they aim at the maintenance of public order, national security and sound development of national economy.

[21] The scope of ISDS is limited to the amount of compensation.

[22] Hamanaka (2017).

negotiations but some preparatory works to be conducted, which should be reported to General Council before the end of 1998. No substantial progress was made at the second WTO ministerial meeting in Geneva in May 1998, and the momentum of dealing with investment at WTO was lost.

After recognizing the stagnant progress of the discussion on investment at both OECD and WTO, Japan started to engage in bilateral negotiation on investment, as a substitute to MAI. In November 1998, Japan agreed to start the negotiation for BIT with Korea. This is earlier than the launch of negotiations of Japan-Singapore EPA for more than 1 year, which implies that the bilateralism of Japan's economic diplomacy started with investment, rather than trade.[23] Signed in 2002, Japan-Korea BIT is the first BIT that belong to the second generation of Japanese BITs. After this, Japan signed a large number of BITs and EPAs with investment chapter (hereafter, International Investment Agreements: IIAs), that belong to the second generation.[24]

The Japanese IIAs that belong to its second generation cover both post-establishment and pre-establishment (for both MFN and NT). However, the MFN provision of some BITs includes exceptions for EPAs/FTAs. The second generation IIAs have two important features. First, because IIAs covers both post-establishment and pre-establishment, the scope of ISDS becomes substantial. Second, the second generation IIAs includes provisions that prohibit the performance requirement encompassing wide range of issues. In principle, those two points hold true for the majority of the second generation Japanese IIAs. In this context, however, two mega IIAs that Japan signed in the late 2010s are noteworthy. First, TPP that was originally based on the US negotiation template does not have substantial coverage on the prohibition of performance requirements, unlike other Japanese IIAs.[25] Second, Japan EU EPA does not have ISDS clauses. Those anecdotes imply that Japan continues to be flexible in negotiating IIAs, without the Model BIT.

4 Commonalities Between China and Japan

4.1 Investment Policy Rather Than Trade Policy

Obviously, both investment and trade policy are the two wheels of external economic policy. However, it seems that investment policy plays the central role in developing national economies of the two countries. This is mainly because investment policy regards how to best mix domestic and foreign capital and technology,

[23] The launch of Japan-Singapore EPA in December 1999 was a reaction to the failed WTO ministerial meeting in Seattle in November 1999.

[24] As of 2020, Japan has around 50 IIAs signed in total.

[25] There items regarding the prohibition of performance requirements not covered by TPP are: location of regional/global headquarters; employment of nationals; research and development.

while trade policy is basically on the conditions for fair competition between domestic and foreign products (the level playing field or not). In other words, the two countries took proactive industrial policies by providing both incentives and disincentives to certain types of investment.

Soon after the WWII, the Japanese import was quite limited because of the shortage of foreign currencies, with the high tariff policy being a secondary policy tool. The room to use tariffs for economic policy tool was further diminished after the 1960s because GATT members' tariffs was cut by around 35% for industrial products, during the Kennedy round. As a result, industrial policy often takes the form of investment policy, where the government decide to which industry the scare capitals to be allocated (both domestic and foreign funds). Investment was also a primary area of Japan's economic diplomacy. Japan was a strong proponent of MAI negotiation conducted at OECD in the 1990s, and the inclusion of investment into the WTO framework. Once those initiatives failed, Japan started to pursue bilateralism, but this started with the investment field, rather than trade.[26]

To a large extent, since its adoption of the opening up policy and economic reform by the end of 1970s, China's economic development has heavily relied on FDI inflow in the past decades, especially before China's accession to the World Trade Organization (WTO) in 2001.[27] Concurrent to its reform process, China has initiated law- and policy-making efforts aiming at attracting FDI. The adoption of the three national FDI laws, namely the Law of Sino-Foreign Equity Joint Ventures (EJVL) of 1979, and the Law of Foreign-Invested Enterprises (FIEL) of 1986, and the Law of Sino-Foreign Cooperative Joint Ventures (CJVL) of 1988, is a clear manifesto of China's such efforts. Upon its WTO accession, China's tariff level was significantly lowered, and this made the room for China to conduct proactive tariff policy diminished. As a result, investment policies continued to be the core of industrial policies.

By the end of the 1990s, China has adopted the "Going Abroad strategy", encouraging Chinese enterprises to invest abroad.[28] Since the implementation of this strategy, China's outward investment has witnessed a rapid increase.[29] More recently, since the 2010s, China has proposed the Belt and Road Initiative (BRI), trying to promote economic connectivity among the many countries in Asia, Africa and Europe, along the ancient Silk Road and Maritime Silk Road.[30] China has taken necessary law-making efforts to facilitate BRI implementation. A key aspect of BRI

[26]Japan started to negotiate BIT with Korea, which was before the launch of its first FTA or EPA, namely Japan-Singapore EPA. For details see Sect. 3.2.

[27]The World Bank (2010).

[28]China Council for the Promotion of International Trade, An Analysis of The Formation and Supporting Policy System of the Going Abroad Strategy, http://oldwww.ccpit.org/Contents/Channel_1276/2007/0327/30814/content_30814.htm (original in Chinese).

[29]See OECD, Outward FDI Flows of China, https://data.oecd.org/fdi/fdi-flows.htm.

[30]The State Council of the People's Republic of China, Action plan on the Belt and Road Initiative, http://english.www.gov.cn/archive/publications/2015/03/30/content_281475080249035.htm.

implementation is promoting Chinese investment in BRI countries.[31] The adoption of the historical Foreign Investment Law (FIL) in 2019 is a notable development, which not only lays down some key rules in China's FDI regulation, but also abolishes the three major national FDI laws.[32]

4.2 Policy Space Rather Than Investment Protection

All states do not want to be bound by BITs to keep its policy space and at the same time want the partners to be bound by BITs to reduce their policy space so that their private sectors' investment in the partner's territory can be better protected. However, because BITs equally bind contracting parties, taking such a "convenient" or "selfish" position is no longer possible. If a state wants the partner to be bound by BIT, it should agree to be bound. Then, the ultimate question that states need to consider is the priority between the policy space for government policies and the protection of investment conducted abroad by private entities.

Despite the fact that Japanese overseas investment significantly increased especially after the Plaza Accord in 1985, it did not have the idea to protect its overseas investment by signing BITs unlike European and North American states. Until 2000, Japan's BIT partners are relatively small economies (say Egypt) and it was partners that requested the signing of BITs. Japan employed non-legal approach to protect its overseas investment such as good political relations and business relations. After 2000, Japan started to sign BITs that have ISDS clause with Asian states, but the its accession into TPP again brought the question of policy space because the then TPP negotiation included the US. Many commentators expressed the view that TPP with ISDS would be harmful because such would reduce the policy space of Japan given that US firms are likely to sue the Japanese government. This is interesting because Japan requested its developing partners to sign BITs with ISDS. While Japan eventually supported the TPP with ISDS, the internal debate in Japan regarding TPP in the 2010 still suggests that policy space was an important issue for Japan.

China uses IIA as a major policy tool for investment protection. Almost all Chinese IIAs have a clear focus on investment protection. This is due largely to the fact that China's early BITs were concluded with European countries that are keen to protect their investment in China, and that China has self-positioned as mainly an FDI importing country before the new millennium. That said, however, China is also experiencing a paradigm shift in IIA-making, and some recent Chinese IIAs also stress the need of maintaining regulatory space, in addition to investment

[31] OECD (2018).

[32] See Article 42 of the Law of the People's Republic of China on Foreign Investment: "This Law shall come into force as of January 1, 2020. *The Law of the People's Republic of China on Chinese-foreign Equity Joint Ventures*, *the Law of the People's Republic of China on Wholly Foreign-owned Enterprises* and *the Law of the People's Republic of China on Chinese-foreign Cooperative Joint Ventures* are repealed simultaneously."

protection. It is particularly the case in light of the fact that China has been repeatedly brought to international arbitration by foreign investors in recent years,[33] and that China has become a major FDI-exporting country in the world.[34] A typical example of such IIAs are the Canada-China BIT and the China-EU CAI, both of which clearly reaffirm that host states shall maintain necessary regulatory space in FDI governance.[35] As states have increasingly realized that IIAs and ISDS could pose profound challenge to their regulatory space, it will not be surprising to see that maintaining state regulatory space will be stressed in China's future IIA-making.

5 Differences Between China and Japan

5.1 Japan "Domestic Industries, not FDI"; China "from FDI to Domestic Industries"

Foreign Direct Investment (FDI) is certainly important for less developed economies that lack domestic investment. FDI brings foreign capital and technology that is useful for national economic development. However, it seems that the long-term goal of the industrial policy of China and Japan was to develop their own domestic industries by themselves. FDI was expected to have positive impact on domestic investment in a long run, and only when such is likely, FDI was welcome by the two countries. In short, for the two countries, FDI was a useful tool to develop infant industries only for a short period.

Immediately after the war, Japan relied on FDI to develop domestic industries. In the case of electronics, under the guidance of Ministry of International Trade and Industries (MITI), joint ventures (JVs) were established between foreign and Japanese firms. The scheme of technology transfer from foreign firms to JVs was also arranged by MITI. Because MITI maintained competitive environment among electronics JVs, they needed to compete with each other. In the case of automobile, Japanese automobile makers technologically assisted by European makers started knock-down production in the 1950s, with a notable exception of Toyota. In general, Japan's basic idea was to impose restriction on inward FDI to protect domestic industries. FDI was permitted only when it was expected to have a good impact on Japanese firms. The goal of Japan's economic policy was not to attract FDI *per se*, but to promote domestic industry, taking advantage of partnership with foreign firms.

---

[33] See *Goh Chin Soon v. People's Republic of China*, ICSID Case No. ARB/20/34; *Macro Trading Co., Ltd. v. People's Republic of China*, ICSID Case No. ARB/20/22; *Hela Schwarz GmbH v. People's Republic of China*, ICSID Case No. ARB/17/19, etc.

[34] OECD, FDI stocks (indicator), https://data.oecd.org/fdi/fdi-stocks.htm.

[35] See, e.g., Section VI, Sub-section 2, Article 4 General Exceptions, China-EU CAI; Article 33 General Exceptions, Canada-China BIT.

Somehow different from Japan, while China's domestic industries have experienced rapid advancement in general since the economic reform, China's economic development heavily relies on the utilization of FDI, which could bring advanced technology and foreign capitals.[36] In recent years, however, China seems to have put much stress in developing its state-owned and/or state-controlled enterprises, which is also described by some as 'state capitalism'.[37] While China's strategy of enhancing state-controlled economy can hardly be said wrong from a policy perspective, it has been observed that, in such a development strategy, the significance of private and foreign enterprises in China's economy is eroding.[38] More recently, the growing tension between China and major developed economies in the world has materially impacted China's FDI inflow and outflow, and China's leadership has declared its policy of 'dual circulation' in economic development, which implies a need to reduce China's reliance on FDI.[39] It remains to be observed how this policy will be implemented and whether it will be successful in the long run.

5.2 *Japan "Technology not Capital"; China "Technology and Capital"*

In the textbook explanations, investment is critically important for the national economy development because it brings both capital and technology. Having said that, the two goal may sometimes compete with each other because technology transfer requirement on investment may impede investment flows. It seems both China and Japan puts emphasis on technology especially during their initial stage of industrialization. Both states impose condition regarding technology transfer, which often takes the form of joint venture requirement. If the import of capital is the ultimate goal, there should have been no conditions attached to inward investment. The common position of the two states was to impose technology transfer conditions even if such reduce the capital inflow.

The postwar Japan faced the shortage of capital. This problem was mainly addressed by Foreign Exchange Law, which basically banned outward investment. Under Foreign Capital Law, capital inflow and repatriation were allowed, although strict technology transfer requirement was imposed (join venture requirement). Despite restriction on capital inflow, Japan did not face serious shortage of capital partly because Japan was able to rely on World Bank loan with relatively low interest

[36] Center for China and Globalization, The Reasons and Prices for China' Reliance on Foreign Investment, http://www.ccg.org.cn/archives/25678 (original in Chinese).

[37] See, generally, Du (2014).

[38] See, e.g., Liebman and Milhaupt (2015).

[39] Xinhua News Agency of 9 November 2020, Scientifically Understanding the New Economic Strategy of Dual Circulation, http://www.xinhuanet.com/politics/2020-11/09/c_1126714546.htm (original in Chinese).

rates. Because infrastructure development was largely financed by the World Bank loans, there was no need for Japan to attract FDI.

China also realizes and stresses the importance of technology in promoting economic development, and technology is a key consideration in China's IIA-, FDI law- and policy-making. For instance, the three national FDI laws explicitly provide that FDI could be in the form of intellectual property, and that China encourages such FDI.[40] In most Chinese IIAs, the term "investment" is broadly defined to cover intellectual property as well.[41] Besides, some recent IIAs include a clause of performance requirements, prohibiting contracting states to impose requirements that could infringe on intellectual property of foreign investors.[42] China's protection of foreign intellectual property has been criticized, especially in recent years. The issue of forced technology transfer has become a contentious trade and investment issue between China and the U.S. and many other states.[43] To respond to the international pressure, law- and IIA-making measures have been taken by China. Notably, the issue of forced technology transfer has been addressed in recent trade and investment agreements, such as the Economic and Trade Agreement between the Government of the United States and the Government of the People's Republic of China (China-U.S. Phase One Agreement),[44] and the China-EU CAI.[45] At the national level, the FIL also explicitly states that forced technology transfer should not be allowed.[46] It may be expected that in the future, the situation of technology transfer could be better regulated, at least from the perspective of China. Yet, whether and to what extent such improvement would appease China's trade partners would remain to be seen.

Perhaps the most critical difference in external environment for the national economy building between China and Japan was the availability of external finance. While Japan took advantage of the World Bank membership and imposed restriction on FDI inflow, China needed to sign IIAs to attract FDI because it faced the shortage of not only technology but also capitals. Thus, unlike Japan, which was able to take advantage of World Bank loan and US financial assistance, China needed to attract FDI mainly from European countries, and IIAs were necessary to facilitate such financial transactions. It was only in the 1980s when China started to have relations with the World Bank. China's participation in ADB also took place only in the mid-1980s.

---

[40] See Article 5 EJVL; Article 3 FIEL; Article 4 and Article 8 CJVL.

[41] See, e.g., Gallagher and Shan (2009).

[42] See, e.g., China-Canada BIT, CAI.

[43] See, e.g., Chi and Qiao (2019), pp. 99–102.

[44] Chapter Two, China-U.S. Phase One Agreement.

[45] Article 3, Section II, China-EU CAI.

[46] Article 22 FIEL.

6 Conclusion

Despite that the two countries achieve economic development in very different external environment, their investment policies fundamentally share more commonalities than differences. Both China and Japan used investment policy as a core components of industrial policies and they regarded investment critically important as a source of technology, in addition to capital. For the two countries, the fundamental goal was to build-up their own national industries and maintenance of policy space for industrial polices was critically important.

However, China needed to rely on FDI unlike Japan that tried to restrict capital inflow. Japan was able to rely on the World Bank loans as the source of capital, while securing technology transfer between private sectors arranged by governments. What Japan needed from foreign firms was technology, not capital. In contrast, China needed both capital and technology. Hence its economic development at an early stage heavily rely on FDI. In order to attract FDI, China signed a large number of IIAs that may restrict policy space, unlike Japan that were indifferent to the signing of IIAs until recently. This does not necessarily mean that China gave up building up its one industries. The Chinese attempt to develop its state-owned and/or state-controlled enterprises, which is also described by some as 'state capitalism' can be understood along this line.

References

Berger A (2013) Investment Treaties and the Search for Market Access in China, Investment Treaty News of 26 June 2013, https://www.iisd.org/itn/2013/06/26/investment-treaties-and-the-search-for-market-access-in-china/

Berger A, Chi M (2021) The EU-China Comprehensive Agreement on Investment: Stuck Halfway?, Columbia FDI Perspectives No. 299, http://ccsi.columbia.edu/files/2021/03/No-299-Berger-and-Chi-FINAL.pdf

Chaisse J, Hamanaka S (2014) The investment version of the Asian noodle bowl: The proliferation of international investment agreements. ADB Working Paper Series on Regional Economic Integration No. 128

Chenggang L (2019) Changes and Prospects of China's Utilization of Foreign Investment since the Forty Years of Reform and Opening up (original in Chinese), http://www.npc.gov.cn/npc/c541/201902/061c546b82e745bb988389f90d346baa.shtml

Chi M, Qiao L (2019) A skeletal review of the Sino-U.S. "trade war": contentious issues, trade multilateralism and policy recommendations. Can Foreign Policy J 26(1):99–107

Du M (2014) China's state capitalism and international trade law. Int Comp Law Q 63(2):409–448

Gallagher N, Shan W (2009) Chinese investment treaties: policies and practices. Oxford University Press, Oxford

Hamanaka S (2016) Insights to great powers' desire to establish institutions: comparison of ADB, AMF, AMRO and AIIB. Global Policy 7(2):288–292

Hamanaka S (2017) China-Japan-Korea trilateral investment treaty: implications for future investment negotiations in Asia. In: Chaisse J, Ishikawa T, Jusoh S (eds) Asia's changing international investment regime. Springer, Singapore, pp 121–139

Hamanaka S (2019) The future impact of trans-pacific partnership's rule-making achievements: the case study of E-commerce. World Econ 42(2):552–563

Lawrence RZ (1993) Japan's low levels of inward investment: the role of inhibitions on acquisitions. In: Froot KA (ed) Foreign direct investment. University of Chicago Press, pp 85–112

Liebman BL, Milhaupt CJ (2015) Regulating the visible hand?: The institutional implications of chinese state capitalism. Oxford University Press, Oxford

OECD (2018) OECD Business and Finance Outlook 2018, The Belt and Road Initiative in the global trade, investment and finance landscape, https://doi.org/10.1787/bus_fin_out-2018-6-en

Pempel TJ (1998) Regime shift, comparative dynamics of the Japanese political economy. Cornell University Press, Ithaca

UNCTAD (2021) World Investment Report 2021: Investing in sustainable recovery. https://unctad.org/webflyer/world-investment-report-2021

World Bank (2010) Foreign Direct Investment – the China Story. https://www.worldbank.org/en/news/feature/2010/07/16/foreign-direct-investment-china-story

Investor Obligations in India's New Bilateral Investment Treaties: Emergence of New Treaty Practice

Prabhash Ranjan

Contents

Abstract Typically, Bilateral investment treaties (BITs) are unidimensional instruments that confer rights on foreign investors and impose obligations on host States. As the backlash against international investment law has intensified in the last few years, this structural aspect has come under increasing scrutiny. The argument is that BITs should also impose obligations on foreign investors to bring a semblance of balance. In view of this, the paper examines the issue of investor obligations in the case of India's new investment treaty practice. After being sued by several foreign investors, India set on the path of developing a new Model BIT with the objective to strike a balance between investment protection and host State's right to regulate. As part of this, India is developing a new treaty practice where obligations are imposed

Some parts of this paper draw from the following work of the author: Prabhash Ranjan, 'Investor's Obligation in Investment Treaties: Missing Text Or A Matter of Application' in Jean Ho and Mavluda Sattarova (Eds) Investor's International Law, 2021, Hart Publishing, an imprint of Bloomsbury Publishing Plc., pp. 125–148.
The author is grateful to Priyadarshani Venkatesh for her assistance.

P. Ranjan (✉)
Jindal Global Law School, O P Jindal Global University, Sonipat, India

M. Chi et al. (eds.), *Asian Yearbook of International Economic Law 2022*,
Asian Yearbook of International Economic Law (2022) 2022: 89–108,
https://doi.org/10.1007/16517_2022_12, Published online: 20 May 2022

on foreign investors. However, these obligations are negative in nature often exist in the form of best endeavour clauses. The paper argues that India should develop its treaty practice so as to impose positive obligations on foreign investors.

1 Introduction

Bilateral Investment Treaties (BITs) – the most important source of international investment law – are treaties concluded for the reciprocal protection and promotion of foreign investment in the territories of the signatory countries. The first modern-day BIT was signed in 1959. Till 31 December 2020, according to the United Nations Conference on Trade and Development (UNCTAD), the total number of BITs stood at 2943.[1] Foreign investors, over the years, have made use of the investor-State dispute settlement (ISDS) mechanism in BITs, to invoke the substantive protections promised in the BITs against the host State. The number of such ISDS claims, by the end of 2020, was more than 1,100.[2]

A large number of BITs, especially in the decades of 70s to 90s, were signed between developed or capital exporting countries and developing or capital importing countries. The primary motivation for developed countries to enter into BITs was the desire to protect their investment in developing countries (the countries that had embraced communism or had newly acquired political independence from erstwhile colonial powers).[3] Developed countries were concerned about several communist and other countries expropriating foreign capital without compensation.[4] Thus, BITs were crafted as a new kind of international instruments that would not only overcome the vagaries of customary international law regarding foreign investment, but would also provide substantive protections to foreign investors by imposing binding constraints on the sovereign rights of developing countries. The ascendancy of neoliberalism in the 1990s especially resulted in the spread and popularity of BITs. While theoretically BITs were reciprocal in nature, in effect they operate in a mono-directional manner conferring rights on 'first world' investors and imposing obligations on 'second' and 'third world' governments.[5]

The proliferating ISDS claims have involved foreign investors challenging a wide array of regulatory measures of the host State such as monetary measures, taxation laws, industrial policies, health and environmental regulations, actions of the

[1] 'Recent Developments in The IIA Regime: Accelerating IIA Reform', UN Doc, 3, IIA Issues Note, 2021. https://unctad.org/system/files/official-document/diaepcbinf2021d6_en.pdf, p. 2.

[2] 'Investor–State Dispute Settlement Cases: Facts and Figures 2020', UN Doc, 4, IIA Issues Note, 2021, https://unctad.org/system/files/official-document/diaepcbinf2021d7_en.pdf, p. 1.

[3] Vandevlede (2010), pp. 45–60.

[4] Vandevlede (2010), pp. 45–60.

[5] Kurtz (2016), p. 55.

judiciary etc. The expansion of BITs and the corresponding rise in ISDS claims covering such a broad spectrum of regulatory issues considered fundamental to host State governance and exercise of public power, has triggered strong reactions and concerns from many States and non-State actors like academics, civil society organisations, and people at large.[6] This contestation has coincided with a backlash against globalisation[7] and against powerful corporations who wield too much power,[8] and whose accountability is challenging to fix under international law.[9] An important constituent of the demand to hold corporations accountable for their actions internationally is to hold them accountable for human rights violations.[10] This demand has gathered momentum in the last decade or so, especially after the publication of the 2011 report of John Ruggie, the UN Special Rapporteur on business and human rights.[11] In 2014, the UN Human Rights Council in Geneva established an open-ended working with the mandate "to elaborate an international legally binding instrument on Transnational Corporations and Other Business Enterprises with respect to human rights".[12] Since then debate and work has begun in all earnest towards developing a business and human rights treaty[13] or finding other ways in which foreign corporations can be made more accountable towards human rights.[14] Recently, the working group came out with its report on human rights-compatible international investment agreements.[15] The report highlights the ingrained imbalances that exist in BITs and urges states to ensure that their investment treaties are compatible with international human rights obligations. An important aspect of the report is its emphasis on investor obligations at the international level.[16]

In this overall context, an important critique that has been advanced against the investment treaties is that they are one-sided international law instruments, which impose obligations on host States, thus constraining their right to regulate, but do not impose obligations on foreign investors.[17] Consequently, while foreign investors benefit from protection of international law against host State's regulatory abuse, it is

---

[6] See Waibel et al. (2010); Franck (2005).

[7] See Rodrik (2011); Stein (2016).

[8] See generally Tepper with Hearn (2018).

[9] Choudhury (2020).

[10] Deva (2012).

[11] 'Guiding Principles on Business and Human Rights: Implementing the United Nations "Protect, Respect and Remedy" Framework' UN Doc A/HRC/17/31, https://www.ohchr.org/documents/issues/business/a-hrc-17-31_aev.pdf.

[12] Business and Human Rights Resource Centre, https://www.business-humanrights.org/en/binding-treaty.

[13] Deva and Bilchitz (2017).

[14] Also see Choudhury (2018).

[15] 'Human rights-compatible international investment agreements' UN Doc A/76/238, https://undocs.org/A/76/238.

[16] *Id.* at 3.

[17] See Choudhury (2020); Ho (2019); Bernasconi-Osterwalder (2020).

difficult to fix accountability of investors or hold them liable for misconduct towards the host States or local communities.[18] This has led some scholars to describe international investment law as investor's international law.[19] In view of this, it has been argued that an important way to correct the ingrained imbalances in investment treaties so that foreign corporations can be held accountable for their actions under international law is by incorporating provisions on investor's obligations in BITs.[20]

In this context, this paper discusses and analyses the presence of provisions on investor obligations in India's new BITs. India, which had one of the biggest BIT programmes once, a few years back, crafted a new investment treaty practice with the aim to reconcile the interests of foreign investors with host State's right to regulate. As an important element of this attempted reconciliation, India incorporated obligations on foreign investors in its new Model BIT of 2016,[21] followed by new BITs that India signed subsequently with Belarus,[22] Taiwan,[23] Kyrgyzstan,[24] and Brazil.[25] In order to make this argument, the paper is divided in five sections. Section 2 sets the background by explaining India's BIT programme in brief and the movement towards the backlash against investment treaties. In Sect. 3, the paper discusses the draft model BIT that India adopted and the investor obligations contained in this draft. Since, this draft contained some interesting provisions on investor obligations, it would be a useful first step towards understanding India's newest treaty practice on this matter. Section 4 discusses the investor obligations in India's final model BIT and in the subsequent BITs that India has signed based on the final model BIT. Section 5 concludes by observing that while India's newest treaty practice imposes binding obligation on the foreign investor on issues such as anti-corruption, the obligations on other issues such as human rights and environment are still in the form of best endeavour clause.

---

[18] Gathi and Puig (2019); Ho (2019).

[19] Sattarova and Ho (2021), pp. 3–4.

[20] Choudhury (2020); Sattarova (2019).

[21] Model Text for the Indian Bilateral Investment Treaty, https://dea.gov.in/sites/default/files/ModelBIT_Annex_0.pdf.

[22] 2018 Treaty Between the Republic of Belarus and the Republic of India on Investment https://dea.gov.in/sites/default/files/BIT%20with%20Belarus.pdf (last accessed 27 September 2021).

[23] 2018 Bilateral Investment Agreement Between The India Taipei Association in Tapei and the Taipei Economic and Cultural Center in India https://dea.gov.in/sites/default/files/BIA%20between%20ITA%20and%20TECC.pdf.

[24] 2019 Bilateral Investment Treaty Between the Government of the Kyrgyz Republic and The Government of the Republic of India https://investmentpolicy.unctad.org/international-investment-agreements/treaty-files/5993/download.

[25] 2020 Investment Cooperation and Facilitation Treaty Between the Federative Republic of Brazil and the Republic of India https://dea.gov.in/sites/default/files/Investment%20Cooperation%20and%20Facilitation%20Treaty%20with%20Brazil%20-%20English_0.pdf.

2 India's BIT Programme: Towards Backlash

From 1994 till the end of 2010, India signed close to 80 BITs and some free trade agreements (FTAs) containing investment chapters.[26] BITs didn't occupy a prominent place in public discourse till the first publicly known BIT arbitral award was issued against India in a case known as *White Industries v India*[27] where an ISDS tribunal found that India violated its obligations under the India-Australia BIT.[28] Things started to change after the issuance of White Industries award in 2011. This change was accelerated as many other foreign investors in 2012 and later brought BIT cases against India challenging a wide range of measures such as the imposition of retrospective taxes,[29] revocation of spectrum licenses,[30] actions of sub-national governments pertaining to withdrawing assurances offered to foreign investors,[31] and denial of refund of taxes.[32]

In 2016, another BIT award was issued against India in a case known as *Devas v India.*[33] This case arose due to India cancelling an agreement concerning the provision of broadband services, where foreign investment was allowed.[34] The ISDS tribunal held that India had violated her obligations under the India-Mauritius BIT.[35] This was followed by several other defeats at investment treaty arbitration forums in cases such as *Deutsche Telekom v India,*[36] *Vodafone v India*[37] and *Cairn Energy v India.*[38]

[26]For a detailed study of India's BITs see Ranjan (2019).

[27]*White Industries Australia Limited v. Republic of India*, UNCITRAL, Final Award (Nov. 30, 2011).

[28]*White Industries v. India*, 16.1.1(a).

[29]Vodafone issued an arbitral notice to India under the India-Netherlands BIT for a retrospective taxation measure, see *Vodafone v. India*, UNCTIRAL, Notice of Arbitration (not public) (Apr. 17, 2014); Cairn Energy also dragged India to arbitration under the India-UK BIT for a retrospective taxation measure. Recently an ISDS tribunal ruled in favour of Vodafone. Likewise, Cairn Energy PLC brought a successful claim against India on the issue of retrospective taxation.

[30]*CC/Devas (Mauritius) Ltd., Devas Employees Mauritius Private Limited, and Telecom Devas Mauritius Limited v. Republic of India,* PCA Case No 2013-09.

[31]*Ras al-Khaimah Investment Authority v. Republic of India* (Rakia v. India), UNCTAD, 2016 https://investmentpolicy.unctad.org/investment-dispute-settlement/cases/767/rakia-v-india.

[32]*Nissan Motor Co., Ltd. v. Republic of India (Nissan v India)*, UNCTAD, 2017 https://investmentpolicy.unctad.org/investment-dispute-settlement/cases/828/nissan-v-india.

[33]*CC/Devas v. India.*

[34]*CC/Devas v. India.*

[35]*CC/Devas v. India.*

[36]Deutsche Telekom AG v Republic of India, PCA Case No. 2014-10, Interim Award, 13 December 2017.

[37]Vodafone International Holdings BV v. Government of India [I], PCA Case No. 2016-35.

[38]Cairn Energy PLC and Cairn UK Holdings Limited (CUHL) v. Government of India, PCA Case No. 2016-7, Award, 21 December 2020.

Due to the cumulative effect of these adverse BIT decisions and BIT arbitration notices, India began the process of reviewing BITs and debating various aspects about BITs, which had not been deliberated upon earlier. These aspects included whether BITs have led to higher foreign investment inflows to India;[39] whether BITs encroach upon India's right to regulate in public interest; whether BITs should contain ISDS provisions;[40] whether the treaty provisions in BITs are too vague and thus susceptible to overly broad interpretations by ISDS arbitral tribunals; whether the ISDS system works in a transparent way, etc.

The review of BITs led to three tangible outcomes. First, India adopted a new Model BIT in 2016.[41] Second, India issued notices of BIT termination to 58 countries.[42] Till date, India has unilaterally terminated more than 75 BITs.[43] Third, India requested 25 of its BIT partner States to issue joint interpretative statements in order to resolve, what India described as 'uncertainties and ambiguities that may arise regarding interpretation and application of the standards contained' in India's BITs.[44]

It is a fact that BIT disputes against India played an important role in India unilaterally terminating several of its BITs. However, this does not mean that BIT claims triggered exit of India from the system. India is still a part of the BIT system as evidenced by the fact that India has developed a new Model BIT, which contains provisions on ISDS moreover, India wishes to renegotiate BITs with its former BIT-partner countries based on the new Model BIT.

3 Draft Model BIT: Sowing the Seeds

The early signs of India's new investment treaty practice on investor obligations were evident in India's draft Model BIT that was released in early 2015 for comments.[45] This draft Model BIT was the precursor to the final Model BIT released

[39] Bhasin and Manocha (2016).

[40] Bhattacharjee (2012).

[41] Model text for the Indian Bilateral Investment Treaty, https://dea.gov.in/sites/default/files/ModelBIT_Annex_0.pdf. Also see Ranjan and Anand (2017).

[42] Government of India, Ministry of Commerce & Industry, Department of Industrial Policy & Promotion (2016) Lok Sabha Unstarred Question No. 1290 (25 July 2016), http://164.100.47.190/loksabhaquestions/annex/9/AU1290.pdf.

[43] See Government of India, Department of Economic Affairs, https://dea.gov.in/bipa (accessed 10 August 2021). For a detailed discussion on India's BITs see Ranjan (2019).

[44] Government of India, Ministry of Finance, Department of Economic Affairs (2016) Office Memorandum – Regarding Issuing Joint Interpretative Statements for Indian Bilateral Investment Treaties (8 February 2016), http://indiainbusiness.nic.in/newdesign/upload/Consolidated_Interpretive-Statement.pdf (hereinafter: JIS Note).

[45] Draft Model Text for the Indian Bilateral Investment Treaty, https://www.mygov.in/sites/default/files/master_image/Model%20Text%20for%20the%20Indian%20Bilateral%20Investment%20Treaty.pdf (hereinafter: Draft Model Indian BIT).

in early 2016. Therefore, before understanding the investor obligations contained in the final Model BIT and the subsequent BITs that India has signed, it will be appropriate to look at the investor obligations in the draft Model BIT. Examining the draft Model BIT provisions is also important because the final Model BIT differed from the draft version as would be explained in the chapter later.

Articles 8 to 12 of the draft Model Indian BIT contained provisions on investor obligations. Article 8.3 said that compliance with Articles 9 to 12 "is compulsory and is fundamental to the operation of this Treaty". It further said that investors and their investments shall benefit from the treaty provisions only if they comply with the investor obligations listed in Articles 9 to 12. Article 8.4 states that a breach by investors and their investments of the investor obligations given in Articles 9 to 12 shall entitle the host State, at its sole discretion and in accordance with its law and Article 14 (investor-State dispute settlement) to seek suitable enforcement, regulatory or other legal action in response to that breach.

Building on this principle further, Article 14.11 allows for counterclaims. Specifically, Article 14.11(i) states that the host State may initiate a counterclaim against the investor or investment for a breach of the obligations given in Articles 9 to 12 before an ISDS tribunal and seek a remedy such as suitable declaratory relief, enforcement action or monetary compensation. Further, Article 14.3(iii) provides that when a foreign investor issues a notice of dispute, it must furnish a self-certified statement "demonstrating compliance with Articles 9, 10, 11 and 12". A combined reading of these provisions reveals that the draft model BIT puts in place a mechanism that not only imposed obligations on the investor but also provided the means to the host State to enforce these obligations through bringing counterclaims.

We will now discuss the obligations that the draft Model BIT imposed on foreign investors. The obligations imposed on foreign investors under Articles 9, 10, 11 and 12 are broadly divided into four categories – obligation against corruption, disclosures, taxation and compliance with the law of the host State respectively. Article 9.1 obligates the foreign investor not to offer, promise, or give any undue pecuniary advantage, gratification or gift whatsoever, either directly or indirectly, to a public servant or to the officials of the host State as an inducement or reward for doing or forbearing to do any official act or obtain or maintain other improper advantage. This obligation extends to the foreign investors both prior and after making the investment.

In recent times, there have been numerous instances where corruption has been an important issue in disputes between foreign investors and States in front of ISDS tribunals.[46] ISDS tribunals have permitted host States to raise corruption as a ground for denial of treaty-protection benefits to the foreign investor. For instance, in *Metal Tech v Uzbekistan*, the tribunal held that since the investment was made through corrupt means, thus it has not been "implemented in accordance with the laws and

[46] See *World Duty Free Company Limited and The Republic of Kenya*, ICSID Case No. ARB/00/7 (Award dated 4 October 2006); *EDF (Services) Limited v. Romania*, ICSID Case No. ARB/05/13 (Award dated 8 October 2009).

regulations of the Contracting Party in whose territory the investment is made" as required by Article 1(1) of the BIT.[47] The tribunal ruled that since the investment has not been made in compliance with the domestic laws of Uzbekistan, the tribunal has no jurisdiction over the dispute.[48] Additionally, questions have often arisen whether investors can be held liable if they are involved in corrupt activities during the making or operation of their investments.[49] Provisions such as Article 9.1 would enable host State to hold foreign investors liable in case they indulge in corrupt practices to derive any kind of benefit for their operations.

Article 10 imposes a number of disclosure requirements on foreign investors. These disclosure obligations relate to foreign investors disclosing accurate and complete information about their business activities, structure, ownership, source and channel of funds, etc. In addition to these regular disclosure requirements, Article 10.6 imposes a supplementary disclosure requirement on foreign investors, "even where not required to do so by law of the host state". Under Article 10.6, investors and investments.

> should develop and comply with policies to ensure timely and accurate disclosure of material information relating, but not limited to matters such as: the financial and operating results of the investment; objectives of the investment; governance structures and policies, in particular, the content of any corporate governance code or policy and its implementation process; remuneration policy for members of the board and key executives; issues regarding employees and other stakeholders; etc.

The Law Commission of India (LCI), which took upon the task of studying the draft Model 2015 BIT, observed in its report that many of the disclosure obligations given in Article 10.6 are

> vague in nature and impose unreasonable obligation to maintain records or make disclosures that are not clearly known to the investor in advance. Provisions such as these can send negative signals to prospective investors, and it is suggested that open-ended requirements of this nature be avoided entirely.[50]

The LCI also pointed out that if the host State wishes to impose disclosure requirements on foreign investors, over and above those enshrined in host State's domestic laws, then these disclosure obligations should be unambiguously defined in the BIT or made known to the foreign investors in advance.[51] Another important aspect missing in Article 10.6 is that while it imposes obligations on the foreign investors to disclose all kinds of information, there is no mention of what the host State would do with this information and whether confidential business information would be protected or not.[52] Accordingly, the LCI recommended that open-ended disclosure

---

[47] *Metal-Tech Ltd. v. Republic of Uzbekistan*, ICSID Case No. ARB/10/3, para. 372.

[48] *Metal-Tech Ltd. v. Republic of Uzbekistan*, para. 373.

[49] Vijayvergia and Belmannu (2020).

[50] LCI Report (2015), p. 31.

[51] LCI Report (2015), pp. 31–32.

[52] LCI Report (2015), p. 32.

requirements given in Article 10.6 should be avoided.[53] The LCI also recommended that the manner in which the host State shall use the information should also be given in the BIT.[54]

Article 11 of the draft model 2015 BIT imposes an obligation on foreign investors related to taxation. Article 11.1 requires investors and their investments to comply with the host State's law on taxation including timely payment of their tax liabilities in accordance with the Law of the Host State. The draft model 2015 BIT refers to taxation at several places. For instance, Article 2.6 (iv) states that the treaty shall not apply to any taxation measures. Article 2.6 (iv) further provides that the determination made by the host State whether or not any conduct on its part is a subject matter of taxation shall be non-justiciable and no arbitration tribunal shall review such determination of the host State. Given the exclusion of taxation matters from the purview of BITs and making host State's determination of a regulatory measure pertaining to taxation non justiciable, obliterates the need to include another provision on taxation as part of investor obligations.

Next, Article 12 imposes an obligation on the foreign investor to comply with the domestic laws of the host State. Specifically, Article 12.1 provides:

> Investors and their Investments shall be subject to and comply with the Law of the Host State. This includes, but is not limited to, the following:
>
> (i) Law concerning payment of wages and minimum wages, employment of contract labour, prohibition on child labour, special conditions of work, social security and benefit and insurance schemes applicable to employees;
> (ii) information sharing requirements of the Host State concerning the Investment in question and the corporate history and practices of the Investment or Investor, for purposes of decision making in relation to that Investment or for other purposes;
> (iii) environmental Law applicable to the Investment and its business operations;
> (iv) Law relating to conservation of natural resources;
> (v) Law relating to human rights;
> (vi) Law of consumer protection and fair competition; and
> (vii) relevant national and internationally accepted standards of corporate governance and accounting practices.

Further, Article 12.2 provides:

> Investors and their Investments shall strive, through their management policies and practices, to contribute to the development objectives of the Host State. In particular, Investors and their Investments should recognise the rights, traditions and customs of local communities and indigenous peoples of the Host State and carry out their operations with respect and regard for such rights, traditions and customs.

The requirement that foreign investors comply with the domestic laws of the host State is found in several BITs. This requirement could be embedded into the definition of investment in the BIT. For instance, Article 1(b) of the India Germany BIT provides that "investment means every kind of asset invested in accordance with

[53] LCI Report (2015), p. 32.

[54] LCI Report (2015), p. 32.

the national laws of the Contracting Party where the investment is made". Several tribunals have held that investments not made in accordance with host State's laws would not enjoy treaty protection. In *Inceysa v El Salvador*,[55] the tribunal held that since *Inceysa's* investment was not made in accordance with the laws of El Salvador i.e. it was illegal, it is 'not included within the scope of consent expressed by Spain and El Salvador in the BIT and, consequently, the disputes arising from it are not subject to the jurisdiction of ICSID'.[56] The objective of asking the foreign investors to comply with domestic law is to ensure that illegal investments do not enjoy treaty protection. However, it is also important to bear in mind that a minor error of a procedural nature will not render the entire investment illegal.[57]

As also pointed out by the LCI report, some of the obligations imposed on the foreign investor by Article 12.1 appear to be of procedural in nature such as information sharing obligations. Since foreign investors have to show compliance with Articles 9, 10, 11 and 12 while submitting a request for an ISDS claim, it is possible that even a minor error of procedural nature or a minor non-compliance with any law, would result in investment not getting treaty protection. Further, the obligation imposed on the foreign investor in Article 12.2 that investors and investments shall strive to contribute to the development objectives of the host State is equivocal in nature. How would it be determined that the foreign investor is contributing to the host State's development? Moreover, the very notion of host State's development is undefined and imprecise.

In view of the above, the LCI recommended that both Articles 11 and 12 be redrafted to first, specify a general requirement of compliance with laws; and second, lay down an exhaustive list of areas in which noncompliance of laws would attract the consequences of foreign investors not enjoying treaty protection.[58] Additionally, instead of imposing an obligation on the foreign investor to furnish a self-certified statement that it has complied with Articles 9, 10, 11 and 12, States should raise investor's non-compliance with domestic laws as a counterclaim.[59]

[55] *Inceysa Vallisoletana SL v. Republic of El Salvador*, ICSID Case No ARB/03/26 (Award) (2 August 2006). Also see *Fraport AG Frankfurt Airport Services Worldwide v. Philippines*, ICSID Case No ARB/03/25 (Award) (16 August 2007).

[56] *Fraport AG Frankfurt Airport v. Philippines*, para. 257.

[57] Schreuer (2013); *Tokios Tokeles v. Ukraine*, ICSID Case No. ARB/02/18 (Decision on Jurisdiction of 29 April 2004 and Dissenting Opinion of President Prosper Weil), paras 83–6).

[58] LCI Report (2015), pp. 35–36.

[59] LCI Report (2015), pp. 35–36.

4 The Final Model 2016 BIT and Subsequent BITs

The final Model BIT 2016 contained investor's obligations in a diluted form as compared to the draft model BIT version discussed above. Chapter III in the final Model BIT contained only two Articles on investor obligations – 11 and 12 as against, five different Articles (8 to 12) in Chapter III of the draft version discussed in the preceding section. While the impact that the LCI report had on revising the draft model BIT is not known, it is quite evident that India decided to scale down some of the investor obligations. In this section we discuss the investor obligations that India adopted in the final model BIT, which have now become part of India's BITs signed with countries like Belarus, Kyrgyzstan, Taiwan, and Brazil. In the final model BIT, investor obligations are contained in Articles 11 and 12. But, before we study these provisions, it is important to make the following points.

First, the final model BIT did away with the requirement imposed in Article 14.3 (iii) of the draft model BIT that required foreign investors to furnish a self-certified statement that they have complied with all the investor obligations while bringing an ISDS claim against the host State. Second, as against Article 14.11 of the draft model BIT that allowed the host State to bring counterclaims against the investor, there is no provision in the final model BIT to bring counterclaims against the investor.[60] The LCI had not recommended doing away with counterclaims. This might raise the question how will the investor obligations given in Articles 11 and 12 be enforced?

Now, let us turn our attention to understanding investor obligations in the final model BIT, which also finds place in other BITs that India has signed based on its model BIT. We divide this discussion under four sub sections. The first two sub sections will discuss the obligations imposed by Articles 11 and 12. Article 11 imposes the obligation on foreign investors to comply with domestic laws. Article 12 mandates the foreign investor to follow corporate social responsibility. The third sub-section will discuss the usefulness of investor obligations in the form of corporate social responsibility since it does not confer direct and binding obligations on foreign investors. Next, in sub-section four, the paper will examine the efficacy of counterclaims as an entry point of investor obligations and whether this would be possible under India's final model BIT and the subsequent BITs. Sub section four will discuss.

4.1 Compliance with Domestic Laws

An important vehicle to impose obligations on foreign investors, apart from imposing direct obligations on them in the treaty or by adopting soft law approaches, is to ensure that the treaty requires the foreign investor to comply with domestic laws.[61]

[60] Footnote 4 of the final model BIT arguably would allow counterclaims. This point is discussed later in the chapter.

[61] Krajewski (2020), pp. 119–120.

Foreign investors are bound by domestic laws. In fact, some ISDS tribunals have concluded that foreign investors have a general obligation to comply with host State laws irrespective of whether the treaty specifies this.[62] However, writing down this requirement in the treaty can elevate a breach of domestic law by the foreign investor to an issue subject to ISDS.[63]

For example, Article 11 of the 2016 Indian model BIT provides:

The parties reaffirm and recognize that:

(i) Investors and their investments shall comply with all laws, regulations, administrative guidelines and policies of a Party concerning the establishment, acquisition, management, operation and disposition of investments.
(ii) Investors and their investments shall not, either prior to or after the establishment of an investment, offer, promise, or give any undue pecuniary advantage, gratification or gift whatsoever, whether directly or indirectly, to a public servant or official of a Party as an inducement or reward for doing or forbearing to do any official act or obtain or maintain other improper advantage nor shall be complicit in inciting, aiding, abetting, or conspiring to commit such acts.
(iii) Investors and their investments shall comply with the provisions of law of the Parties concerning taxation, including timely payment of their tax liabilities.
(iv) An investor shall provide such information as the Parties may require concerning the investment in question and the corporate history and practices of the investor, for purposes of decision making in relation to that investment or solely for statistical purposes.

Similar provisions exist in the India-Belarus BIT,[64] the India-Taiwan BIT,[65] the India-Kyrgyzstan BIT,[66] and the India-Brazil BIT.[67] This requirement to comply with domestic laws is mentioned as a separate requirement, independent of the definition of a protected investment. The key characteristics of this provision are as follows. First, when compared with the version that existed in Article 12 of the draft model BIT, the language of Article 11 is precise. Unlike Article 12 of the draft model BIT that left the issue of compliance with domestic laws vague and open-

---

[62] *Cortec Mining Kenya Ltd et al v. Kenya*, Award, ICSID Case No. ARB/15/29 (22 October 2018), para. 333; *Plama Consortium Limited v. Republic of Bulgaria*, ICSID Case No. ARB/03/24, Award (27 August 2008), paras. 138–139. Also see Choudhury (2020).

[63] Krajewski (2020), p 119.

[64] Article 11 India-Belarus BIT.

[65] Article 11 India-Taiwan BIT.

[66] Article 11 India-Kyrgyzstan BIT. See also Article 7(1) of the 2019 Netherlands Model BIT, which provides: "investors and their investments shall comply with domestic laws and regulations of the host State, including laws and regulations on human rights, environmental protection and labour laws." The content of the obligations imposed on foreign investors will depend on the content of domestic laws. If domestic laws contain weak provisions on human rights or environmental protection, for example, then the corresponding obligations on the foreign investors will also be weak.

[67] Article 11 of India-Brazil BIT.

ended, Article 11 clearly delineates what the investor's obligations are as regards compliance with domestic laws. Second, the investor obligations against corruption, and on taxation, given in Articles 9 and 11 of the draft model BIT; have been subsumed in Articles 11(ii) and 11(iii). India's new investment treaty practice on anti-corruption obligation is different from what we find in several other new generation BITs, where the anti-corruption obligation is woven into the CSR provisions. For instance, Article 16 of the Canada-Burkina Faso BIT states that countries should 'encourage' enterprises operating within its territory to incorporate internationally recognised CSR standards and 'principles' that address issues such as anti-corruption.[68] Article 11(2) of the Nigeria-Singapore BIT also talks of addressing issues such as anti-corruption by encouraging enterprises to incorporate internationally recognised CSR standards and principles.[69]

The key difference between India's new investment treaties and other BITs that contain anti-corruption provision as part of CSR on the other hand is that the former treaties impose a binding obligation on the foreign investor. Whereas, in the other set of treaties, the anti-corruption obligation exists in the form of a best endeavour clause. Furthermore, in these latter treaties, the obligation is on the States to 'encourage' foreign investors to incorporate internationally recognised CSR standards, including those on anti-corruption.

4.2 Corporate Social Responsibility

Article 12 of the final Model BIT talks of corporate social responsibility. Article 12 provides:

> Investors and their enterprises operating within its territory of each Party shall endeavour to voluntarily incorporate internationally recognized standards of corporate social responsibility in their practices and internal policies, such as statements of principle that have been endorsed or are supported by the Parties. These principles may address issues such as labour, the environment, human rights, community relations and anti-corruption.

Similar provision exists in India's BITs with Belarus,[70] Kyrgyzstan,[71] and Taiwan.[72] Important issues such as human rights are present in these treaties as part of the investor's corporate social responsibility. Human rights have attracted considerable attention in the context of investor obligations. The core issue is whether or not

---

[68] Article 16 of Agreement between the Government of Canada and the Government of Burkina Faso for the Promotion and Protection of Investments.

[69] Article 11(2) of Investment Promotion and Protection Agreement Between the Government of the Federal Republic of Nigeria and the Government of the Republic of Singapore. Also see Article 16 of the Canada-Guinea BIT; Article 15(3) of the Canada-Mali BIT.

[70] Article 12 of India-Belarus BIT.

[71] Article 12 of the India-Kyrgyz Republic BIT.

[72] Article 12 of the India-Taiwan BIT.

foreign investors are bound by human rights obligations. This issue has arisen in cases like *Urbaser v Argentina.*[73] The *Urbaser* tribunal ruled that corporations can be subjects of international law[74] and are under a duty not to engage in activities that harm or destroy human rights.[75] However, as regards the question of whether the foreign investor was under an international law obligation to provide drinking water and sanitation services to the population living on the territory of the Concession, the tribunal held that only States have a positive obligation to meet the human right to water whereas corporations only have a negative obligation in this regard unless specific human rights obligations are imposed on the foreign investor say as part of the BIT.[76] In other words, investors would have human rights obligations only if they are established through incorporating direct investor obligations in investment treaties.[77]

However, the presence of human rights as part of the foreign investor's corporate social responsibility does not impose any positive or direct obligations on the foreign investor. Article 12 in the final model BIT and in other Indian BITs are couched in the best endeavour language. In the same vein, Article 12.2(a) of the India-Brazil BIT provides that investors and their investments shall "endeavour" to comply with voluntary principles and standards such as contributing to the economic, social and environmental progress, aimed at achieving sustainable development.[78] In other words, as long as the foreign investor can show that they endeavoured to address human rights principles, they cannot be held liable for breach of human rights obligations. Similar language also exists in other BITs signed by Brazil where investors, in respect of CSR obligations, are required to develop best efforts to "respect the human rights of those involved in the companies' activities, consistent with the international obligations and commitments of the Host Party".[79]

A better formulation in on the issue of human rights exists in the Nigeria-Morocco BIT. Article 18(2) of this BIT provides that 'investors and investments shall uphold human rights in the host state'. Interestingly, this provision imposes a direct and binding obligation on both the 'investor' and the 'investments'. Furthermore, as per Article 18(4): investors and investments shall not manage or operate the investments in a manner that circumvents international human rights obligations to which the host state and/or home state are Parties. In other words, international

[73] *Urbaser S.A. and Consorcio de Aguas Bilbao Bizkaia, Bilbao Biskaia Ur Partzuergoa v. The Argentine Republic*, ICSID Case No. ARB/07/26, 8 December 2016.

[74] *Urbaser v. Argentina*, para. 1194.

[75] *Urbaser v. Argentina*, para. 1199. For a critique of the reasoning employed by the *Urbaser* tribunal see Abel (2018), pp. 84–88.

[76] *Urbaser v. Argentina*, paras. 1208 and 1210.

[77] Choudhury (2017), pp. 469–470; Sattarova (2019), p. 24; Krajewski (2020).

[78] Same formulation exists in some other Brazilian BITs such as Article 15(2) of the Brazil-UAE BIT and Article 15(2) of the Brazil-Guyana BIT.

[79] See Article 9(2) of the Brazil-Malawi BIT.

human rights obligations that are binding on both the home and the host State would fall within the ambit of Article 18(2).

4.3 Usefulness of BITs Providing Investor Obligations

Some may argue that the utility of providing investor obligations in the form of corporate social responsibility in BITs is limited because most of these obligations, as discussed above, employ soft law or hortatory language, and are not binding on foreign investors. Thus, these provisions do not really help in holding foreign investors accountable under international investment law. Although some BITs impose binding obligations on foreign investors, which can act as a gateway to holding investors accountable, it is true that a majority of them park investor obligations in best endeavour clauses. Hortatory language will not be very effective in holding the foreign investors to account. Thus, one may be sceptical of the proposition that some scholars make especially vis-à-vis human rights obligations, that the incorporation of human rights obligations on foreign investors amounts to the 'hardening' of the soft law on business and human rights.[80]

However, there is another dimension that should be kept in mind. Investor obligations, even if they are expressed in best endeavour language, can play an important role in altering the manner in which ISDS tribunals have often viewed investment treaties. For instance, ISDS tribunals have looked at BITs largely as instruments for the promoting and protecting foreign investment.[81] In other words, ISDS tribunals have given preference to investment protection over other compelling objectives.[82] Thus, the presence of investor obligations, even in non-binding language, would play an important role in being part of the overall context of the investment treaty, and thus signalling a reframing of the objectives of the treaty.[83] This could be seen as part of the broader reform project in international investment law, which aims to recalibrate investment treaties into international instruments that go beyond the simplistic goal of providing protection to foreign investors.

The ISDS tribunal shall have to take this new set of objectives into account while interpreting the any BIT provision.[84] In other words, the presence of these investor obligations can be conducive to addressing the asymmetrical design of BITs. They can ensure that ISDS tribunals interpret the key substantive provisions of the BIT while keeping in mind the fact that treaties impose obligations on foreign investors

---

[80] Choudhury (2017).

[81] *Siemens AG v. The Argentine Republic*, ICSID Case No ARB/02/8, Decision on Jurisdiction (3 August 2004), para. 81. Also see Gudgeon (1986).

[82] See e.g. *Azurix Corp v. The Argentine Republic*, ICSID Case No. ARB/01/12, Award (14 July 2006), 261.

[83] See Sattarova (2019).

[84] See Vinuales (2017), p. 368; Choudhury (2020).

too (not just States), rendering investor conduct a significant aspect of the interpretative matrix.[85]

4.4 Counterclaims as an Entry-Point for Investor Obligations

Some new generation BITs or investment treaties specifically provide for counterclaims[86] that can be made against foreign investors by host States. These counterclaims could be an entry point for investor obligations.[87] A good example of this is Article 28(9) of the Common Market for Eastern and Southern Africa Investment Agreement 2007 (COMESA).[88] Article 28(9) provides:

> A Member State against whom a claim is brought by a COMESA investor under this Article may assert as a defence, counterclaim, right of set off or other similar claim, that the COMESA investor bringing the claim has not fulfilled its obligations under this Agreement, including the obligations to comply with all applicable domestic measures or that it has not taken all reasonable steps to mitigate possible damages.

Thus, Article 28(9) allows the host State to bring a counterclaim against a foreign investor if the investor has not complied with its obligations under the treaty.

Likewise, Article 43(1) of the Draft Pan African Investment Code (PAIC), as part of the chapter on ISDS, provides:

> Where an investor or its investment is alleged by a Member State party in a dispute settlement proceeding under this Code to have failed to comply with its obligations under this Code or other relevant rules and principles of domestic and international law, the competent body hearing such a dispute shall consider whether this breach, if proven, is materially relevant to the issues before it, and if so, what mitigating or off-setting effects this may have on the merits of a claim or on any damages awarded in the event of such award.

Article 43(2) of the Draft Pan African Investment Code provides:

> A Member State may initiate a counterclaim against the investor before any competent body dealing with a dispute under this Code for damages or other relief resulting from an alleged breach of the Code.

Thus, Article 43(2) clearly allows the host State to bring a counterclaim against a foreign investor. Article 43(1) provides that in case the foreign investor has failed to comply with the obligations imposed, the ISDS arbitration tribunal shall taken such breaches into account to decide whether such breaches have any mitigating or

[85] For more on how context can play a role in interpretation of investment treaties see *Adel A Hamidi Al Tamimi v. Sultanate of Oman*, ICSID Case No. ARB/11/33, Award (3 November 2015), paras. 387–390; *David R. Aven and others v. Republic of Costa Rica*, ICSID Case No. UNCT/15/3, Award, 18 September 2018, para. 412.

[86] See also *Urbaser v. Argentina*; *David R. v. Costa Rica.*

[87] Choudhury (2020).

[88] Article 28(9) of the Common Market for Eastern and Southern Africa Investment Agreement.

off-setting effects either on the merits of the claim made by the foreign investor or on the damages awarded.

Turning our attention to India's final model BIT and the subsequent treaties on the issue of counterclaims. As pointed out earlier, they do not specifically recognise or allow for host States bringing counterclaims. So, does it imply that the host State under these treaties cannot bring counterclaims against the foreign investor? In answering this question it would be pertinent to carefully look at footnote 4 to Article 26.3 of the final model BIT. Article 26.3 provides:

> for the calculation of monetary damages, the tribunal shall also reduce the damages to take into account any restitution of property or repeal or modification of the measure, or other mitigating factors.

Then, it provides a footnote, which states that

> mitigating factors can include, current and past use of the investment, the history of its acquisition and purpose, compensation received by the investor from other sources, any unremedied harm or damage that the investor has caused to the environment or local community or other relevant considerations regarding the need to balance public interest and the interests of the investor.

Similar provision is present in India's BITs with Belarus,[89] Taiwan,[90] and the Kyrgyz Republic.[91]

Scholars argue that the mitigating factors mentioned in the footnote would allow for the reintroduction of counterclaims through the back door.[92] As per footnote 4, the tribunal will have to take into account mitigating factors while calculating monetary damages to be paid to the foreign investors. Furthermore, footnote 4 gives wide discretion to the ISDS tribunal to determine mitigating factors.[93] Given the breadth of these mitigating factors, it would give opportunities to the host State to make submissions about any harm, say environmental harm that the investor may have caused. Here, the host State would surely advance the argument of the harm based on breach of domestic laws or other obligations imposed on the foreign investor in the BIT. Thus, in these Indian BITs, the host State has the opportunity to bring counterclaims against the foreign investor indirectly and not directly.

---

[89] See Article 26.3 of India-Belarus BIT 2018.

[90] See footnote 1 of Article 25.3 of the Bilateral Investment Agreement between the Indian Taipei Association in Taipei and The Taipei Economic and Cultural Center in India, 2018.

[91] See footnote 4 to Article 26.3 of the India-Kyrgyz Republic BIT.

[92] Hepburn and Kabra (2017), pp. 98–99.

[93] Hepburn and Kabra (2017), p. 99.

5 Conclusion

One of the major criticisms that the international investment law regime has received is its asymmetrical character where host States are under obligation whereas foreign investors enjoy rights. India's newest BIT practice has tried to address this asymmetry by providing for investor obligations in investment treaties. There are two ways to theorize the presence of investor obligations in BITs – either as part of the recalibration project aimed at balancing investment protection and host State's right to regulate in BITs; or as part of a project that aims to make foreign or transnational corporations accountable for their actions under international law and not just as part of the domestic legal systems in which they operate, where recalibrating treaties is a side point.

If the recalibration theorization is accepted, where the objective is to strike a balance between investment protection and host State's right to regulate, then the provisions on investor obligations could be seen as the normativity of embedded liberalism, something which has been missing in the first generation BITs.[94] John Gerard Ruggie, an American political scientist, conceptualised the post-World War II international economic order as a case of 'embedded liberalism'[95] – a multilateral economic order predicated upon domestic interventionism.[96] Ruggie argued that the post-World War II international economic order shows how "power and legitimate social objectives become fused to project political authority into the international system."[97] 'Embedded liberalism' represented compromise between free market and the State intervening in favour of political and social stability.[98] Thus, imposing specific obligations on foreign investors can be seen as part of building a new BIT template premised on embedded liberalism.

The discussion in the chapter shows that while India has started inserting investor obligation provisions in the newly signed BITs, provisions in most BITs employ soft law or hortatory language, thus framing investor obligations as non-binding best endeavours. This is especially true for provision on corporate social responsibility. These provisions appear to be more a part of the recalibration project, than a part of holding transnational corporations accountable under international law. They also reveal a certain degree of reluctance to impose binding obligations on foreign investors. Perhaps, India and its treaty partner countries appear to be more comfortable with imposing best endeavour clauses on investors. Consequently, the criticism that many make that BITs are essentially neoliberal instruments that are resistant to tweaks has merit.

In sum, it can be said that the surest way of holding foreign investors accountable is by imposing direct and binding obligations on investors as part of the text of the

[94] See Kalderimis (2010); Titi (2014), p. 56.

[95] Ruggie (1982). Also see Lang (2006); Lang (2011).

[96] Lang (2011), p. 393.

[97] Lang (2011), p. 382.

[98] Harvey (2007). Also see Ruggie (1982).

treaty. The provisions in India's BITs that impose the compliance requirements on foreign investors follow this template. Especially on the question of anti-corruption obligation, there is a direct and a binding obligation impose on foreign investors. In this regard, India could consider the treaty templates of other BITs such as the Nigeria-Morocco BIT, the Draft PAIC and few other BITs that are promising. It is critical that India and other countries undertake these treaty reforms, not just as an important step in recalibrating investment treaties but also to address the concern that corporations wield too much power without accountability under international law. These reforms are doable. The incorporation of the best endeavour clauses on investor obligations is a progressive step, which should lead to the next logical step of binding obligations on foreign investors. These reforms are critical to build, what Joseph Stiglitz describes as 'progressive capitalism'.[99]

References

'Analysis of the 2015 Draft Model Indian Bilateral Investment Treaty' Law Commission of India Report No. 260., https://lawcommissionofindia.nic.in/reports/Report260.pdf

Abel P (2018) Counterclaims based on international human rights obligations of investors in international investment arbitration. Brill Open Law 1(1):61–90

Bernasconi-Osterwalder N (2020) Inclusion of investor obligations and corporate accountability provisions in investment agreements. In: Chaisse J, Choukroune L, Jusoh S (eds) Handbook of international investment law and policy. Springer, Cham

Bhasin N, Manocha R (2016) Do bilateral investment treaties promote FDI inflows? Evidence from India. Vikalpa: J Decis Mak 41(4):275–287

Bhattacharjee S (2012) India seeks treaty revision to Deal with corporate suits. The Indian Express of 4 April 2012, http://archive.indianexpress.com/news/india-seeks-treaty-revisions-to-deal-with-corporate-suits/932195/

Choudhury B (2017) Spinning straw into gold: incorporating in business and human rights agenda into international investment agreements. Univ Pa J Int Law 38(2):425–481

Choudhury B (2018) Balancing soft and hard law for business and human rights. Int Comp Law Q 67(4):961–986

Choudhury B (2020) Investor obligations for human rights. ICSID Rev Foreign Invest Law J 35(1–2):82–104

Deva S (2012) Regulating corporate human rights violations: humanising business. Routledge, London

Deva S, Bilchitz D (2017) Building a treaty on business and human rights: context and contours. Cambridge University Press, Cambridge

Franck SD (2005) The legitimacy crisis in investment treaty arbitration: privatizing public international law through inconsistent decisions. Fordham Law Rev 73:1521–1625

Gathi J, Puig S (2019) Introduction to the symposium on investor responsibility: the next frontier in international investment law. AJIL Unbound 113:1–3

Gudgeon K (1986) United States bilateral investment treaties: comments on their origin, purposes, and general treatment standards. Int Tax Bus Lawyer 4(1):105–135

Harvey D (2007) A brief history of neoliberalism. Oxford University Press, Oxford

[99] Stiglitz (2019).

Hepburn J, Kabra R (2017) India's new model investment treaty: fit for purpose? Indian Law Rev 1(2):95–114
Ho J (2019) The creation of elusive investor responsibility. AJIL Unbound 113:10–15
Kalderimis D (2010) Investment treaties and public goods. Transnatl Disp Manage J 1(2010)
Krajewski M (2020) A nightmare or a Noble dream? Establishing investor obligations through treaty-making and treaty-application. Cambridge University Press, Cambridge
Kurtz J (2016) The WTO and international investment law: converging systems. Cambridge University Press, Cambridge
Lang ATF (2006) Reconstructing embedded liberalism: John Gerard Ruggie and constructivist approaches to the study of the international trade regime. J Int Econ Law 9(1):81–116
Lang ATF (2011) World trade law after neoliberalism. Re-imagining the Global Economic Order. Oxford University Press, Oxford
Ranjan P (2019) India and bilateral investment treaties. Oxford University Press, Oxford
Ranjan P, Anand P (2017) The 2016 model Indian bilateral investment treaty: a critical deconstruction. Northwest J Int Law Bus 38(1):1–54
Rodrik D (2011) The globalisation paradox. Oxford University Press, Oxford
Ruggie JG (1982) International regimes, transactions, and change: embedded liberalism and the postwar economic order. Int Organ 36(2):379–415
Sattarova M (2019) Investor responsibilities from a host state perspective: qualitative data and proposals for treaty reform. AJIL Unbound 113:22–27
Sattarova M, Ho J (2021) Introduction. In: Ho J, Sattarova M (eds) Investor's international law. Hart, pp 3–4
Schreuer C (2013) Investments, International Protection. Max Planck Encyclopedia of Public International Law
Stein A (2016) The great trilemma: are globalization, democracy, and sovereignty compatible? Int Theory 8(2):297–340
Stiglitz J (2019) People power and profits: progressive capitalism for an age of discontent. Penguin Random House
Tepper J, Hearn D (2018) The myth of capitalism. John Wiley
Titi C (2014) The right to regulate in international investment law. Hart, Oxford
Vandevlede KJ (2010) Bilateral investment treaties: history, policy and interpretation. Oxford University Press, Oxford/New York
Vijayvergia C, Belmannu P (2020) Exploring the prospects of host-state counterclaims in corruption disputes. Arbitr Int 36(4):583–600
Vinuales JE (2017) Investor diligence in investment arbitration: sources and arguments. ICSID Rev Foreign Invest Law J 32(2):346–370
Waibel M, Kaushal A, Chung K-H, Balchin C (2010) The backlash against investment treaty arbitration: perceptions and reality. Kluwer, Hague

Latest Developments of China's Foreign Investment Policy and Law

Nanying Tao

Contents

Abstract In the wake of US-China tensions and global economic recession, China redesigned wide array of policies and laws to attract and maintain foreign direct investment in China. The most significant reform is the adoption of negative list approach plus pre-establishment national treatment, which further liberalizes foreign investors' access to the Chinese market. This new policy was first tested in Shanghai Pilot Free Trade Zone. After Shanghai's success, China boosted the confidence in rebuilding its entire foreign investment regime. Domestically, it enacted the Foreign Investment Law whose key features include the nationwide application of negative list plus pre-establishment national treatment, the principle of equality between domestic and foreign investment and some relevant administrative reforms. China's foreign investment regime is further upgraded by the recent signing of the Regional Comprehensive Economic Partnership (RCEP) and the EU-China Comprehensive Agreement on Investment (CAI). Therein lies China's tendency towards the "new development philosophy" in international investment. In despite of the new advancements, there are still issues to be clarified, especially the investor-state dispute settlement (ISDS).

N. Tao (✉)
Shanghai University of Finance and Economics, Law School, Shanghai, P.R. China
e-mail: taonanying@mail.shufe.edu.cn

M. Chi et al. (eds.), *Asian Yearbook of International Economic Law 2022*,
Asian Yearbook of International Economic Law (2022) 2022: 109–126,
https://doi.org/10.1007/16517_2022_11, Published online: 11 May 2022

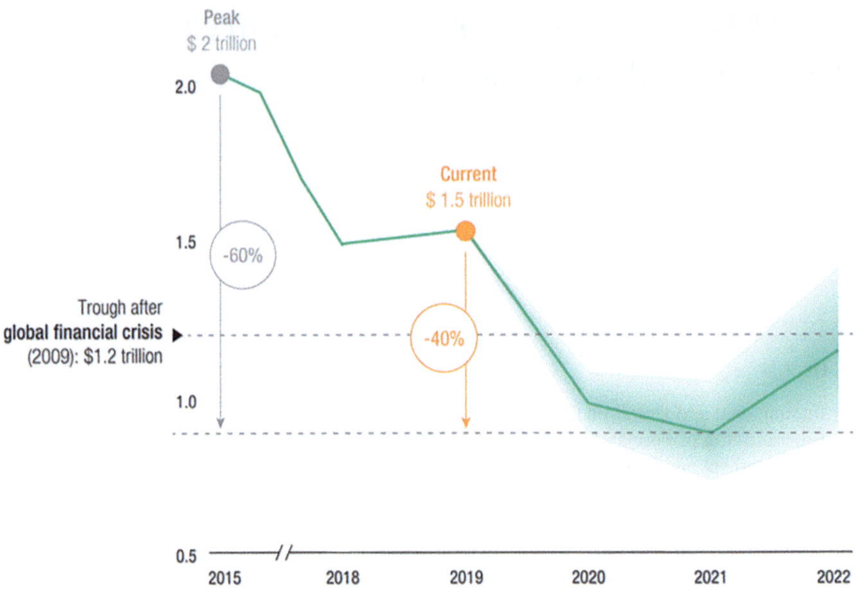

Fig. 1 Global FDI inflows 2015–2019 and 2020–2022 forecast (Trillions of dollars). Source UNCTAD

With the ongoing US-China tensions, China's current and future attitude towards foreign direct investment (FDI) raises wide attention of the international community. Many observers are wondering if China will restrict, or even expropriate foreign investment in China due to the increasing Western (mostly the U.S.) hostility. This concern is not unreasonable. Since its inception, the policies and laws in the People's Republic of China concerning foreign investment have swayed between extremes of restriction and openness, largely depending on the Western attitude towards China. Prior to 1978, FDI in China was highly restricted due to the ideological tension between China and the West in the Cold War era. In the 1980s when the Cold War was waning, China began to relax restrictions on FDI into its domestic economy. Since its accession to the WTO, China has gradually liberalized FDI and become the world's second largest FDI recipient.[1] Based on this history, it is no wonder that people would worry about the future of FDI in China—if the current tensions lead to a "new Cold War", will China discontinue its process of investment liberalization? This paper tries to reply this concern by presenting recent developments in China's legal framework and policies towards FDI.

[1]Chen (2011), pp. 33–50.

1 International and Domestic Contexts

China's policies and laws towards FDI are, first of all, made in consideration of international circumstances. Recent years have witnessed a slowdown in the global economy. An obvious indicator is the lasting decline of global FDI flows in recent and maybe future years. According to the World Investment Report 2020, Global FDI flows reach their peak value in 2015 and decrease in the following 5 years. Especially in 2020, they are forecasted to decrease by up to 40 per cent from the value of $1.54 trillion, bringing FDI below $1 trillion for the first time since 2005.[2] And the trend is expected to remain, decreasing by a further 5 to 10% in 2021 (see Fig. 1).[3]

The decay is of course caused by the COVID-19 pandemic which broke out in early 2020 and will last in the near future. Policies and measures taken by governments during the pandemic, such as lockdown and international travel restrictions, were significantly slowing down or even damaging existing investment projects, and the deep recession following the pandemic will negatively affect the willingness to invest in the future years.

But COVID-19 is not the only culprit, rather, it can be regarded as the last straw breaking the back of the global economy. Even before the outbreak of the pandemic, the global FDI flows had already been stagnant as a result of the so-called reverse globalization.[4] Since 2016, economic nationalism and protectionism has grown to an unprecedented height and created turbulences including the Brexit referendum, trade wars, and the WTO Appellate Body crisis.[5] The arrival of COVID-19 appears to accelerate the trend towards reverse globalization, as we can see the global surge of economic nationalism as well as the escalation of US-China tensions in 2020. In brief, the prospect of global economy is highly uncertain, depending on the effectiveness of policy interventions to mitigate the effects of reverse globalization and on the duration of the pandemic. Accordingly, investors are projected to be more reluctant to expand their business abroad.[6]

Facing an overall decline in the global FDI flows, China is under severe pressure in attracting and maintaining FDI inflows into its domestic economy. Previously, China could successfully absorb FDI because of its cheap labor costs, comparatively rich resources, stable political situations and preferential policies to foreign

[2] UNCTAD (2020), p. X.

[3] UNCTAD (2020), p. 2.

[4] See e.g. Frieden (2019), pp. 43–52.

[5] The proximate reason for the World Trade Organization (WTO) crisis is the dwindling number of Appellate Body members, the result of the US blocking new appointments as the terms of sitting members expire. In April 2020, China, the EU and other WTO members have formally notified the "Multi-party interim appeal arbitration arrangement" (MPIA) to the WTO. See World Trade Organization (2020).

[6] UNCTAD (2020), p. X.

investment.[7] But now it is less competitive as an investment destination: the labor costs are increasing as workers are demanding higher wage partly in order to compensate for rising inflation that is eroding their purchasing power, the long-term overexploitation of raw materials and energy brings about environmental and social problems which in turn jeopardize the sustainable development of economy, and the ongoing US-China tensions raise wide concern about the security of investing in China.[8] Recent years some companies have already left China and relocated in other cheaper Asian sites such as Thailand, the Philippines and Vietnam; and some even returned to their home countries.[9]

In face of the current international and domestic circumstances, China feels an urgent need to upgrade its preferential policies concerning FDI in order to enhance the competitiveness in the global market and maintain its status as an economic power. The following will demonstrate how China reformulates its policies and laws to respond the newly emerging challenges and problems.

2 Liberalization of Foreign Investment: Negative List Approach

With the global growth of economic nationalism and protectionism, what has been easily overlooked is China's recent liberalization of its policies concerning foreign investors' merge and acquisition activities in China. A salient indicator is reducing restrictions on foreign investors' entry into certain industries, known as the adoption of negative list approach.

Investment liberalization largely depends on the effective removal of restrictions on investment in certain areas. In practice the restrictions can be revealed by the adoption of either a positive or a negative list approach in the investment catalogue. A positive list permits investment in only those areas expressly stated on the list whereas a negative list permits investment in all areas except those on the list. From this point of view, the negative list approach is thought to be a more liberal policy towards FDI.[10]

For a long term, China had used a positive list, notably the Catalogue of Industries for Guiding Foreign Investment, to delineate the areas where foreign investment was

[7] Chen (2006), p. 919.

[8] Zhong (2019), pp. 138–139.

[9] According to the UNCTAD report, in 2019, FDI flows into developing Asia declined by 5%, to $474 billion, but in South-East Asia, inflows grew 5% to a record level of $156 billion, propelled by strong investment in countries such as India, Indonesia and Vietnam. In meanwhile as the impact of the 2017 tax reforms in the United States waned, FDI flows to developed economies rose by 5%, to $800 billion, from their revised level of $761 billion in 2018. Supra UNCTAD (2020), pp. 11 and 38.

[10] Hu (2017), p. 229.

encouraged, allowed, and prohibited.[11] This approach is perhaps based on China's mentality as a capital-importing state, the lack of strength of China's nascent economy vis-a-vis its international counterparts, and the attempts to maintain the "socialist nature" of Chinese economy.[12] Therefore in many early Sino-foreign bilateral investment treaties (BITs),[13] we can find that foreign investors did not enjoy full-fledged national treatment: unlike local investors, they had no freedom to establish investments in certain sectors (e.g. financial industry, education industry and telecommunication industry), and national treatment was only conferred after the investment had been approved by the Chinese government.

China's move towards the negative list approach started from the negotiations between China and the United States for the conclusion of BIT. A focal point for the BIT negotiation was whether China could, at the request of the United States, provide foreign investors with treatment that is no less favorable than domestic investors when they both entry a market and establish investments, known as the pre-establishment national treatment.[14] In other words, the U.S. wanted China to apply the negative list approach and to remove hurdles in market access as much as possible. A nationwide debate on the future tendency of China's FDI management regime then was carried out: should China incrementally liberalize investment with the existing positive list approach, or should it radically shift to the negative list approach?[15] Eventually the government chose the latter. In July of 2013, China during the fifth ground of US–China Strategic and Economic Dialogue conceded that the negotiations could continue with the condition of pre-establishment national treatment.[16] To fulfill the concession, it soon promised to grant foreign investors market access based on the negative list instead of the existing positive list.[17]

China's acceptance of the negative list approach is not merely under the U.-S. pressure; rather, it is based on pragmatism. While negotiating with the United States, the Chinese government has already realized the rising costs and foreign competition in low-end manufacturing and is upgrading industry in order to replace labor-intensive and resource-intensive manufacturing facilities with capital-intensive and technology-intensive industries.[18] The transformation of economy of course requires the endeavor of domestic firms, but the process will be smooth with the addition (or maybe the guidance) of foreign technologies brought by investment. Now the fourth industrial revolution is taking shape, represented by the global

[11] Liu (2018), p. 288.

[12] Sauvant and Nolan (2015), p. 922; Shan and Chen (2016), p. 225.

[13] For example, China-Sweden BIT (effective 29 March 1982), the very first Chinese BIT, contained neither national treatment nor investor-state dispute settlement provisions.

[14] Shan and Chen (2016).

[15] Cui and Cai (2019), p. 15.

[16] People News (2013) The fifth ground of the US–China Strategic and Economic Dialogue is Closed. http://world.people.com.cn/n/2013/0712/c1002-22180761.html.

[17] Shan and Chen (2016), pp. 229–230.

[18] Zhong (2019), pp. 143–144.

development of artificial intelligence (AI), 5G technology, nanotechnology, autonomous vehicles (AV), blockchain, gene therapy, virtual reality, 3D printing and others that blur the lines among the physical, digital, and biological spheres. To catch up with the trend, not only China, but also all stakeholders of the global polity, from the public to private sectors, are seeking and attracting the providers of intellectual and physical capital, be it innovators or shareholders, investors or whoever. In this sense, the U.S. request for pre-establishment national treatment was a momentum for China to release its control over certain high-tech industries and actively absorb relevant investment. By 2020, China has completely opened up its financial sector and, substantially, liberalized many manufacturing industries including the pharmaceutical, petrochemical, petroleum, and equipment manufacturing industries.[19]

3 Establishment and Development of Pilot Free Trade Zones

Since it is a first try, China in practice faced significant problems in applying the negative list approach, ranging from risk control to implementation measures. The resolution is trial and error, manifested by establishing pilot free trade zones (PFTZs) around the country. The idea of PFTZ may be derived from the Special Economic Zone (SEZ) practice. In the 1980s, China abandoned its ideological constraints in the economic strategy and progressed in its efforts to attract foreign investment through offering five SEZs, namely Shenzhen, Zhuhai, Xiamen, Shantou and Hainan, special and preferential policies (e.g. the removal of tariffs on imported goods for re-export).[20] From 1980 the five SEZs, especially Shenzhen, grew at a phenomenal rate as a tremendous amount of foreign capital was invested there, igniting the lust of Chinese people for wealth and attracting a huge population across the country flowing into. Based on the experience gained from the SEZs, the Chinese government decided to select several areas as test beds for the negative list approach which, depending on the performance, may eventually be implemented nationally. To minimize the economic fluctuations and other unpredictable consequences brought by the radical shift, China in 2013 chose Shanghai, the country's most mature and experienced market, as the first PFTZ.[21]

Unlike the free trade area or customs union under the General Agreement on Tariffs and Trade (GATT), Shanghai PFTZ is still subject to the overall authority of

[19] Special Administrative Measures (Negative List) for the Access of Foreign Investment (2020). https://www.ndrc.gov.cn/xxgk/zcfb/fzggwl/202006/P020200624549035288187.pdf.

[20] Chen (2011), p. 36.

[21] The China (Shanghai) Pilot Free Trade Zone Administration (Shanghai PFTZ) is built on the four existent customs supervision areas: Shanghai Waigaoqiao Bonded Zone, Waigaoqiao Bonded Logistics Zone, Yangshan Bonded Port, Shanghai Pudong Airport Free Trade Zone, and part of Pudong New Area, with the area of 120.72 km^2 in total. See http://en.china-shftz.gov.cn/2020-04/08/c_263780.htm.

the Chinese government. The PFTZ Management Committee, which coordinates and administers the operation of Shanghai PFTZ, serves as the agent of the Shanghai Municipal People's Government.[22] But Shanghai PFTZ enjoys some extent of autonomy as the State Council, authorized by the Standing Committee of the National People's Congress (Chinese top legislature), conferred it with the power to temporarily suspend and adjust relevant laws and regulations in the zone.[23] For example, to implement the negative list approach, the administrative approval items prescribed in the Law of the People's Republic of China on Foreign-Funded Enterprises, the Law of the People's Republic of China on Chinese-Foreign Equity Joint Ventures, and the Law of the People's Republic of China on Chinese-Foreign Contractual Joint Ventures (hereafter "Three Investment Laws") were suspended for three years in the zone,[24] paving the path for Shanghai to explore new rules and measures regulating foreign investment.

In the first three years, the governments formulated and promulgated series of regulations to construct a new foreign investment regime in the PFTZ. Overall speaking, the construction contains two parts: liberalizing market access and transforming government functions. For the first part, the State Council in 2013 issued a Framework Plan for Shanghai PFTZ ("Frame Plan"), where it stated that "the fields of financial services, shipping services, commerce and trade services, professional services, cultural services, and social services shall be selected for expanded opening-up, and access restriction measures (except for banking institutions and information and communication services), such as the qualification requirements for investors, equity ratio restrictions, and restrictions on business scope, shall be suspended or cancelled, so as to create a market environment favorable to the equal access of various investors".[25] The Shanghai municipal government soon detailed the Frame Plan and announced the Special Management Measures for Access of Foreign Investment to China (Shanghai) Pilot Free Trade Zone (Shanghai Negative List) in 2014. However, it seems that the first negative list did not significantly relax market access for foreign investment, as it included 139 restricting measures in 89 fields ranging from agriculture to entertainment.[26] One reason for it may be that China in the early years still took prudential attitude

[22]Ibid.

[23]Decision of the Standing Committee of the National People's Congress on Authorizing the State Council to Temporarily Adjust the Relevant Administrative Approval Items Prescribed in Laws in China (Shanghai) Pilot Free Trade Zone [Expired] (Effective 1 October 2013).

[24]Ibid.

[25]Notice by the State Council of Issuing the Framework Plan for China (Shanghai) Pilot Free Trade Zone (Effective 18 September 2013), http://www.gov.cn/zwgk/2013-09/27/content_2496147.htm.

[26]Special Management Measures for Access of Foreign Investment to China (Shanghai) Pilot Free Trade Zone (Effective 30 June 2014). See http://www1.shanghaiinvest.com/cn/viewfile.php?id=8306.

towards the new approach, maintaining the shift in an incremental and controllable way.[27]

Constructing a new foreign investment regime needs not only the opening-up of market but also an administrative reform which guarantees the opening-up. Conventionally, foreign investors were required to go through a complicated and time-consuming approval process before doing business in China. First, they should prepare an application including a letter of intent, approval documents from the Environment Protection Department, an energy conservation rating from the Energy Conservation Department and others, and submit the application to the Development and Reform Commission (DRC) for verification. Even after the investment was approved, investor should also, depending on the amount of investment, obtain approval for the form of foreign investment enterprise business vehicle by sending a joint venture contract or articles of association to the Commission of Commerce (COFCOM) or Ministry of Commerce (MOFCOM). After obtaining the above approvals, investor must then request a business license from the State Administration of Industry and Commerce (SAIC).[28] These restrictive and complicated procedures were essentially discriminations as they were not applied to the domestic investors—at least the domestic investors did not need the approval for the form of enterprise business vehicle from the COFCOM or MOFCOM. Moreover, the approval procedures were often arbitrary and confidential, as the various authorities involved could set the criteria of whether the project was in line with national development plans and industrial policies without reasoning.[29] This further increase the costs and risks of investing in China.

To guarantee the pre-establishment national treatment, Shanghai PFTZ, through several regulations and administrative orders, streamlined the procedures for establishing investment. Article 13 of the Regulations on China (Shanghai) Pilot Free Trade Zone stipulates that

> for areas falling outside the Negative List, on the principle of same treatment for foreign investors and domestic investors, recordation will apply for foreign investment projects; the establishment and change of foreign investment projects will be subject to recordation. . .[30]

Thanks to the cancellation of approval procedure, most foreign investors who seek to establish projects in the PFTZ are only required to go through a simple recording procedure with the PFTZ Administrative Commission. The recording procedure is further simplified by a "One Window" model. Under the new model, investors could

---

[27] In a report concerning the Regulations on China (Shanghai) Pilot Free Trade Zone, Wei Ding, the vice dean of the Law Committee, pointed that, to deal with the relationship between reform and stability, the Committee in the law-making process had left room for future institutional innovations. Committee of Legislative Affairs of Shanghai Municipal People's Congress (2014).

[28] Potter (1995), p. 171.

[29] Villalta Puig and Tsam Tai (2017), pp. 680–681.

[30] Article 13 of the Regulations on China (Shanghai) Pilot Free Trade Zone (effective 1 August 2014), http://www.china-shftz.gov.cn/PublicInformation.aspx?GID=94d49ae8-08ef-4c96-8151-b5686394d2f8&CID=953a259a-1544-4d72-be6a-264677089690&MenuType=1&navType=1.

submit applications to the Authority for Industry and Commerce (AIC). After receiving all materials, the AIC then issues all relevant licenses and certificates (e.g. business license, enterprise code certificate, and tax registration certificate) to the investors.[31] The speed of establishing investment in the PFTZ is thus significantly fast: while it may take at least 29 days to set up a business elsewhere in China, the time in Shanghai PFTZ is only 4 days.[32]

Besides the reform of establishment procedures, Shanghai PFTZ also accelerated the transformation of government functions in other fields, with an aim to build a new management system compatible with the negative list approach. For instance, the aforementioned "One Window" model was later developed into a new administrative mechanism featuring "all-in-one acceptance, integrated approval, and efficient operation."[33] In the meanwhile the government strengthened data exchange and information sharing between relevant departments so that they can effectively coordinate.[34] Moreover, Shanghai PFTZ sought more channels to protect the rights of foreign investors. In April of 2014, the Shanghai International Arbitration Center officially issued the China (Shanghai) Pilot Free Trade Zone Arbitration Rules (the "FTZ Arbitration Rules") which included a lot of bold attempts and innovation for better settling the commercial disputes among foreign investors.[35]

With the new foreign investment regime, Shanghai during 2013 to 2016 attracted 40,000 companies to the PFTZ.[36] This early success encouraged the Chinese government to roll out PFTZ nationwide, and the speed quickened due to the continuing changes in domestic and international circumstances. In 2015 China added three more PFTZs,[37] seven in 2017,[38] one in 2018[39] and further six in 2019.[40] Whilst the first generation of PFTZs are centered around coastal areas with sea ports, most of the following zones are located inland, indicating a push to attract foreign investment to China's interior. In the meanwhile, Shanghai PFTZ was expanded to the Lingang New Area. Major foreign investments, such as the new

[31] Villalta Puig and Tsam Tai (2017), p. 682.

[32] Palmioli and Heal (2014), p. 6.

[33] The "One Window" model cuts all unnecessary bureaucratic steps for application, approval and management. To register and undertake business in China, foreign-funded enterprises will be able to submit a single application to a single office, rather than register separately with various government offices. Accordingly, the office after accepts application will issue all licenses to the applicants. See fn. 25.

[34] Since 2013, Shanghai has built series of information platforms, including the Public Service Information Platform, Shanghai Data App, and Credit Shanghai.

[35] Shanghai International Arbitration Center (2015).

[36] Yang (2017).

[37] They are China (Guangdong) Pilot Free Trade Zone, China (Tianjin) Pilot Free Trade Zone and China (Fujian) Pilot Free Trade Zone.

[38] They are China Pilot Free Trade Zones in Liaoning, Zhejiang, Henan, Hubei, Chongqing, Sichuan and Shanxi.

[39] China (Hainan) Pilot Free Trade Zone.

[40] They are in Shandong, Jiangsu, Guangxi, Hebei, Yunnan and Heilongjiang.

Tesla car factory, have already operated therein. The development of PFTZ culminated in 2020, marked by the building of Hainan Free Trade Port (FTP). In June of 2020, the State Council announced the Overall Plan for the Construction of Hainan Free Trade Port.[41] In order to develop the southern island province into a globally-influential high-level free trade port, Hainan FTP was said to target the highest level of investment liberalization. A representative move is granting market access to foreign investors who make a prior commitment. The "prior commitment" mechanism abandons the administrative approval requirement in principle and concentrates on the interim and ex post regulation. In other words, foreign investors, even those invest in restricted fields, could skip the recordation procedure and operate their business directly in Hainan FTP if a commitment regarding the lawfulness of investment has been made.[42]

Successful experiments in the PFTZs reinforced China's determination to apply the negative list approach nationwide. In June of 2017, the DRC and the MOFCOM jointly unveiled China's first national negative list: Special Administrative Measures for Foreign Investment Access. Compared to the aforementioned Shanghai Negative List, the national version shortened the restricted and prohibited fields (35 and 28 respectively).[43] And the tendency continued—the latest 2020 National Negative List has cut the number of special measures to 33.[44]

4 The Chinese Foreign Investment Law

While formulating liberal policies and regulations on FDI, China felt that it was necessary to provide the liberalization with a stable, unified and transparent legal framework. Thus in 2015, China drafted the Foreign Investment Law of the People's Republic of China (FIL) and released for comments and revisions. However, the law-making plan was put on hold until 2019. In a matter of months, the Chinese government on 15 March 2019 officially passed the FIL and announced that the existing foreign investment legal regime represented by the Three Investment Laws would be repealed when the new law came into effect on 1 January 2020.[45] The speedy reform of China's foreign investment legal regime can be attributed to many factors, such as the outbreak of China-US trade wars, the sufficient experience gained from the PFTZs, and the national promotion of the negative list approach.

[41] Master Plan for the Construction of Hainan Free Trade Port (effective 1 June 2020), http://www.gov.cn/zhengce/2020-06/01/content_5516608.htm.

[42] Ibid.

[43] The National Development and Reform Commission and the Ministry of Commerce of the People's Republic of China (2017) Catalogue of Industries for Guiding Foreign Investment [Expired] (effective 28 June 2017), http://www.gov.cn/xinwen/2017-06/28/content_5206424.htm.

[44] See fn. 19.

[45] Investment Law of the People's Republic of China, http://www.chinalaw.gov.cn/Department/content/2019-03/18/592_230773.html.

One highlight of the FIL is that China in Article 4 of the law commits to maintaining the negative list approach plus pre-establishment national treatment for foreign investment and it for the first time defines the scope: "pre-establishment national treatment refers to the treatment given to foreign investors and their investments during the investment access stage, which is not lower than that given to their domestic counterparts; negative list refers to special administrative measures for the access of foreign investment in specific fields as stipulated by the State. The State shall give national treatment to foreign investment beyond the negative list. The negative list will be issued by or upon approval by the State Council."[46]

Compared to the previous administrative regulations, the FIL is more advanced as it offers foreign investors national treatment in a comprehensive sense, including not only national treatment before establishment but also that during and after establishment. Article 9, for example, states that "foreign-invested enterprises may, in accordance with the law, equally enjoy the State policies concerning the support of enterprise development". Article 15 and 16 further stipulate that foreign-invested enterprises have equal access to the standard-setting work and government procurement in accordance with the law.

Also, from the text we can find that the government's role in the investment management system has shifted from a supervisor to a server. The law expresses that "the State establishes and improves a system serving foreign investment to provide consultation and services to foreign investors and foreign-invested enterprises on laws and regulations, policy measures, and investment project information",[47] and "the people's governments at all levels and their relevant departments shall, in accordance with the principles of facilitation, efficiency and transparency, simplify procedures, improve efficiency, optimize government services, and further improve the level of foreign investment services."[48]

Some may, at this point, conclude that China, through the new legal regime, could create a stable, transparent, and predictable investment environment for foreign investors. This may be true, but it is too early to say so. As is often the case with national legislations, the FIL only lays out a basic framework for the new foreign investment legal regime, leaving many gaps to be filled by separate implementation regulations, rules and measures.

For example, China's policy towards the typical structure of investment protection known as ISDS is ambiguous. To settle disputes between state and foreign investors, Article 26 of the FIL provides a "foreign investment complaint mechanism". This is an administrative complaint and settlement mechanism for foreign-invested enterprises. "If a foreign-invested enterprise or its investors believe that the administrative actions of the administrative organ and its staff infringe upon their

[46]Investment Law of the People's Republic of China, Article 4.

[47]Investment Law of the People's Republic of China, Article 11.

[48]Investment Law of the People's Republic of China, Article 19.

legitimate rights and interests, they may apply for a coordinated solution through the complaint and settlement mechanism for the foreign-invested enterprise".[49]

The establishment of complaint mechanism may have a far-reaching implication for China's attitude towards ISDS. It is well known that China used to favor abandoning ISDS altogether, leaving foreign investors to the vicissitudes of domestic law and court procedures in the host state, or of any inter-state process under customary international law or as agreed in investment treaties.[50] Since 1998 China gradually liberalized foreign investors' access to international arbitration, as many new BITs and re-negotiated BITs stipulated access to the International Centre for Settlement of Investment Disputes (ICSID) and other international arbitration mechanisms on a wide range of investment-related issues.[51] Recently China began to waver. The most recent BITs provide access to international arbitration, but they set domestic administrative procedure as preconditions for ISDS. For instance, the Annex C.21 of China–Canada BIT (2012) states that:

> Upon receipt of the Notice of Intent or at any time prior, China shall require that an investor make use of the domestic administrative reconsideration procedure. If the investor considers that the dispute still exists four months after the investor has applied for the administrative reconsideration, or where no such remedies are available, the investor may submit its claim to arbitration.[52]

Apparently, the complaint mechanism contained in the FIL confirms the hesitation. This move seems to deviate from investment liberalization and promotion. Emphasizing the prior recourse to administrative settlement may somewhat prolong the whole settlement process as investors have to go through long and costly administrative settlement before resort to arbitration. Moreover, the impartiality and independence of administrative settlement may be doubted as the domestic institutions in China are believed to be hardly a sufficient bulwark against governmental interferences.[53]

5 China's Recent Treaty Practice in International Investment Law

While reforming its foreign investment legal regime, China never stops making new international investment agreements (IIAs) with other states although there appeared no likelihood of any deal being done due to the pandemic and China-US tensions. Then things suddenly changed for the better, featured with the conclusion of RCEP and the EU-China CAI in the end of 2020. RCEP is a free trade agreement (FTA)

[49] Investment Law of the People's Republic of China, Article 26.

[50] Wang (2011), pp. 204–225; Willems (2011); Chi and Wang (2015).

[51] Chi and Wang (2015), pp. 883–888.

[52] Annex C.21 (1), China–Canada BIT (effective 1 October 2014).

[53] Schill (2007), pp. 73–91.

among 15 Asia-Pacific states, namely China, Australia, Brunei, Cambodia, Indonesia, Japan, Laos, Malaysia, Myanmar, New Zealand, the Philippines, Singapore, South Korea, Thailand, and Vietnam. Representing about 30% of the world's population and 30% of global GDP as of 2020, RCEP is marked as the largest regional trade bloc outside the WTO.[54] Soon after the signing of RCEP, China finished its seven-year-long negotiations with the European Union and reached in principle a comprehensive agreement on investment, known as the EU-China CAI. When implemented, the two agreements will help anchor China in international investment, serving as a potential counterweight to disruptions from trade tensions and the pandemic. Besides the significance in realpolitik, the two newly signed treaties, from the perspective of international investment law, are valuable. First, they demonstrate the internationalization of China's negative list approach, and second, they imply China's promotion of the "new development philosophy" in international investment.

One key feature in RCEP and the EU-China CAI is that they both adopt negative list approach to market access, though at different levels. According to Article 10.3 of RCEP, national treatment shall be conferred in principle to foreign investors when they establish, acquire, expand, manage, conduct, operate or sell investments in the contracting states.[55] The negative list approach is provided by Article 10.8, where states that the request of national treatment shall not apply to sectors listed by contracting states in their Schedules of Reservations and Non-Conforming Measures for Services and Investment (RCEP Annex III).[56] Notwithstanding all 15 contracting states adopted negative list approach for investment, the level of openness in each state varies. For example, whereas China's schedule of reservations largely resembles its national negative list (2019 Edition) and runs to only 28 pages,[57] the number of pages in Myanmar's is 53,[58] suggesting significant obstacles to investment are likely to remain. Page counts alone of course do not tell the whole story, as Article 10.8 (b) and (c) allow the renewal and amendment of reservations, indicating that the negative list approach will incrementally lead to greater access.[59]

Like RCEP, the CAI also grants foreign investors national treatment with respect to establishment and operation (Article 4) except the reservations China listed in

---

[54] RCEP: Asia-Pacific countries form world's largest trading bloc, https://rcepsec.org/2020/11/26/rcep-asia-pacific-countries-form-worlds-largest-trading-bloc/.

[55] Legal Text of the RCEP Agreement, https://rcepsec.org/wp-content/uploads/2020/11/Chapter-10.pdf, Article 10.3.

[56] RCEP Agreement, Article 10.8.

[57] Legal Text of the RCEP Agreement, Indonesia – Schedule of Reservations and Non-Conforming Measures for Investment. https://rcepsec.org/wp-content/uploads/2020/11/China-Schedule-of-Reservations-and-Non-Conforming-Measures-for-Investment.pdf.

[58] Legal Text of the RCEP Agreement, Myanmar – Schedule of Reservations and Non-Conforming Measures for Investment. https://rcepsec.org/wp-content/uploads/2020/11/Myanmar-Schedule-of-Reservations-and-Non-Conforming-Measures-for-Investment.pdf.

[59] RCEP Agreement, Article 10.8.

Annex I,[60] but the level of market access is higher than that provided by RCEP. For instance, China in RCEP requires the shareholding percentage of the Chinese party in automobile manufacture to be more than 50%, while it in the CAI stipulates that "after 2022, investments by foreign investors in the manufacture of passenger cars will not be subject to restrictions on shareholding percentage."[61] Another typical reflection is the liberalization of financial service. In the CAI China for the first time makes an international commitment to the entry of foreign financial institutions into the Chinese banking, securities, future and insurance market, albeit some restrictions on the nature of investors and on the percentage of shareholding.[62] Additionally, we can find from the CAI that many sectors traditionally monopolized by local investors are increasingly open to foreign investors, such as telecommunication services, education, medicine and press.[63]

Besides the internationalization of negative list approach, the treaties China recently concluded also imply a potential paradigm shift in the Chinese investment policy: from seeking investment liberalization to promoting comprehensive development in international investment, known as the "new development philosophy". Proposed by Chinese President Xi Jinping for China's Five-Year Plan, the conception of "new development philosophy" refers to innovative, coordinated, green, open and shared development.[64] More specifically, innovative development focuses on the drivers of growth while coordinated development aims to solve the imbalance in development, green development highlights the harmony between human and environment, open development stresses interactions between China and the international community, and shared development underpins social equality and justice.[65] The "new development philosophy" preliminarily aims to address challenges and problems arising from China's road to modernization. In the years filled by unprecedented uncertainties and pandemic-induced challenges coupled with headwinds of protectionism and unilateralism, it seems that China attempts to put the policy on the international table for answering broad skepticism about its commitment to market opening and international rules and norms.

A slew of provisions in the two treaties epitomize the "new development philosophy", although each lays emphasis on different aspects. Taking more account of the uneven levels of development among the contracting states, RCEP stresses more on equality and justice. For developing and least developed country parties, additional flexibilities and provisions for special and differential treatment are offered. For

---

[60] EU-China Comprehensive Agreement on Investment (CAI), https://trade.ec.europa.eu/doclib/docs/2021/january/tradoc_159343.pdf, Article 4.

[61] EU-China Comprehensive Agreement on Investment (CAI), China's schedule of commitments and reservations.

[62] Ibid.

[63] Ibid.

[64] Xinhuanet (2016) Leading Development with New Development Philosophy, http://www.xinhuanet.com//politics/2016-04/29/c_128943741_2.htm.

[65] Ibid.

instance, to respect the desire to control the country's economy and protect key domestic industries from foreign capital, Article 10.1 specifically points out in the footnotes that investment in Malaysia, Thailand, Cambodia, Indonesia, and Viet Nam means those specifically approved or registered in writing by competent authorities in accordance with their respective laws, regulations, and policies.[66] Moreover, measures concerning investment facilitation among the contracting states, such as organizing meetings between respective competent authorities aimed at exchanging knowledge and approaches to better facilitate investment, are also included in order to enhance the parties' (especially the developing Parties) capability to attract and maintain FDI.[67]

With the addition of "Section IV: Investment and sustainable development", it appears that the CAI focuses more on coordinated and green development. Integrating sustainable development, especially the protection of environment and labor rights, into IIAs is not uncommon for the European Union if we look at investment treaties it signed in recent years.[68] For a long term China is thought to avoid grand gesture in sustainable development especially international labor standards and climate change: that's why the EU-China BIT negotiations had gone at a snail pace.[69] Surprisingly China at this time agreed to ambitious provisions on sustainable development. According to the rules, China is undertaking several commitments in the areas of labor and environment, including promoting corporate social responsibility, effectively implementing the Paris Agreement on climate change, facilitating and encouraging investment in environmental goods and services, fulfilling the obligations under the International Labor Organization Conventions (ILO) it has ratified, and working towards the ratification of the ILO fundamental Conventions on forced labor. The enforcement of these commitments is relatively solid, subject to a specific working group known as independent panel of experts who will address sustainable development matters with a high degree of transparency and participation of civil society.[70]

Obviously the two treaties, especially the CAI, are the most ambitious IIAs that China has ever concluded. They may be a bellwether of China's future attitude towards international investment: from investment liberalization to comprehensive development. Yet it is still too hard to see how China will present its "new development philosophy" on the international stage, since the two treaties are not yet ratified (in 2022 RCEP took effect for the ratifying countries) and their finer details, such as the design of ISDS, are still up for debate. Apparently both treaties only establish a quasi-WTO mechanism for the settlement of state-state dispute,

[66] RCEP Agreement, Article 10.1.

[67] RCEP Agreement, Article 10.17.

[68] See for example Chapter 20 of the Comprehensive and Progressive Agreement for Trans-Pacific Partnership (CPTPP), chapter 22–24 of the Comprehensive Economic and Trade Agreement (CETA).

[69] See e.g. Shan and Wang (2015), pp. 263–264; Devadason (2014).

[70] EU-China Comprehensive Agreement on Investment (CAI), Subsection 4.

while the provisions with regard to the settlement for investor-state dispute are absent, which is relatively rare in China's IIA practice. Many reasons can be attributed to the absence, such as the international criticism against ISDS, the European promotion of the controversial investment court, the huge differences among RCEP contracting states concerning the acceptance of ISDS, and also China's recent policy preference to administrative settlement. Given these uncertainties, China is thought to take an early harvest approach with future upgrades when negotiating the treaties.[71] Both treaties contain a commitment to try to complete negotiations on investment dispute settlement within certain years, indicating that some thorny issues such as whether the investor-state disputes should be settled in the context of arbitration or an investment court will be addressed or renegotiated at a later stage.

6 Conclusion

Against the backdrop of US-China tensions and global economic recession, China is, with the gradual adoption of negative list approach and the "new development philosophy", cultivating a more liberal, more friendly and more equitable environment in the hope of raising the possibility of further FDI. The implementation of FIL and the conclusion of RCEP and the EU-China CAI of course signify a milestone in China's policy and laws on foreign investment, manifesting not only the determination to liberalize market access but also a tendency to rebalance several relations arising from international investment (e.g. investor-state, developing-developed, human-nature). But these moves are only a starting point. To achieve a stable, transparent and predictable investment environment, many more commitments, legislations, regulations and measures are needed. This is a huge project, and recent events, such as US-China tensions in which the United States aggressively sought to discourage FDI into China, and the COVID-19 pandemic which has cast a cloud over the world's FDI prospects in at least the short to medium term, may make it harder for China to proceed the project.

References

Chen A (2006) Should the four great safeguards in Sino-Foreign BITs be hastily dismantled? J World Invest Trade 7(6):899–933

Chen C (2011) Foreign direct investment in China: location determinants, investor differences and economic impacts. Edward Elgar, Cheltenham

Chi M, Wang X (2015) The evolution of ISA clauses in Chinese IIAs and its practical implications. J World Investment Trade 16(5–6):869–898

[71] Wang (2017).

Committee of Legislative Affairs of Shanghai Municipal People's Congress (2014) Report on the Review of the Regulations on China (Shanghai) Pilot Free Trade Zone. http://www.spcsc.sh.cn/shrdgzw/node5/node48/n1709/u1ai58047.html

Cui F, Cai K (2019) An initial discussion on China's foreign investment law. J SUIBE 3:14–24

Devadason ES (2014) The Trans-Pacific Partnership (TPP): the Chinese perspective. J Contemp China 23(87):462–479

Frieden J (2019) The Backlash against globalization and the future of the international economic order. In: Diamond P (ed) The crisis of globalization: democracy, capitalism, and inequality in the twenty-first century. I.B. Tauris, London, pp 43–52

Hu J (2017) A retrospective view on the first three years of China (Shanghai) Pilot Free Trade Zone. Chinese Econ 50(4):225–237

Liu M (2018) The new Chinese foreign investment law and its implication on foreign investors. Northwest J Int Law Bus 38(2):285–306

Palmioli G, Heal A (2014) Structural economic reform in China: the role of the Shanghai Free Trade Zone. ESCAP Trade Insights:Issue No. 3

Potter P (1995) Foreign investment law in the People's Republic of China: Dilemmas of state control. China Q 141:155–185

Sauvant KP, Nolan MD (2015) China's outward foreign direct investment and international investment law. J Int Econ Law 18(4):893–934

Schill SW (2007) Tearing down the great wall: the new generation investment treaties of The People's Republic of China. Cardozo J Int Comp Law 15(1):73–118

Shan W, Chen H (2016) China-US BIT negotiation and the emerging Chinese BIT 4.0. In: Lim CL (ed) Alternative visions of the international law on foreign investment: essays in Honour of Muthucumaraswamy Sornarajah. Cambridge University Press, Cambridge, pp 223–252

Shan W, Wang L (2015) The China–EU BIT and the emerging 'Global BIT 2.0'. ICSID Rev 30(1):260–267

Shanghai International Arbitration Center (2015) The China (Shanghai) Pilot Free Trade Zone Arbitration Rules. http://www.shiac.org/upload_files/file/2020/20200813142126_1384.pdf

UNCTAD (2020) World Investment Report 2020. https://unctad.org/en/pages/PublicationWebflyer.aspx?publicationid=2769.

Villalta Puig G, Tsam Tai SL (2017) China (Shanghai) Pilot Free Trade Zone investor-state dispute settlement: an uncertain experiment. J World Investment Trade 18(4):673–711

Wang G (2011) Chinese mechanisms for resolving investor-state dispute. Jindal J Int Aff 1(1):204–233

Wang H (2017) The RCEP and its investment rules: learning from past Chinese FTAs. Chinese J Glob Gov 3(2):160–181

Willems JY (2011) The settlement of investor state disputes and China new developments on ICSID Jurisdiction. South Carolina J Int Law Bus 8(1):1–62

WTO (2020) Statement on a Mechanism for Developing, Documenting and Sharing Practices and Procedures in the Conduct of WTO Disputes (JOB/DSB/1/Add. 12), https://trade.ec.europa.eu/doclib/docs/2020/april/tradoc_158731.pdf

Yang X (2017) Shanghai Government Work Report. https://www.shanghai.gov.cn/nw12336/20200813/0001-12336_1192582.html

Zhong C (2019) Transformation of China's opening-up mode from Chinese foreign investment law. Wuhan Univ J (Philosophy Soc Sci) 72(5):138–147

Part III
Special Focus: Competition Neutrality

From a White Paper to a Proposal for a Regulation on Foreign Subsidies: Filling a Regulatory Gap in Protecting the EU Internal Market

Filip Krenek and Eddy De Smijter

Contents

Abstract In recent years, there has been an increased concern that companies receiving foreign subsidies may have an unfair advantage when they perform economic activities in the EU, which undermines fair competition in the EU internal market. Different from aid granted by Member States, which is subject to EU State

The information and views set out in this article are those of the authors and do not necessarily reflect the official opinion of the European Commission.

F. Krenek (✉) and E. De Smijter
DG Competition, European Commission, Brussels, Belgium
e-mail: Filip.Krenek@ec.europa.eu; Eddy.De-Smijter@ec.europa.eu

M. Chi et al. (eds.), *Asian Yearbook of International Economic Law 2022*,
Asian Yearbook of International Economic Law (2022) 2022: 129–148,
https://doi.org/10.1007/16517_2021_3, Published online: 12 January 2022

aid control, foreign subsidies currently go largely unchecked. To launch a debate on possible solutions to address this regulatory gap, the European Commission published in June 2020 a 'White Paper on levelling the playing field as regards foreign subsidies'. After an extensive consultation of the ideas proposed in the White paper, the European Commission adopted in May 2021 a proposal for a Regulation on foreign subsidies distorting the internal market. This article explores the subject of these two documents, describes the development of the legislative proposal and explains the rationale behind the proposed actions.

1 Introduction

On 17 June 2020, the European Commission published a 'White Paper on levelling the playing field as regards foreign subsidies'[1] ("White Paper"). Announced in the Commission Communication 'New Industrial Strategy for Europe' in March 2020,[2] the White Paper aimed to address long-standing concerns across EU Member States and industry that there may be a gap in both the international and European legal framework, which makes the EU unable to effectively address distortions to the EU internal market caused by third-country subsidies. Even before the pandemic, there have been incidences in which foreign subsidies appear to have distorted the internal market. However, due to the significant economic downturn caused by the COVID-19 pandemic, there is an increased risk that subsidised companies can get an unfair advantage that undermines fair competition in the EU market.

Following the adoption of the White Paper, a 14-week public consultation had been launched. The Commission received 150 contributions from a wide range of stakeholders, including 17 from public authorities of Member States, 24 submissions from third-country stakeholders, and more than 100 contributions from business and industry associations as well as individual companies.[3] The feedback received in the consultation process confirmed the need for a legislative proposal to ensure that businesses compete on a level playing level in the internal market. As a result, the Commission confirmed in its Work Programme for 2021 the intention to put forward a legislative proposal on levelling the playing field as regards foreign subsidies.[4]

[1] European Commission, White Paper on levelling the playing field as regards foreign subsidies, COM(2020) 253 final, 17 June 2020.

[2] European Commission, A New Industrial Strategy for Europe, COM(2020) 102 final, 10 March 2020.

[3] European Commission, Summary of the responses to the public consultation on the White Paper on levelling the playing field as regards foreign subsidies. October 2020, https://ec.europa.eu/competition/international/overview/WP_foreign_subsidies2020_summary_public_consultation.pdf.

[4] European Commission, Commission Work Programme 2021, COM(2020) 690 final, 19 October 2020, Annex 1.

In October 2020, the Commission published an Inception impact assessment for the initiative, which outlined broader policy options to address the issue, and to which the Commission received 22 responses.[5] Throughout October 2020-January 2021, the Commission also carried out targeted consultation of key stakeholders, including representatives of EU businesses and industry associations active in sectors which seem to be more prone to distortive foreign subsidies.[6] The feedback from the stakeholders has been instrumental in the process of shaping the legislative proposal.

On 5 May 2021, the European Commission adopted a proposal for a Regulation on foreign subsidies distorting the internal market.[7] The proposal aims at addressing a regulatory gap whereby foreign subsidies distorting the internal market currently go unchecked, while aid granted by Member States is subject to EU State aid rules. The proposed Regulation captures all market situations where subsidies distort competition in the EU, but it focuses particularly on concentrations of companies (mergers and acquisitions) and participation in EU public procurement procedures.

2 Political Context

The existence of a regulatory gap as regards the distortive effect of foreign subsidies on the EU internal market has already been acknowledged in the March 2019 Joint Communication of the Commission and the High Representative 'EU-China: A strategic outlook' and in a 2020 report of the European Court of Auditors, which stressed that the different treatment between State aid given by Member States and subsidies granted by third-countries may distort competition in the EU.[8]

Both EU co-legislators have also acknowledged the need for levelling the playing field as regards foreign subsidies and called on the European Commission to follow-up on the White Paper by means of a legislative proposal.

Already in its February 2020 report on competition policy,[9] the European Parliament called on the Commission to explore "appropriate investigative tools in cases where a company is deemed to have engaged in distortionary behaviour due to government subsidies or to have made excessive profits based on a dominant market position in its home country". After the adoption of the White Paper by the

[5]European Commission, Feedback received on: Trade & investment – addressing distortions caused by foreign subsidies, October 2020, https://ec.europa.eu/info/law/better-regulation/have-your-say/initiatives/12621-Trade-investment-addressing-distortions-caused-by-foreign-subsidies/feedback?p_id=8607947.

[6]DG Competition (2021).

[7]European Commission, Proposal for a Regulation on foreign subsidies distorting the internal market COM(2021) 223 final, 5 May 2021.

[8]European Court of Auditors (2020), p. 47.

[9]European Parliament, Report on competition policy – annual report 2019, A9-0022/2020, 25 February 2020.

Commission, the Parliament expressed its view on the initiative in the resolution on the Trade policy review from November 2020,[10] in which the European Parliament "welcomes the White Paper on Foreign Subsidies as a necessary complementary tool to trade defence measures, and looks forward to a legislative proposal from the Commission".

In the September 2020 conclusions,[11] also the EU Council has stressed that "operators competing from third countries in the Single Market should operate under the same conditions and rules as their European counterparts while ensuring that the EU remains an attractive business environment for foreign investments" and "looks forward, in that respect, to discussing the White Paper on levelling the playing field as regards foreign subsidies". This view has also been supported by the Special European Council meeting in October 2020,[12] which concluded that "further instruments to address the distortive effects of foreign subsidies in the Single Market [should be] developed".

3 Economic Context

With almost EUR 6 trillion in goods and services traded in 2019, the EU is the largest trading block in the world, accounting for about 16% of total global trade.[13] The openness of the EU market is a great strength that spurs competitiveness, innovation and provides jobs. Trade accounts for 35% of EU GDP and 35 million jobs in the EU depend on exports.[14] The EU is also one of the top providers and destinations of foreign direct investment. In 2019, the EU accounted for a 25% of global inward FDI stocks, or about EUR 7 trillion, and 32% of global outward stocks.[15]

Over the past decades, the European economy has become ever more closely integrated with the economies of many third countries, as evidenced by increasing trade flows, but also flows in finance and in investment. Between 2009 and 2019, EU exports in goods and services grew by 6.4% annually, while total imports grew by an

[10] European Parliament, Resolution on the EU Trade Policy Review, P9 TA(2020)0337, 26 November 2020.

[11] Council of the European Union, Conclusions on a deepened Single Market for a strong recovery and a competitive, sustainable Europe, 10698/20, 11 September 2020.

[12] European Council, Special meeting of the European Council (1 and 2 October 2020) – Conclusions, EUCO 13/20, Brussels, 2 October 2020.

[13] DG Trade Statistical Guide, August 2020, excluding intra-EU trade, https://trade.ec.europa.eu/doclib/docs/2013/may/tradoc_151348.pdf.

[14] European Commission, EU trade agreements: delivering new opportunities in time of global economic uncertainties, Press release IP/19/6074, 14 October 2019.

[15] UNCTAD (2020).

average 5.6% per year. Meanwhile, EU inward and outward FDI stocks respectively have grown by 6.6% and 6.4% annually between 2013 and 2019.[16]

Simultaneously, there have been increased concerns that the growth in trade and investment flows may also be coupled with subsidies by third states that could distort the internal market. A foreign subsidy may provide an unfair advantage to its beneficiary and thus lead to a distortive effect on the EU internal market. The list below illustrates some of these distortions:

- A subsidy may be used to finance operations of a company that would otherwise not be viable in the market. Such a subsidy may lead to overcapacity, loss of innovation potential and a long term loss for consumers in terms of price or quality.
- A subsidy may be used to dissuade competitors from entering a market. The subsidised company may, for example, keep artificially low prices as barriers for new entrants or maintain its market share by temporarily sustaining losses, financed by subsidies. This may dissuade competitors from engaging in the market since the market they could potentially reach is artificially diminished. It may also prevent competitors from acquiring a large enough market share to benefit from economies of scale.
- A foreign subsidy may be used to increase the market share of a company, among others, by means of mergers and acquisitions or a successful participation in public procurement procedures. A company benefiting from a subsidy may overbid in acquisition tenders or undercut in public procurements. This has a direct effect on its competitors, but by increasing its market share, it may also reach a dominant position that allows the company to use other forms of anti-competitive behaviour, such as excessive or predatory pricing. In such a case, the subsidies may have been necessary for the company to reach a dominant position, but may no longer be needed to sustain it due to economies of scale.

Evidence suggests a global increase in the use of subsidy measures (see Fig. 1). This trend is likely to continue given the size of financial support packages that countries around the world have put in place as a response to the economic crisis caused by the COVID pandemic. The World Bank estimates that the size of the fiscal stimulus measures in 2020 is about double the amount used during the crisis in 2008–2009.[17] Moreover, the subsidy measures are also likely to persist well into the future, as evidence from the Global financial crisis of 2008–2009 shows that around one third of discriminatory measures put in place in 2009 are still in place today.[18]

Subsidy amounts notified to the World Trade Organization (WTO) have also increased in recent years. The EU's main trading partners notified the following subsidy amounts for 2018: China-EUR 520 billion, US-EUR 17 billion, Russia-EUR

[16] Eurostat (bop fdi main, bop fdi flow), accessed on 24 March 2021.

[17] World Bank (2021), p. 7.

[18] Evenett and Baldwin (2020).

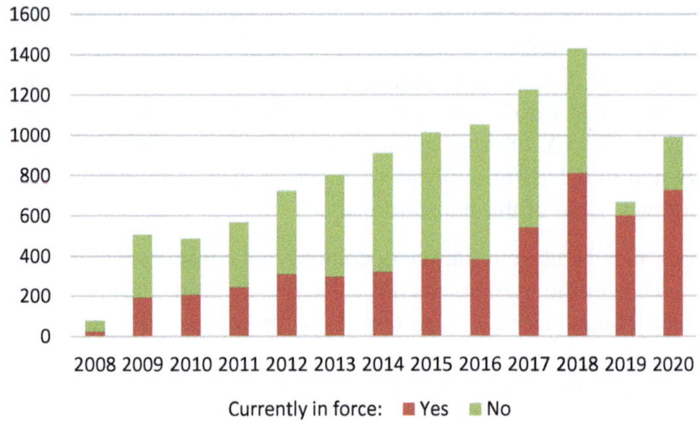

Fig. 1 Number of new subsidy measures (worldwide) per year. Source: Authors own construction based on Global Trade Alert (GTA) (GTA provides data on trade-distortive measures taken globally since November 2008. GTA uses the UNCTAD Multi-Agency Support Team (MAST) taxonomy. The MAST chapter L provides information on subsidy measures. [Data extracted on: 22/6/2021]; Source: https://www.globaltradealert.org/)

3.8 billion, the UK-EUR 0.9 billion and Switzerland-EUR 0.7 billion.[19] However, these figures only include schemes and not individual subsidy grants and therefore likely underestimate the total amounts of subsidies granted.

Other reports estimate that China, as a trading partner with the highest notified amounts, provided direct and indirect subsidies to its state-owned enterprises in the range of 1.3–1.6% GDP in 2018, with the total amount of subsidisation likely being higher as one third of direct subsidies is said to be granted to private companies.[20] While these figures provide a similar magnitude of subsidy amounts as what was reported to the WTO, they also show discrepancies and point to a lack of reliable data and of transparency.

In terms of sectors most affected by distortive foreign subsidies, the Impact Assessment report accompanying the proposed Regulation,[21] stakeholder replies to the consultation on the White Paper[22] and several OECD reports[23] refer to the following ones: aluminium, automotive, aviation, construction, energy, railway, semiconductors, shipbuilding, steel, telecommunications and transport

[19] European Commission, Impact Assessment accompanying the Proposal for a Regulation on foreign subsidies distorting the internal market, SWD(2021) 99 final, 5 May 2021.

[20] Business Europe (2020).

[21] European Commission, Impact Assessment accompanying the Proposal for a Regulation on foreign subsidies distorting the internal market, SWD(2021) 99 final, 5 May 2021.

[22] European Commission, Summary of the responses to the public consultation on the White Paper on levelling the playing field as regards foreign subsidies, https://ec.europa.eu/competition/international/overview/WP_foreign_subsidies2020_summary_public_consultation.pdf.

[23] OECD (2019a); OECD (2019b); OECD, Subsidies in the steel sector: A stocktaking note, 2017, DSTI/SC (2017)11.

infrastructure. This has also been confirmed in the targeted consultation that took place between October 2020 and January 2021.[24]

4 Regulatory Gap

Despite the limited evidence caused by a general lack of transparency, the steady increase of uncontrolled subsidy measures around the globe is likely to have already caused distortions in the internal market. However, European and national authorities were so far unable to counter those distortions, since they currently have no powers to detect and to appropriately address foreign subsidies.

The White Paper provides an analysis of the extent to which existing instruments can be used to deal with foreign subsidies in different areas. In the area of competition, it looks at the antitrust rules, the State aid rules, and the merger rules. But in none of the existing instruments, there is a specific possibility or intention to deal with foreign subsidies. If rules exist that deal with foreign subsidies, for example in free trade agreements, these are usually limited to certain transparency obligations. Such agreements typically only contain very limited, if any, rules on which types of subsidies may or may not be allowed. As for subsidy rules under the WTO, the Agreement on Subsidies and Countervailing Measures (SCM Agreement)[25] is limited to the import of subsidised goods, but does not cover services, investment or other financial flows.

4.1 EU State Aid Rules

Introduced already with the Treaty of Rome in 1957, the EU has a sophisticated system of State aid control, which regulates aid granted by EU Member States. One of the main goals of the State aid control system is to ensure that the aid is "well-designed, targeted at identified market failures and objectives of common interest, and the least distortive".[26]

Over more than 60 years of experience, EU State aid rules have been developed for granting aid in various contexts, such as regional aid, aid for environmental protection and energy, aid for rescue and restructuring, etc. In all of these areas, EU State aid rules provide strict subsidy disciplines that aim to prevent distortions in the

[24] DG Competition (2021).

[25] Agreement on Subsidies and Countervailing Measures (SCM Agreement), April 15 1994, Marrakesh Agreement Establishing the World Trade Organization, Annex 1A, 1869 UNTS 14. [Not reproduced in ILM].

[26] European Commission, Fitness check of the 2012 State aid modernisation package, SWD(2020) 257 final, PART 1/4, p. 56.

internal market by subsidy races between the Member States, where "for every State aid measure, Member States must demonstrate, that it is kept to the minimum to change the behaviour of companies and if the same change in behaviour could have been obtained with less aid".[27]

State aid rules also require a high level of transparency: "By providing publicly accessible information on State aid interventions that might have potentially distortive effects on competition and intra-EU trade, the transparency requirements foster market discipline and assist in ensuring that Member States target their support measures in line with the applicable State aid rules".[28] In addition, the Transparency Directive[29] subjects certain public undertakings to increased requirements on transparency, i.e. by keeping separate accounts and providing for a reporting system to check financial flows between public authorities and the companies owned by the Member States.

At present, however, there are no equivalent rules in the EU for foreign subsidies. This difference in treatment between aid granted by Member States and subsidies granted by third countries creates an uneven playing field. Companies supported by third-country governments are therefore able to enjoy an unfair advantage that may not be available to their competitors.

4.2 *Other EU Competition Tools*

The EU also has a well-developed system of merger control,[30] which uses an ex-ante notification system to assess mergers and acquisitions of companies above a certain EU turnover. The focus of the assessment is on the resulting market structure in a given market and the concentration may only be approved and declared compatible with the internal market if it is considered not to lead to a significant impediment to effective competition. However, the EU merger control does not take specifically into account how the merger or acquisition has been financed and whether, for instance, foreign subsidies have been used to finance the acquisition or to increase the financial strength of the acquiring party.

Enshrined in Articles 101 and 102 of the Treaty on the Functioning of the European Union (TFEU), EU antitrust rules apply to all types of anticompetitive behaviour that stems from a position of market dominance or an agreement between

---

[27] European Commission, Fitness check of the 2012 State aid modernisation package, SWD(2020) 257 final, PART 1/4, p. 77.

[28] European Commission, Fitness check of the 2012 State aid modernisation package, SWD(2020) 257 final, PART 1/4, p. 78.

[29] Commission Directive 2006/111/EC of 16 November 2006 on the transparency of financial relations between Member States and public undertakings as well as on financial transparency within certain undertakings, OJ L 318 17.11.2006.

[30] Council Regulation (EC) No 139/2004 of 20 January 2004 on the control of concentrations between undertakings, OJ L 24, 29.1.2004.

undertakings in the market. While certain forms of anti-competitive behaviour may be enabled or facilitated by foreign subsidies, antitrust rules do not allow the Commission or Member States to take this into account when investigating a possible infringement of Article 101 or 102 TFEU.

4.3 WTO Rules and the SCM Agreement

There are also subsidy rules and disciplines embedded in international agreements under the WTO, to which the EU and its Member States are members. These are in particular the General Agreement on Tariffs and Trade (GATT)[31] and the SCM Agreement, which are, however, limited to trade in goods. The definition of a subsidy under the SCM Agreement contains three basic elements: (i) a financial contribution (ii) by a government or any public body within the territory of a WTO member (iii) which confers a benefit. Financial contributions include grants, loans, guarantees, equity injections, foregone tax, provision or purchase of goods of services.

The SCM Agreement sets out a category of prohibited subsidies, which include subsidies for the export of goods (export subsidies) or subsidies that are contingent upon using domestic inputs (import substitution subsidies). For this category, a distortion of trade is presumed, and the subsidies can be directly remedied if not withdrawn. Subsidies that are ‘specific’ to certain enterprises, industries, or their groups and cause adverse effects (injury, serious prejudice, nullification or impairment) are considered actionable. All actionable subsidies can be challenged at multilateral level through the WTO Dispute Settlement Mechanism, but countervailing measures can only be taken against subsidies causing an injury.

The SCM Agreement also provides an obligation on WTO members to notify subsidy measures granted or maintained within their territory. However, the level of compliance with this obligation is generally low. By October 2020, less than a half of all 164 WTO members have submitted their full subsidy notifications for 2019, more than a year after the deadline.[32] The EU along with several other WTO members is therefore pursuing to increase transparency on subsidies at the WTO level.[33] The EU has been also been engaged in trilateral talks with the US and Japan to improve multilateral cooperation, including in the area of industrial subsidies.[34]

[31] General Agreement on Tariffs and Trade (GATT) 1994, April 15 1994, Marrakesh Agreement Establishing the World Trade Organization, Annex 1A, 1867 UNTS 187, 33 ILM 1153.

[32] WTO, Chair cites “chronic” low compliance with subsidy notification requirements, 27 October 2020, https://www.wto.org/english/news_e/news20_e/scm_27oct20_e.htm.

[33] WTO, Council for Trade in Goods, Procedures to enhance transparency and strengthen notification requirements under WTO Agreements, JOB/GC/204/Rev.4, 24 November 2020.

[34] Joint Statement of the Trilateral Meeting of the Trade Ministers of Japan, the United States and the European Union, Washington, D.C., 14 January 2020, https://trade.ec.europa.eu/doclib/docs/2020/january/tradoc_158567.pdf.

While the scope of application of GATT and the SCM Agreement are limited to trade in goods, the area of service subsidies is covered by the WTO General Agreement on Trade in Services (GATS).[35] The GATS sets out a non-discrimination obligation and includes a mandate to negotiate rules for services subsidies, but no such disciplines have been developed yet. In addition, it does not set out the possibility to impose countervailing duties to effectively remedy the distortion. Finally, the GATS also does not cover non-service investment and other financial flows.

4.4 Trade Defence Instruments

The EU anti-subsidy rules[36] are based on the provisions of the SCM Agreement. Specifically, the EU anti-subsidy Regulation allows a remedial action, such as imposing a countervailing duty to offset any subsidy granted for the manufacturing, production, export or transport of goods that are imported into the EU.

An anti-subsidy investigation needs to determine the existence of the subsidy and an injury to the EU industry as well as a causal link between the two. Finally, the investigation includes a 'Union interest test' to assess whether the imposition of remedies is in the interest of the EU industry. If these conditions are met, the EU can impose countervailing duties.

Since the EU anti-subsidy Regulation only provides for an action against subsidised imports of goods from third countries, it does not address situations where the subsidised company is already established within the territory of the EU. It also does not cover trade in services, investment and other financial flows, which may benefit from foreign subsidies and cause harm in the internal market.

4.5 FDI Screening Regulation

The EU investment screening Regulation[37] applies to foreign direct investment (FDI) that may have an adverse effect on security or public order within the EU. Specifically, the FDI screening mechanism looks at the potential impact of such an investment on critical infrastructure (incl. energy, transport, health, finance,

---

[35] General Agreement on Trade in Services (GATS), April 15 1994, Marrakesh Agreement Establishing the World Trade Organization, Annex 1B, 1869 UNTS 183, 33 ILM 1167.

[36] Regulation (EU) 2016/1037 of the European Parliament and of the Council of 8 June 2016 on protection against subsidised imports from countries not members of the European Union, OJ L 176, 30.6.2016.

[37] Regulation (EU) 2019/452 of the European Parliament and of the Council of 19 March 2019 establishing a framework for the screening of foreign direct investments into the Union, OJ L 79I, 21.3.2019.

etc.), critical technologies (incl. artificial intelligence, robotics, quantum and nuclear technologies, etc.), supply of critical inputs (incl. energy, raw materials and food security), access to sensitive information and the freedom and pluralism of the media.

When determining whether the investment is likely to affect security or public order, the Member State affected by the foreign investment and the Commission may take into consideration whether the foreign investor is controlled by a third country, including through ownership or the provision of significant funding. While this screening mechanism may thus consider certain types of subsidies, the assessment of foreign funding in the context of the FDI screening is solely to establish whether this amounts to a control by a third-country government. Moreover, the assessment carried out under the FDI screening mechanism is designed to address risks to security or public order, not threats to competition or possible distortions of the internal market.

4.6 *Public Procurement*

With regards to public procurement, the proposal for an International Procurement Instrument (IPI)[38] aims to open up third-country procurement markets, but does not address the effects of foreign subsidies in the internal market. The instrument would allow investigations into cases of possible discrimination against EU companies in third-country markets. Where an investigation would find that a foreign country applies barriers to the participation of EU companies in its procurement tenders, the Commission could impose price adjustment measures on products, services or bidders from that country. However, the instrument, if adopted, will not resolve the issue of subsidised bids in EU public procurement procedures.

The existing rules on EU public procurement set out in the relevant Directives[39] include provisions on so-called abnormally low tenders. These provisions allow a contracting authority to reject a tender if it establishes that the abnormally low price

[38] European Commission, Amended proposal for a Regulation of the European Parliament and of the Council on the access of third-country goods and services to the Union's internal market in public procurement and procedures supporting negotiations on access of Union goods and services to the public procurement markets of third countries, COM(2016) 34 final, 29 January 2016.

[39] Directive 2014/23/EU of the European Parliament and of the Council of 26 February 2014 on the award of concession contracts, OJ L 94, 28.3.2014, p. 1–64. Directive 2014/24/EU of the European Parliament and of the Council of 26 February 2014 on public procurement and repealing Directive 2004/18/EC, OJ L 94, 28.3.2014, p. 65–242. Directive 2014/25/EU of the European Parliament and of the Council of 26 February 2014 on procurement by entities operating in the water, energy, transport and postal services sectors and repealing Directive 2004/17/EC, OJ L 94, 28.3.2014, p. 243–374. Directive 2009/81/EC of the European Parliament and of the Council of 13 July 2009 on the coordination of procedures for the award of certain works contracts, supply contracts and service contracts by contracting authorities or entities in the fields of defence and security, and amending Directives 2004/17/EC and 2004/18/EC, OJ L 216, 20.8.2009, p. 76–136.

is a result of technically, economically or legally unsound assumptions or practices. Such a consideration is a part of the overall assessment of the viability of the offer, and may in principle lead to a rejection as described in the Commission guidance on the participation of third country bidders.[40] The contracting authority may, for instance, reject an abnormally low tender if the tenderer has obtained aid from an EU Member State, but is unable to prove that the aid in question is compatible with the internal market. But where the abnormally low price is caused by a foreign subsidy, the contracting authority does not have an equal ground to reject such a bid. The existence of a foreign subsidy may only be taken into consideration as part of the overall viability of the offer.

The guidance also acknowledges that third country bidders are not necessarily subject to strict rules similar to EU State aid control and that the application of the provisions on abnormally low tenders may not be sufficient to address the issue of foreign subsidies.

5 Overview of the Proposed Regulation

5.1 Scope

The definition of a foreign subsidy in the proposed Regulation on distortive foreign subsidies is similar to that of State aid under EU State aid rules, but is also aligned with the subsidy definition provided in the SCM Agreement.

In the proposed Regulation, 'foreign subsidy' is defined as a financial contribution originating directly or indirectly from the government of a non-EU country that confers a benefits to a company engaging in an economic activity in the internal market, and which is selective, i.e. limited to an individual company or industry or to several companies or industries. A financial contribution in the meaning of the Regulation includes capital injections, grants, loans, guarantees, foregone tax revenue and the provision or purchase of goods and services. Unlike the SCM Agreement, the proposed Regulation suggests that subsidies may also have a cross-border effect. Such subsidies may thus be granted to a beneficiary, which is located outside the territory of the country granting it.

Due to their specific nature, the financial relations between state-owned enterprises and public authorities may be more complex, which is also the reason for having Transparency Directives with regard to EU State aid. To address the issue of opacity, the proposed Regulation suggests that if a company, whether or not owned by a foreign state, fails to provide information to demonstrate otherwise, it may be deemed to have received a benefit by means of a financial contribution.

[40] Communication from the Commission, Guidance on the participation of third country bidders and goods in the EU procurement market, C(2019) 5494 final, 24 July 2019.

The White Paper and the proposed Regulation make no distinction as to the nationality of the beneficiary of the foreign subsidy. The instrument neither targets any particular economic sector nor considers specifically the ownership of the company. This is a clear difference from the FDI Screening Regulation, where state-ownership may amount to control by a third country and subsequently lead to the prohibition of an investment. The FDI Screening Regulation also lists, if not exhaustively, certain sectors and areas which are targeted as so-called "critical infrastructures" or strategic sectors. The proposed Regulation aims to ensure a level playing field in the whole internal market and therefore it applies equally to all sectors of the economy. It acknowledges that some sectors may be more prone than others to distortions caused by foreign subsidies and the proposal therefore sets out a possibility to conduct market investigation into specific sectors, types of economic activity or subsidy instruments.

The proposed Regulation would allow the Commission to investigate financial contributions granted by non-EU countries to companies engaging in an economic activity in the EU and to redress their distortive effects. As already suggested in the White Paper, also the proposed Regulation introduces two notification-based tools and a general market investigation tool.[41] Different from the White Paper, the proposal refines the notification-based tools for concentrations and public procurement to target the potentially most distortive subsidies while preserving the flexibility of the ex-officio review:

- A notification-based tool to investigate concentrations involving a financial contribution by a non-EU government, where the EU turnover of the company to be acquired (or of at least one of the merging parties) is €500 million or more and the foreign financial contribution is at least €50 million;
- A notification-based tool to investigate bids in public procurements involving a financial contribution by a non-EU government, where the estimated value of the procurement is €250 million or more; and
- A tool to investigate all other market situations and smaller concentrations and public procurement procedures, which the Commission can start on its own initiative (ex-officio).

As a general rule, the proposed Regulation also sets a threshold of €5 million over 3 years on the subsidy amount, below which subsidies are deemed unlikely to distort the internal market.

[41] The White Paper also covered the issue of EU funding, which is partially addressed in the proposed Regulation. If a company competes for support from the EU budget, it needs to demonstrate the financial viability of the proposed project. By having received a foreign subsidy, the company may be in a better position to obtain that funding compared to its competitors. Where EU funding is distributed through procurement procedures under shared management, the mechanisms developed in the Regulation would also apply. EU funding distributed through direct or indirect management, however, is not addressed by the proposed Regulation. In order to deal with the issue, the Commission will explore the possibility to propose amendments to the Financial Regulation (Regulation (EU, Euratom) 2018/1046, OJ L 193, 30.7.2018, p. 1–222).

5.2 Procedure

The investigative procedure envisaged in the Regulation consist of a preliminary review and, if there are indications of the existence of a subsidy, an in-depth investigation.

With respect to concentrations and public procurements, the acquirer (or the merging parties) or the bidder would be subject to a mandatory notification of financial contributions granted by third country authorities in the three years prior to the transaction. The concentration could not be completed and the investigated bidder could not be awarded the contract while the Commission's review is pending.

With regards to notifiable concentrations, the proposed Regulation addresses both acquisition and mergers with a lasting change of control,[42] or the creation of a joint venture. Unlike the White Paper, which used a secondary 30% threshold of voting right to establish control, the definitions used in the proposal are better aligned with the way the concept of control is applied in EU merger rules and thus create more legal certainty. In terms of time limits, the Regulation proposes 25 working days for a preliminary review and 90 working days for an in-depth investigation in the case of notified concentrations, in line with the time limits set out in the EU Merger Regulation.

For public procurement, the proposed time limits are set at 60 and 200 days respectively since procurement procedures would typically take longer to conclude and the Commission may have to assess more than one bidder in a given public procurement. In order not to delay the procurement procedures, the evaluation of the different bids would go ahead, in parallel to the assessment of the financial contribution, and could even be concluded if the award goes to a bid that has not received any financial contribution. However, if the winning bid is potentially subsidised, then the assessment of that subsidy would have to be concluded first.

The general market investigation tool will allow the Commission to review on its own initiative (ex-officio) other market situations (e.g. greenfield investment, operating subsidies) as well as potentially subsidised concentrations and bids below the notification thresholds. The proposal also includes a possibility to request an ad-hoc notification, when the Commission suspects that a foreign subsidy may be involved, which would trigger the corresponding notification-based procedure.

The White Paper also proposed to include qualitative thresholds alongside the quantitative ones to capture sectors with a high growth potential (i.e. start-ups). However, the use of qualitative criteria was criticised in the public consultation as the criteria seemed too vague or unclear. Instead, the Regulation proposes the use of an ad-hoc notification requirement to cater for situations of so-called killer acquisitions, which may impede innovation by eliminating future competitors by absorbing or discontinuing their project development. This ad-hoc notification would have the

[42] Guidance on the notion of "control" can be found in the Commission Consolidated Jurisdictional Notice under Council Regulation (EC) No 139/2004 on the control of concentrations between undertakings, OJ C 95, 16.4.2008, p. 1.

same suspensive effect as that for notified concentrations and public procurement bids, and could thus prevent such harmful takeovers.

5.3 *Assessment of the Distortion*

To comply with the non-discrimination principle and the national treatment obligation under WTO rules, foreign subsidies would in principle have to be assessed similarly as, or at least not worse than State aid under the European rules.

The Commission would need to establish whether a financial contribution is a foreign subsidy within the meaning of the Regulation and whether it distorts the internal market. The Regulation proposes a number of subsidy categories and a non-exhaustive list of indicators to assess whether a foreign subsidy is distortive.

The categories of subsidies which are likely to be distortive include unlimited state guarantees, subsidies to an ailing company without a restructuring plan, subsidies directly facilitating an acquisition or subsidies facilitating the submission of an unduly advantageous tender. There is a high likelihood that such subsidies are distortive and therefore would not require a detailed assessment based on indicators. These subsidies would generally not be allowed under EU State aid rules, and some of these subsidies are also prohibited under the WTO rules. However, the company concerned could still demonstrate that the subsidy in question does not distort the internal market.

In all other cases, the Commission will assess the distortion based on indicators, which include the amount of the subsidy (both absolute and relative size), the nature of the subsidy, the purpose and conditions attached to the subsidy, as well as its actual use in the internal market. For instance, a subsidy is more likely to be distortive if it covers a substantial part of the purchase price when acquiring a company or a large part of the procurement contract value. Or, an operating subsidy may be more distortive than an investment subsidy of the same size. The indicators also include the situation of the company and the markets concerned as well as the company's level of economic activity on the internal market. For example, a subsidy which sustains otherwise economically unviable assets and creates overcapacity may be more distortive, particularly when the market concerned already has high barriers to entry. By contrast, a subsidy may be less distortive if granted to a small and medium-sized enterprise (SME) or a company with a low-degree of activity in the EU.

5.4 *Balancing and Redressive Measures*

Despite the distortive character of the subsidy, either by falling within one of the categories or established through the indicators, it could still have a positive impact. Where warranted, the Commission would therefore also consider the possible positive effects of the foreign subsidy and balance them against the distortion to determine appropriate redressive measures to remedy the distortion. Such balancing, in the White Paper referred to as EU interest test, would be similar to what the Commission can do under the EU State aid rules in case of aid that contributes to achieving a common objective.[43]

The proposed Regulation includes a range of structural or behavioural remedies that can be imposed by the Commission or proposed by the company to remedy the distortion. These include divestment of certain assets, the reduction of capacity or market presence, providing access to a certain infrastructure, prohibition of a specific market conduct or publication of research and development (R&D) results.

Inspired by the recovery obligation under EU State aid rules, the repayment of a foreign subsidy is also envisioned as a possibility in the proposed Regulation. However, before accepting such remedy, the Commission will have to be convinced that it will be really effective. It might be difficult to trace back whether the subsidy has been paid back to the granting state and has not been channelled back in some other way to the beneficiary. The repayment would therefore only be accepted as a remedy if it can be ascertained that the repayment effectively remedies the distortion and is done in a transparent way.

In case of notified transactions, the Commission will also have the power to prohibit the subsidised acquisition or the award of the public procurement tender to the subsidised bidder.

5.5 *Sectoral Legislation*

While there are currently no instruments to deal with foreign subsidies that distort the EU internal market in general, there are already rules that apply to certain specific sectors. The proposed Regulation on foreign subsidies therefore clearly sets out how the possible overlaps will be addressed.

The Regulation on safeguarding competition in air transport[44] allows the Commission to conduct investigations if it finds evidence of a practice distorting competition among EU air carriers and in the air transport services markets. It also covers subsidies to non-EU country air carriers, but not other actors in the aviation chain such as ground handling companies and it does not contain specific rules on public procurement or subsidised acquisitions of EU targets. The proposed Regulation would therefore apply only in these instances that are currently not covered.

In the area of maritime, the Regulation on protection against injurious pricing of vessels[45] would also allow the EU to act against the sale of vessels that are sold

[43] Article 107(2) and (3) TFEU.

[44] Regulation (EU) 2019/712 of the European Parliament and of the Council of 17 April 2019 on safeguarding competition in air transport, and repealing Regulation (EC) No 868/2004, OJ L 123, 10.5.2019, p. 4–17.

[45] Regulation (EU) 2016/1035 of the European Parliament and of the Council of 8 June 2016 on protection against injurious pricing of vessels, OJ L 176, 30.6.2016, p. 1–20.

below normal price and cause injury to the Union industry. However, this Regulation will only become applicable once the OECD Shipbuilding Agreement[46] has entered into force. Awaiting that, the Regulation on foreign subsidies is therefore proposed to take precedent until the sectoral one becomes applicable.

Finally, there is the Regulation on unfair pricing in the maritime transport,[47] but this Regulation has only been applied once in its 35 years of existence, as it has turned out difficult to prove the existence of a dumping price under the Regulation. The Regulation on foreign subsidies is therefore also proposed to take precedent.

6 From the White Paper to the Proposed Regulation

There are a number of notable differences between the approach set out in the White Paper and the proposal for a Regulation. Some of these changes are cross-cutting, others apply to the individual three parts of the legislation. This section compares the two and explains some of the notable changes, which were very often informed by the feedback received during the public consultation process.

In the public consultation on the White Paper, stakeholders have stressed that the notification requirement under Modules 2 and 3 should not create unnecessary administrative burden on companies and public authorities. Stakeholders have also underlined that it will be key to ensure access to the relevant information on foreign subsidies in order to make the instrument effective. Finally, there have also been concerns about a possible chilling effect that a legislative initiative on foreign subsidies might have on foreign investment in the EU.

6.1 Administrative Burden and Enforcement Powers

To limit the administrative burden on companies, the proposed Regulation uses relatively high notification thresholds to deal with potentially subsidised concentrations and bids. This limits the number of notified cases to only the largest transactions, where subsidies may have the potentially most distortive effects. The administrative burden on both companies and public authorities is also further limited by the €5 million per 3 years threshold on the subsidy amount, below which subsidies are unlikely to be distortive. This threshold is 25 times higher than the *de minimis* applied in State aid and proposed in the White Paper. It provides ex-ante legal certainty, which in State aid is guaranteed by the various block

[46] Agreement respecting Normal Competitive Conditions in the Commercial Shipbuilding and Repair Industry, OECD/LEGAL/0277.

[47] Council Regulation (EEC) No 4057/86 of 22 December 1986 on unfair pricing practices in maritime transport, OJ L 378, 31.12.1986, p. 14–20.

exemptions and the fact that Member States first notify aid to the Commission before implementing it. It also reduces the burden on companies and particularly small and medium-sized enterprises (SMEs) that would usually fall below this threshold.

As regards the enforcement of the instrument, the White Paper suggested a division of competence between the Commission and national authorities for the so-called Module 1 (ex-officio review) inspired by the shared enforcement in antitrust.[48] Based on the feedback received in the public consultation, it is proposed that the Commission would be exclusively competent to enforce the Regulation to ensure uniform application across the EU. The Commission may also benefit from the experience in enforcing State aid rules and applying trade defence instruments, which are closest in nature to the proposed rules with regards to foreign subsidies.

The review of potentially subsidised concentrations under the Regulation as well as the Module 2 of the White Paper have both been proposed to be enforced exclusively by the Commission. This has been supported by stakeholders, who saw a benefit in having a one-stop-shop for notified concentrations of high transaction value that would typically have an EU dimension, and would anyway require notification in multiple Member States. Having the Commission as the sole enforcer would further reduce administrative burden since notified concentrations above €500 million EU turnover would usually also trigger a notification under EU merger control. The two processes would run in parallel, but there may be synergies that decrease the burden on companies.

For the enforcement of the former Module 3, which addressed distortions in EU public procurement, the White Paper also suggested a system of shared competence. The notification of a potentially subsidised bid would have to be filed with the contracting authority that has organized the tender. However, as these contracting authorities may be quite small (i.e. local administrations, towns, regions), they may not be able to assess whether there is a distortive foreign subsidy. The contracting authority would therefore pass on that part of the assessment of a tender to the competent national supervisory authority, which would inform EU authorities to ensure consistency of application across the EU. The resulting assessment of the foreign subsidy would be passed back to the contracting authority, which would take this information into account in the assessment of the different bids.

Various stakeholders have stressed that such a system is unnecessarily complex and inefficient as the contracting authorities may not have the necessarily skills or capacity to assess the existence of a subsidy. The proposed Regulation therefore simplifies this procedure by requiring the contracting authority only to transmit the information on the potentially subsidised bid to the Commission, who would assess the existence of the subsidy and the distortion. The assessment of the distortion would run in parallel to the evaluation of the different bids. If the Commission finds that a bid is unduly subsidised, it can prohibit the contracting authority from awarding the contract to that bidder. If, however, the contracting authority decides

[48] See Council Regulation (EC) No 1/2003 of 16 December 2002 on the implementation of the rules on competition laid down in Articles 81 and 82 of the Treaty, OJ L 1, 04.01.2003, p. 1.

to award the contract to another bidder, the assessment could be stopped before the Commission concludes whether or not the bid was subsidised.

6.2 *Collection of Necessary Information*

The combination of the ex-ante and ex-officio tools provides an effective combination to gather the necessary information to effectively enforce the Regulation. To effectively collect information, the notification system is complemented by deterrent sanctions in case companies refuse to submit complete and accurate information, similarly to what currently exists in EU merger control. If a company does not notify a subsidised concentration or bid meeting the thresholds, the Commission will be able to impose fines and review the transaction as if it had been notified.

In ex-officio cases, the initial information can come from the market, including competitors, business associations or other interested parties. The Commission will also be able to conduct on-site inspections, ask companies to supply relevant information and impose fines and penalties if they refuse. If, however, it is not possible to gather all necessary information, the Regulation would give the power to the Commission to decide on the case on the basis of the facts available.

The proposed Regulation also sets out the possibility to carry out market investigations into specific sectors, types of economic activity or a specific type of a subsidy instrument.

6.3 *Effects on Foreign Investment*

The proposed Regulation ensures that companies in the EU can compete in a market open to investment, which is fair and competitive. Currently, companies may face unfair competition, which results from foreign subsidies that provide an advantage to their recipients. As a result, companies—even if they are more efficient or more innovative—are at risk of being crowded out. Even if subsidies may provide a short-term benefit to consumers in the form of lower prices, foreign subsidies may have detrimental effects in the long run by reducing the choice of products and services. It may also harm innovation as the more efficient or more innovative companies might be forced to leave the market.

The proposed set of tools will allow the Commission to tackle foreign subsidies that distort the level playing field in the internal market. It may also deter subsidised investment or the participation of subsidised bidders in EU public procurement procedures. By doing so, the Regulation aims to restore the level playing field so that business decisions are based on efficiencies and commercial opportunities rather than financial support. The improved competition in the market should instead have a 'crowding-in effect' and attract non-subsidised investment, both foreign and EU that would otherwise be directed elsewhere.

7 Outlook

The European Parliament and the Council will now discuss the Commission's proposal in the context of an ordinary legislative procedure. Once adopted, the Regulation will be directly applicable across the EU.

References

Business Europe (2020) The EU and China: Addressing the Systemic Challenge. A comprehensive EU strategy to rebalance the relationship with China, January 2020

DG Competition (2021) Foreign subsidies, https://ec.europa.eu/competition/international/overview/foreign_subsidies.html

European Court of Auditors (2020) The EU's reponse to China's state-driven investment strategy, Review 03. https://www.eca.europa.eu/Lists/ECADocuments/RW20_03/RW_EU_response_to_China_EN.pdf

Evenett SJ, Baldwin R (2020) Revitalising Multilateralism: Pragmatic Ideas for the New WTO Director-General, CEPR, https://voxeu.org/content/revitalising-multilateralism-pragmatic-ideas-new-wto-director-general

OECD (2019a) Measuring distortions in international markets: the semiconductor value chain, OECD Trade Policy Papers, No. 234, OECD Publishing Paris

OECD (2019b) Measuring distortions in international markets: the aluminium value chain, OECD Trade Policy Papers, No. 218. OECD Publishing Paris

UNCTAD (2020) World Investment Report 2020, Statistical Annex

World Bank (2021) Global Economic Prospects. January 2021. https://www.worldbank.org/en/publication/global-economic-prospects

Filip Krenek works as an International Relations Officer in the Task Force Foreign Subsidies of DG Competition, European Commission.

Eddy De Smijter is head of the International Relations Unit in DG Competition.

Third-Country State Aid Regulation: The European Debate on Foreign Subsidies

Necessity and Possibilities of a Reform

Jürgen Kühling, Thomas Weck, and Philipp Reinhold

Contents

Abstract Open markets and international competition are one of the political goals of Western market economies such as the European Union (EU). The EU expects further positive developments regarding the EU internal market, especially in its exchanges with Asia. At the same time, however, the EU increasingly emphasizes that competition should not only be free, but that it must also "fair". European and foreign companies should be subject to the same competitive conditions, especially within the internal market. An impairment of such a "level playing field" is seen, among other things, in the provision of foreign subsidies. The European

The article is based on chapter IV of the XXIII Biennial Report ("Competition 2020") of the German Monopolies Commission. Nevertheless, it only reflects the personal views of its authors.

J. Kühling
University of Regensburg, Chair for Public Law, Real Estate Law, Infrastructure Law, and Information Law, Regensburg, Germany
e-mail: Juergen.Kuehling@jura.uni-regensburg.de

T. Weck (✉)
Monopolies Commission, Bonn, Germany
e-mail: thomas.weck@monopolkommission.bund.de

P. Reinhold
Saarland University, Chair of Public Law, International Law and European Law of Prof. Dr. Marc Bungenberg, Saarbrucken, Germany
e-mail: reinhold@europainstitut.de

M. Chi et al. (eds.), *Asian Yearbook of International Economic Law 2022*,
Asian Yearbook of International Economic Law (2022) 2022: 149–162,
https://doi.org/10.1007/16517_2021_4, Published online: 5 December 2021

Commission set out its initial thoughts on the issue in June 2020, and published a regulatory proposal in May 2021. This contribution looks at the reasons as well as the proposed solutions to deal with foreign subsidies in the EU. At best, a European regulation will lead to a further development of international subsidy law. In any case, companies will most likely soon have to adjust to changed conditions for competition in the EU.

1 Introduction

A characteristic of globalization is that the West and the East of the world are establishing more and more ties between each other. For the EU, specifically, the fast-growing trade relations with China are of particular importance. After the USA, China is already the EU's second largest trading partner and the EU is China's largest trading partner today.[1] As a result of constant mutual market openings based on agreements within the framework of the WTO, the internal structures of both parties and their interaction are becoming increasingly important. From the perspective of the European Union, this interaction is characterized by two dimensions: The outside dimension is that both partners have to develop their external relationship based on the ideas of reciprocity. The inside dimension is that the EU itself has to make sure that its guiding principles are safeguarded within its internal market, one of which is the existence of a level playing field in competition.

The economic relations between the EU and China have given rise to lots of debate in recent years. The discussions do not only concern competition, but also industrial and, to some extent, security policy. In fact, the State has a different—direct and indirect—influence on the market in China from what we are used to in Europe. The Monopolies Commission therefore decided to examine Chinese State capitalism and its significance for the protection of competition in the EU more closely in its Biennial Report No. XXIII. However, the relevant issues do not come up in the relationship between the EU and China only. Instead, these issues can come up in the relationship between the EU and any other third country or between other countries in general depending on the role of state influence into the economy.

The following contribution builds on the main findings of the report and at the same time aims to contribute to a better understanding of the reform discussions in the EU. To this end, the importance of State aid control for competition in the EU will first be discussed (2). Then it will be shown why an amendment to the existing EU rules is necessary (3). In the next section, the reform proposal of the European Commission and the partly divergent proposals of the Monopolies Commission will be presented in comparison (4). Finally, the possible reactions of and long-term benefits for third countries such as China will be addressed (5).

[1] Monopolies Commission (2020), para. 570.

2 State Aid Law as Fundamental Element of EU's Economic Order

The European single market is today composed of 27 different national economies and cultural areas. The rules laid down in the European treaties serve the purpose of integrating the 27 economies into an area of freedom, security and justice without internal frontiers (Art. 3(2) TEU). For the European common market, the EU Treaties make a decision in favour of an open, highly competitive, social market economy with free and undistorted competition (Art. 3(3) TEU and Protocol No. 27 on the internal market and competition).[2] This systemic decision is implemented through a number of basic principles that are likewise ingrained in the EU Treaties themselves.[3]

Within the common market, the individual autonomy of all market participants is protected in terms of legal personality, freedom of action, and equality.[4] Moreover, as an objective corollary to these individual freedoms, all participants operate in a single market without internal borders, to which the "system of undistorted competition" applies.[5] Since the early days of the EU, the European fundamental freedoms[6] as well as the rules of competition and have reduced trade barriers by individual Member States, thus enabling the free economic movement within the EU. By claiming their individual freedoms vis-à-vis the EU Member States, market participants have been able to unleash the economic dynamics of the internal market and at the same time contributed to the close integration of the Member States.

For the free economic movement within the internal market, European competition law lays down specific rules that are intended to prevent concentrations of power and at the same time to ensure equal opportunities. In this respect, the aim is to ensure efficient competition contributing to the well-being of consumers. On the one hand, all companies are subject to the ban on cartels (Art. 101 TFEU) as well as abuse and merger control (Art. 102 TFEU and EC Merger Regulation[7]). On the other hand, Member States are subject to the provisions of the EU treaties, including Art. 106, 107 et seq. TFEU and Art. 4(3) TEU, when intervening in the market. This

---

[2]Protocol (No 27) on the internal market and competition, OJ C 115, 9.5.2008, p. 309. See Monopolies Commission (2020), paras. 596 et seq. regarding the system decision and function guarantees of European economic order.

[3]On the following see in particular Hatje (2009), pp. 801–853 as well as Monopolies Commission (2020), sec. 2.1 and 2.2 as well as paras. 605 et seq.

[4]See Art. 34 et seq. TFEU (fundamental freedoms) and the EU Charta on Fundamental Rights.

[5]See again Protocol (No 27) (fn. 2) and Art. 101 et seq. TFEU.

[6]The EU fundamental freedoms consist of the free movement of goods (Art. 28, 34, 35 TFEU), free movement of workers (Art. 45 TFEU), freedom of establishment (Art. 49 TFEU), free movement of services (Art. 56 TFEU) and free movement of capital (Art. 63 TFEU).

[7]Council Regulation (EC) No 139/2004 of 20 January 2004 on the control of concentrations between undertakings (the EC Merger Regulation), OJ L 24, 29.1.2004, p. 1 (ECMR).

means, for example, that Member States may only subsidize individual companies if such support is compatible with the State aid rules.[8]

At the heart of existing EU State aid law is the so-called "market investor test", which makes it possible to distinguish non-market interventions from mere State participation in competition.[9] The addressee is the State in all its subdivisions, also along federal structures. In principle, the test can be applied to measures adopted by a State both against individual companies (= selective) and entire sectors of the national economy. It also does not matter whether the measure has a direct effect on competition or not as even indirect effects are addressed. However, for the test to apply, it is crucial that the State acts as an economic operator and not in a sovereign capacity. Where the State participates in economic transactions, it must be examined whether the State action is carried out under normal market conditions, i.e., in conformity with market principles. In case of an economic transaction, it is decisive that it would be carried out by public authorities and private market participants on equal terms ("*pari passu*") or, that it consists in the sale or purchase of assets, goods and services by means of a competitive, transparent, non-discriminatory and unconditional procurement procedure. In the absence of an economic transaction, any general State measures that might lead to production conditions not in conformity with market principles as a whole are not covered, but can be examined to determine whether an objective recognized under EU law is being pursued and whether the State limits market intervention in order to achieve this objective to appropriate and necessary measures (proportionality).

Art. 107(1) TFEU provides that selective aid is prohibited as a principal matter. However, the provision does not set up an absolute ban on State aid. Art. 107(2) and (3) TFEU as well as the secondary legislation adopted on the basis of Art. 109 TFEU contain a number of reasons which allow subsidies to be granted under certain conditions, because there are legitimate purposes behind them such as combating social imbalances and natural disasters or the promotion of art and culture.[10] This differential treatment mirrors, to some extent at least, the economic perspective, which considers subsidies not to be harmful in all cases.[11] On the one hand, indeed, it is assumed that subsidies can even produce positive effects on the market in cases of market failure.[12] For example, they can be used to counter negative externalities or to provide public goods.[13]

On the other hand, however, subsidies are often used by countries for protectionist reasons and, in this context, represent a non-tariff trade restriction on imports

[8] State aid control has been enshrined in the EU Treaties from the earliest days onwards; see already Art. 4(c) of the Treaty Establishing the European Coal and Steel Community, 18 April 1951, 261 U.N.T.S. 140.

[9] See on this Monopolies Commission (2020), paras. 609–613.

[10] For an overview see https://ec.europa.eu/competition/state_aid/legislation/legislation.html.

[11] Cif. Lehner and Meiklejohn (1991), p. 19; Buelens et al. (2007), p. 6.

[12] Lehner and Meiklejohn (1991), p. 19 et seq.; Buelens et al. (2007), p. 6 and 10 et seq.

[13] Lehner and Meiklejohn (1991), p. 19 et seq.

from other countries.[14] In addition, the use of subsidies by one country leads to an incentive for other countries to resort to subsidies themselves.[15] This so-called "subsidy race" has a negative impact on the budget of countries and may increase the imbalance between countries that have large financial resources and those that have limited financial means.[16]

Hence, not only between EU Member States, but also when looking at the individual State in isolation, the differentiating control of State aid appears justified.[17] It strengthens budgetary discipline and leads to lower spending.[18] At the same time, it reduces the risk of inefficient and harmful misspending due to government failures.[19] By means of effective State aid control, EU Member States are forced to look at the effect of selective aid, and the damaging influence of lobbying on administrative action is also limited.[20]

3 Reasons for a New Approach to Foreign Subsidies in the EU

According to the Treaties, support for companies from third countries is not subject to any control that is completely comparable with EU State aid law. Hence, there has been an increasing debate about the need to amend either foreign trade or competition law. That being said, the influence of third countries on the economy is already subject to other rules under EU law, and the gaps are consequently not as glaring as one might think.

In cross-border trade, unfair trade practices in the form of third-country influence can be addressed by the existing anti-dumping and anti-subsidy instruments.[21] EU anti-dumping law already takes into account that prices for imported goods may "not result from the free play of market forces".[22] At the same time, EU anti subsidy law

[14]Lehner and Meiklejohn (1991), p. 23; Buelens et al. (2007), p. 6.

[15]Lehner and Meiklejohn (1991), p. 24; Buelens et al. (2007), p. 6.

[16]Buelens et al. (2007), p. 6 et seq.

[17]Buelens et al. (2007), p. 7 et seq.

[18]Buelens et al. (2007), p. 8.

[19]Buelens et al. (2007), p. 8.

[20]Buelens et al. (2007), p. 8.

[21]Monopolies Commission (2020), paras. 635 et seq. and 703 et seq.

[22]Art. 2(6a)(b) of the Anti-Dumping Regulation 2016/1036 of the European Parliament and of the Council of 8 June 2016 on protection against dumped imports from countries not members of the European Union (codification), OJ L 176, 30.6.2016, p. 21, as amended by Regulation (EU) 2017/2321 of the European Parliament and of the Council of 12 December 2017, OJ L 338, 19.12.2017, p. 1 and Regulation (EU) 2018/825 of the European Parliament and of the Council of 30 May 2018, OJ L 143, 7.6.2018, p. 1.

is directed towards the provision of a financial contribution by a third country, if a benefit is thereby conferred and damage to the union industry can be proven.[23] However, it must be noted that, on the one hand, anti-dumping law is basically only directed against price discrimination by private companies and, on the other hand, the instrument is not only used for competitive purposes, but also for reasons of industrial policy. Anti-subsidy law is directly directed against state subsidies, however, industrial policy considerations also play a role in this context. Moreover, anti-subsidy law can only regulate cases where goods are imported into the EU. However, European companies also complain about unfair competition from foreign companies established in the internal market as well as by companies providing services.[24]

Apart from EU trade law, the European competition rules apply to both EU and non-EU companies when they are active on the internal market. The EU competition rules are not directly applicable to measures of third countries. However, in the assessment of the market position of undertakings (in abuse and merger control), it can also be taken into account that a third country is behind those undertakings. That being said, the question of whether the *behavior of undertakings* (seated in the EU or outside) violates the prohibition of cartels or abuses (Art. 101 or Art. 102 TFEU) must be answered solely on the basis of the constituent elements of the relevant provisions.[25] As regards changes in *market structure*, merger control is in place to protect consumers against market power.[26] Even if, for example, the enhancement of financial strength through state support can be taken into account, the market share and the competitive behavior of the companies are primarily considered in merger control, without specifically looking at existing or future subsidies.

Merger control must be regarded separately from investment control. Investment control has been tightened more and more in recent years. The EU has adopted a framework regulation to create common rules in the EU and to establish exchanges between Member States.[27] Member States that have not yet introduced investment controls are encouraged to do so and to notify the rules to the EU.[28] While reference

[23] Regulation (EU) 2016/1037 of the European Parliament and of the Council of 8 June 2016 on protection against subsidised imports from countries not members of the European Union, OJ L 176, 30.6.2016, p. 55, as amended by Regulation (EU) 2017/2321 of the European Parliament and of the Council of 12 December 2017, OJ L 338, 19.12.2017, p. 1 and Regulation (EU) 2018/825 of the European Parliament and of the Council of 30 May 2018, OJ L 143, 7.6.2018, p. 1.

[24] See Monopolies Commission (2020), paras. 636–683 and 703–741.

[25] Monopolies Commission (2020), paras. 684 et seq.

[26] Monopolies Commission (2020), paras. 826 et seq.

[27] Regulation (EU) 2019/452 of the European Parliament and of the Council of 19 March 2019 establishing a framework for the screening of foreign direct investments into the Union, OJ L 79I, 21.3.2019, p. 1. See Monopolies Commission (2020), paras. 805–825.

[28] See the List of screening mechanisms notified by Member States (Last update: 16 February 2021), https://trade.ec.europa.eu/doclib/docs/2019/june/tradoc_157946.pdf.

is occasionally made to investment control as a protective instrument,[29] investment control is not about competition, but about public safety and order.[30]

Finally, public procurement law allows the authorities responsible for the tender to consider also criteria other than those strictly relevant for the award of contracts ("*vergabefremde Kriterien*"). In addition, the authorities can exclude unusually low bids from the procedure. This allows to take into account the influence which third countries exercise through financial support for individual foreign bidders or other strategic measures that interfere with tender procedures.[31]

Even though, as has been demonstrated, various rules can be applied to situations in which unfair competitive conditions may arise due to state support, European State aid law (Art. 107 et seq. TFEU) itself is only applicable to Member States.[32] There is thus a legal asymmetry when it comes to regulating aid from Member States and from third countries. The principle of equal competitive opportunities is thus violated. This is particularly evident with regard to the gaps already identified in the context of anti-subsidy law in relation to EU-based companies and in relation to trade in services. This problem is further exacerbated by the fact that, pursuant to Art. 106 TFEU, the European competition rules also apply in relation to the state-owned enterprises (SOEs) of the Member States. This provision is also not applicable to foreign SOEs.[33]

This legal asymmetry has recently led to discussions within the EU as to how this regulatory gap could best be closed. Different mechanisms are conceivable to eliminate the contradiction between the (limited) internal orientation of EU State aid law and the (limited) outside orientation in the treatment of foreign subsidies. In the end, however, what is needed is an instrument protecting the competitive "level playing field" in the EU's internal market. In this regard, a particularly promising approach would be to introduce a new instrument complementing existing EU State aid law as State aid law has developed a relatively elaborate system to handle State support measures already.

4 The Current Reform Proposals

There is more or less a common understanding that problems may arise because the existing rules do not provide for fully equivalent treatment of EU Member State aid and foreign subsidies.[34] This is also the result of the European Commission's

[29] BDI (2019), p. 17.

[30] Monopolies Commission (2020), paras. 805 et seq.

[31] Monopolies Commission (2020), paras. 790–791.

[32] Monopolies Commission (2020), paras. 742 et seq.

[33] Monopolies Commission (2020), paras. 777 et seq.

[34] Some participants in the discussion argue that the issues have a broader span; see, e.g., Netherlands, Non-Paper strengthening the level playing field on the internal market, undated, https://www.

problem analysis,[35] and the German Monopolies Commission shares the European Commission's views in that regard.

Some differences exist in how to best align EU Member State aid and foreign subsidies control in the future.[36] However, these differences should not be overstated. Both the European Commission and the Monopolies Commission take the view that we need a new legal instrument to deal with the competition effects of foreign subsidies, and that this new legal instrument should be geared towards protecting the "level playing field" within the EU internal market.

The main difference is that the European Commission proposes a toolbox including three tools whereas the Monopolies Commission proposes just one tool, but with a corresponding scope of application. The reason for this divergence lies in where the instruments would apply and how they would be shaped. The European Commission favors a general screening instrument allowing for *ex officio* investigations. In addition, a merger instrument and a procurement instrument would be embedded in merger and procurement procedures under the existing rules. The Monopolies Commission, in contrast, proposes one stand-alone instrument, which would be oriented a lot at the existing rules for State aid control. However, the instrument would, at the same time, be subordinate to existing rules. Under this instrument, market participants operating in the EU with foreign subsidies would have to notify the State support they receive. In general, however, they could pursue their activities notwithstanding this notification. The competent authority would only have the right to intervene if this is necessary to protect competition. A standstill obligation, as it is known from State aid law, would only apply in merger and procurement cases, to avoid that foreign aid is passed on to other private or public beneficiaries.

When it comes to the details, the European Commission initially favored a definition of foreign aid according to the standards of EU anti-subsidy law and the EU Regulation on safeguarding competition in the air transport sector,[37] but recently proposed a definition which seems to be more aligned with the criteria of EU State aid law.[38] In any event, the central intervention criterion would be the existence of a distortion. The European Commission considers to define certain categories of

---

permanentrepresentations.nl/binaries/nlatio/documents/publications/2019/12/09/non-paper-on-level-playingfield/Dutch+nonpaper+on+Level+playing+field.pdf; which has been commented in: Monopolies Commission (2020), paras. 903 et seq.

[35] European Commission, White Paper: On levelling the playing field as regards foreign subsidies, COM(2020) 253 final, 17 June 2020 (hereinafter: White Paper), pp. 9 et seq. On this basis the European Commission has recently published its "Proposal for a Regulation of the European Parliament and of the Council on foreign subsidies distorting the internal market, COM(2021) 223 final. See for the evolution of the European Commission's proposal the contribution by Krenek and De Smijter in this volume.

[36] See European Commission, White Paper, COM(2020) 253 final, pp. 13 et seq.; Monopolies Commission (2020), paras. 864 et seq., and particularly the comments in para. 885.

[37] Regulation 2019/712 of the European Parliament and of the Council of 17 April 2019 on safeguarding competition in air transport, and repealing Regulation (EC) No 868/2004, OJ L 123, 10.5.2019, p. 4.

[38] Art. 2 of the European Commission's proposal, COM(2021) 223 final.

subsidies that are "most likely to distort the internal market".[39] Subsidies not falling into those categories would be subject to an overall competitive assessment involving the market structure and behavior, but also the market openness of the third country.[40] This approach is somewhat similar to the distinction between prohibited and countervailable subsidies under the WTO Agreement on Subsidies and Countervailing Measures. The distortive effects would have to be balanced with possible positive effects.[41] The European Commission initially had proposed a Union interest test at this juncture, along the lines of the anti-dumping and anti-subsidy regulations. It now favors a balancing process that is kept more open. If subsidies fall foul of the rules, the competent authority could either order repayment or impose other remedial measures.[42]

The current European Commission proposal converges with ideas which the German Monopolies Commission set forth in its most recent Biennial Report.[43] The Monopolies Commission, however, orientates its proposal even more at the existing State aid rules. The legal test would be designed as an equal treatment clause. A financial contribution that violates Art. 107 TFEU as a Member State measure would be considered incompatible with the internal market and would open up the possibility of intervention. But also regarding the finding of a distortion of competition and the available remedies, the Monopolies Commission would align the new rules with Art. 107 et seq. TFEU on State aid to the widest extent possible. The reason is that this brings equal treatment between EU and third countries to the fore. Also against the background of WTO rules, it is necessary to clarify that the instrument should be aimed solely at equal treatment. To allow for flexibility and to facilitate things in practice, however, the Monopolies Commission would also foresee the possibility to recognize international aid control systems. The EU-Singapore FTA is a good example for a more common understanding on subsidies between the EU and a trading partner. In addition, States could have or introduce their own subsidy control systems that are at least comparable to the one of the EU. The European Commission should have the option of issuing a recognition decision in cases where national subsidy control exists or a reciprocal obligation has been agreed in a free trade agreement. Aid that is permissible according to such a system would not be considered incompatible with the EU interest. Free trade agreements can also contribute to a common understanding on possible justifications for the provision of subsidies. The EU-Singapore FTA has also inspired us with regard this aspect, as it has integrated the exceptions known from State aid law into an international context. Apart from international rules, a subsidy should also not constitute an impairment of the level playing field if European competitors receive aid from the EU or its Member States. When it comes to aid that fails the test, the

[39] Art. 4 of the European Commission's proposal, COM(2021) 223 final.

[40] Art. 3 of the European Commission's proposal, COM(2021) 223 final.

[41] Art. 5 of the European Commission's proposal, COM(2021) 223 final.

[42] Art. 6 of the European Commission's proposal, COM(2021) 223 final.

[43] Monopolies Commission (2020), paras. 551 et seq., especially paras. 924 et seq.

Monopolies Commission would favor the remedies of EU State aid law, i.e., repayment obligations. SOEs should additionally be subjected to transparency obligations.

In practice, the two proposals of the European Commission and the Monopolies Commission are likely to lead to similar results in most cases. The widest practical divergence originally existed between the ideas for the organizational setup. The European Commission initially proposed a partly decentralized system, except for merger cases which should be handled by the Commission only. In contrast, the Monopolies Commission spoke out for a centralized system, with the EU Commission enforcing the new instrument alone. In this respect, the Monopolies Commission took into consideration that the European Commission has built up central expertise in both State aid control and international trade matters. This expertise is not available to the same extent at national level. In addition, having several authorities involved would increase the burden for the undertakings concerned. Indeed, it would not contribute to the international acceptable of the new instrument if it leads to discriminatory treatment or increase the regulatory burden for foreign market entrants in a deterrent fashion. In this respect, it seems that a number of contributors have expressed similar views. In any case, the European Commission is now also proposing a centralized system, as it had been advocated by the Monopolies Commission before.

5 Possible Third-Country Reactions and Long-Term Benefits

The reform proposals discussed before militate in favour of a novel instrument that would subject third-country subsidies provided to companies operating in the EU to a control similar to Member State aid control. If the European Union were to introduce such an instrument, this instrument might have a strong impact particularly on the trade relationship between the EU and China, as China is today one of the largest trading partners of the EU.[44]

That being said, the new instrument would not constitute a protectionist instrument, different from other new trade policy measures which enjoy increasing popularity on the international arena (i.e., import restrictions such as punitive tariffs, political use of investment control). Such protectionist instruments are characterized above all by the fact that they impede market access from third countries. They harm those affected and can lead to mutual retaliation which not only negatively impacts on the parties involved but which harms global trade in general. In contrast, the new instrument discussed here would aim at levelling the playing field. To this end, it

[44] See also the contribution by Wambach in this volume.

would merely impose conditions designed to prevent companies from third countries from entering the EU single market under auspices that would give them advantages and eliminate equal competition to the detriment of companies already active in the single market. However, the protection of the domestic economy against external threats of damage is in itself a generally recognized legitimate interest.

This does not exclude that a large trading partner, such as China, would introduce similar mechanisms to establish some sort of counterpart control vis-à-vis foreign companies entering the Chinese market. Indeed, chapter 5 of the Chinese Antimonopoly Law,[45] which contains regulations to combat the abuse of State administrative power for non-competitive purposes, might already provide a basis for such type of control under existing law. Chapter 5 generally prohibits State authorities from causing disadvantages to individual companies in the movement of goods through their decisions (Art. 32). In addition, is prohibits, among other things, State measures that hinder the market entry of non-locally produced goods or create other obstacles to the free movement of goods (Art. 33 Var. (iv) and (v): "creating burdens or other methods to limit the entry of non-local commodities" and "other conducts that block free regional commodity circulation"). It also prohibits preferential treatment of local companies in procurement procedures (Art. 34).

If the introduction of a European level playing field instrument were to activate a similar mechanism in China, however, this should not be seen critical from the European perspective. On the contrary, it would have to be welcomed in principle. Such a development would bring the European and Chinese economic systems closer together in regulatory terms and broaden the basis for a level playing field between the two systems. Moreover, any new instrument neutralizing foreign state subsidies would establish competition on equal terms between foreign and domestic companies in the respective internal market. This would reduce competitive distortions and free competitive potential within the market, thus ultimately benefiting consumers.

6 Conclusions and Outlook

It has been shown what role State aid law plays for competition in the European internal market. However, in a globalized world trade with open markets, a gap remains for the European competition system, which impedes the maintenance of the level playing field in the internal market. This has led a large number of market participants to demand a reform of competition law. First proposals have now been published. China is one of the largest trading partners of the EU and would be

[45] "Chapter 5 Abuse of Administrative Power to Eliminate or Restrict Competition". An English translation of the Chinese Antimonpoly Law can be found under https://www.wipo.int/edocs/lexdocs/laws/en/cn/cn099en.pdf.

affected by a reform to a substantial extent, but the impact would also be felt by other countries that provide selective support to companies and industries.

The investment agreement negotiated between the EU and China includes general obligations for the behavior of State-owned enterprises and comprehensive transparency rules for subsidies.[46] Thus, it may provide a starting point to find a minimum compromise on how to define foreign subsidies that may be subject to additional instruments, and perhaps even on how to shape these instruments. If the EU and China agree on how this toolbox is going to look like, this may be better for China than if the EU decides on this alone. In the Monopolies Commission's view, however, the agreement is no substitution for a new instrument effectively protecting the competitive level playing field within the EU internal market.[47] In addition, the EU and China should discuss how procedures in the EU can be streamlined with a view to reducing the regulatory burden on third-country investors.

In any case, it must be stressed that subsidies should be approached the same way regardless of whether they are granted by EU Member States or by foreign countries, and in the latter case, irrespective of which foreign country is concerned. Further, if both Europeans and the home countries of EU-external market participants could agree that foreign subsidies are a challenge of its own—regardless of the country concerned—then we should also go into one direction to meet this challenge. The introduction of an instrument for third-party aid, which would put third-country subsidies and Member State aid on an equal footing as far as possible would be the first right step on this path from the perspective of the European Union.

References

BDI (2019) Grundsatzpapier China. Partner und systemischer Wettbewerber – Wie gehen wir mit Chinas staatlich gelenkter Volkswirtschaft um?, https://bdi.eu/publikation/news/china-partner-und-systemischer-wettbewerber/

Buelens C, Garnier G, Meklejohn R, Johnson M (2007) The economic analysis of state aid: some open questions. European Economy No. 286

Hatje A (2009) Wirtschaftsverfassung im Binnenmarkt. In: von Bogdandy A, Bast J (eds) Europäisches Verfassungsrecht: Theoretische und dogmatische Grundzüge, 2nd edn. Springer, Heidelberg, pp 801–853

Lehner S, Meiklejohn R (1991) Fair Competition in the internal market: Community State aid policy. European Economy No. 48

Monopolies Commission (2020) Chinese state capitalism: A challenge for the European market economy (English translation of Chapter IV of the XXIII. Biennial Report). https://monopolkommission.de/images/HG23/Main_Report_XXIII_Chinese_state_capitalism.pdf

[46] EU – China Comprehensive Agreement on Investment (CAI), https://trade.ec.europa.eu/doclib/press/index.cfm?id=2115.

[47] See already Monopolies Commission (2020) paras. 864 et seq., and particularly the comments in para. 984.

Jürgen Kühling LL.M. is holding the Chair for Public Law, Real Estate Law, Infrastructure Law, and Information Law at the University of Regensburg, Germany, and is Chairman of the German Monopolies Commission.

Thomas Weck LL.M. works as a Senior Legal Analyst.

Philipp Reinhold was Legal Analyst at the Monopolies Commission and works currently as a research assistant at the Chair of Public Law, International Law and European Law of Prof. Dr. Marc Bungenberg, LL.M. at Saarland University.

Upgrading Subsidy Norms for the Digital Age: EU White Paper's Contribution and Remaining Questions

Jaemin Lee

Contents

Abstract In the context of the pending WTO reforms, amendment of the subsidy rules contained in the SCM Agreement has become one of the top priorities. Most notably, the present subsidy rules have not been able to capture various circumventive and indirect subsidization measures. Also, the dividing line between legitimate government support measures and illegal subsidies has been murky, stoking intense confrontation among Members. New subsidy rules should be able to address these outstanding issues. In this respect, the recent endeavor of the EU through the 2020 Subsidy White Paper is both important and timely. The White Paper sets forth a new framework for future subsidy norms, which will offer a critical benchmark for the global community to rely upon in future subsidy discussions. That said, there are several questions that may deserve careful attention in elaborating the proposals contained in the White Paper. These questions concern structural issues between the new norms adopted by individual WTO Members in the interim such as those envisaged by the White Paper and the present SCM Agreement, and between the new norms and international investment agreements. Careful consideration of

J. Lee (✉)
School of Law, Seoul National University, Seoul, Korea
e-mail: jaemin@snu.ac.kr

M. Chi et al. (eds.), *Asian Yearbook of International Economic Law 2022*,
Asian Yearbook of International Economic Law (2022) 2022: 163–180,
https://doi.org/10.1007/16517_2021_5, Published online: 8 December 2021

these structural issues may ensure smooth transition to new subsidy rules without triggering unnecessary legal challenges.

1 Introduction

The Agreement on Subsidies and Countervailing Measures ("SCM Agreement") annexed to the Marrakesh Agreement Establishing the World Trade Organization provides the following definition of a "subsidy": "a financial contribution by a government or [a] public body[1] (Article 1.1(a)(i)) that confers a benefit[2] (Article 1.1(b)) to a specific enterprise or industry[3] (Article 1.2)". This simple definition notwithstanding, disputes and controversies have persisted since the inception of the World Trade Organization ("WTO"). All three components (i.e., financial contribution, benefit, and specificity) have invited debates and arguments, and WTO members are still not entirely clear about the exact meaning and contours of a subsidy, hence the scope of the SCM Agreement.

These ambiguities and uncertainties have also posed significant challenges for Korea as it has faced a series of critical subsidy disputes at the WTO dispute settlement proceedings.[4] Needless to say, the WTO regime has achieved some clarity as regards these critical terms in the SCM Agreement over the past 26 years through the Appellate Body and panel decisions. At the same time, however, each dispute has also raised its own share of ambiguities and uncertainties one way or

[1] As regards financial contribution, Article 1.1(a) of the SCM Agreement provides as follows: 1.1 For the purpose of this Agreement, a subsidy shall be deemed to exist if: (a)(1) there is a financial contribution by a government or any public body within the territory of a Member (referred to in this Agreement as "government"), i.e. where: (i) a government practice involves a direct transfer of funds (e.g. grants, loans, and equity infusion), potential direct transfers of funds or liabilities (e.g. loan guarantees); (ii) government revenue that is otherwise due is foregone or not collected (e.g. fiscal incentives such as tax credits); (iii) a government provides goods or services other than general infrastructure, or purchases goods; (iv) a government makes payments to a funding mechanism, or entrusts or directs a private body to carry out one or more of the type of functions illustrated in (i) to (iii) above which would normally be vested in the government and the practice, in no real sense, differs from practices normally followed by governments; or (a)(2) there is any form of income or price support in the sense of Article XVI of GATT 1994; [. . .].

[2] Article 1.1(b) of the SCM Agreement provides as follows regarding benefit: 1.1 For the purpose of this Agreement, a subsidy shall be deemed to exist if: [. . .] (b) a benefit is thereby conferred.

[3] Article 2 of the SCM Agreement provides detailed rules to determine specificity as follows: 2.1 In order to determine whether a subsidy, as defined in paragraph 1 of Article 1, is specific to an enterprise or industry or group of enterprises or industries (referred to in this Agreement as "certain enterprises") within the jurisdiction of the granting authority, the following principles shall apply: [. . .].

[4] Lee and Yoo (2011), p. 129 (in Korean); Lee (2010), p. 381 (in Korean).

another, rendering many states either wondering or unsatisfied. If anything, this less-than-optimal outcome on the SCM Agreement front may underpin the intensifying confrontation between the United States and China.

Such being the case, whatever subsidy regulation schemes the global community is exploring at the moment in the context of the WTO reform, Free Trade Agreement (FTA) negotiations, or unilateral domestic endeavors (such as EU White Paper of May 2020), the focus should be placed on clarification of the critical terms: in other words, how to define the core elements of the subsidy norms reflecting the lessons of the WTO members for the past 26 years and the demand from the market with the advent of the digital economy and artificial intelligence. Otherwise, the global community will see more disputes between the United States and China, between the EU and China, and between other countries.[5] Clarification of key terms is critical in amending the SCM Agreement or otherwise upgrading subsidy norms in the global community. Clarification will help states adjust their national policies in a subsidy norm-compliant manner and thus reduce disputes among states.

2 Outdated and Sidelined Norms

Many people would agree that the current subsidy norms are outdated.[6] The absence of the preamble of the SCM Agreement reflects the controversy at the time of the conclusion of the negotiations at the Uruguay Round ("UR"). The gap between the norms in the SCM Agreement and the reality in the market has been growing over the years. As a matter of fact, the essence of the current norms was drafted in the early stage of the UR, namely between 1986 and 1988. Now, in 2021, the global community is witnessing the drastically changed landscape in trade and investment: the US-China confrontation is intensifying, and the COVID-19 pandemic is engulfing the entire world.[7] Even before the latest challenges, the global financial

[5] See Capital Trade Incorporated (2009), p. 121.

[6] For instance, Japan, the EU, and the US proposed a trilateral initiative on the WTO reform, which focused on subsidies, state enterprises, and 'forced' technology transfer. It emphasizes that the SCM Agreement needs to provide a more guidance in determining 'serious prejudice', as well as to enlarge the scope of prohibited subsidies. Howse (2020), pp. 371–389.

[7] New Zealand Government, Unite against COVID-19, https://covid19.govt.nz/business-work-and-money/financial-support/financial-support-for-businesses/; Kim & Chang,COVID-19: Government Relief for Companies Impacted by COVID-19 in Korea, Newsletter of 23 April 2020, https://www.kimchang.com/en/insights/detail.kc?sch_section=4&idx=21265; Irish Tax and Customs, Information about the Temporary Wage Subsidy Scheme (TWSS), https://www.revenue.ie/en/employing-people/twss/information-about-twss/index.aspx; Government of Canada, Canada Emergency Wage Subsidy (CEWS), https://www.canada.ca/en/revenue-agency/services/subsidy/emergency-wage-subsidy.html; German Chambers of Commerce, Covid-19: German Federal Support Measures, https://www.dihk.de/resource/blob/27920/a6591ae8f2f43dcf37ff9e4bec50fb72/support-measures-corona-data.pdf.

crisis about 10 years ago,[8] and the climate change threats[9] signaled the upcoming changes or the need for changes in the global trade regime. What stands out in these changes is how to understand the proper role of a government in national emergency situations, which strikes the core portion of the SCM Agreement. While many states feel the necessity for new norms for the changed circumstances, the subsidy norms still remain static with the failure of the Doha Development Agenda ("DDA") negotiations. States still have to operate under the same old subsidy norms drafted in late 1980s.

Most importantly, in the past 26 years of the WTO regime, states have realized the complexity of subsidy disputes; they have seen a number of circumventive measures, direct or indirect subsidization, disguised support schemes and the like. The regulatory net of the SCM Agreement is not able to identify and capture these instances, stoking the dissatisfaction of interested states. Such being the case, it seems to be a right time to explore upgrades, elaboration and fine-tuning of the subsidy norms.[10] These endeavors can take place in diverse fora including both the WTO and FTA frameworks.

3 Elements of Prospective Norms

Obviously, there are many issues that deserve attention and discussion. Perhaps not all these issues will be able to be taken up due to the logistical constraints. States might want to canvass outstanding issues to prioritize only those that require immediate attention and discussion. One such priority topic would be "public body"[11] appearing in the SCM Agreement. There have been long debates about the meaning of the term "public body"—how is it (not) different from "state enterprises" "state trading enterprises", or "state-owned enterprises (SOE)"?[12] More fundamentally, how do we distinguish a public body from a government agency?

[8] See OECD (2009), p. 18.

[9] Government of Canada, Government Announces Climate Action Incentive Payments for 2021, https://www.canada.ca/en/department-finance/news/2020/12/government-announces-climate-action-incentive-payments-for-2021.html; Canada Drives, Carbon Taxes & Rebates Explained (Province by Province), https://www.canadadrives.ca/blog/news/carbon-taxes-and-carbon-tax-rebates-in-canada-explained.

[10] Regulating subsidies is more complicated than tariffs, as constraints on domestic subsidies can prevent countries from using the first-best economic policies. Furthermore, the economic scope of the subsidy problem is not clearly defined. See Brown and Hillman (2019), pp. 557–578. In addition, Hoekman and Nelson (2020) argue that because subsidy measures can take a variety of forms depending on the type of economy, it is necessary to develop subsidy norms to reflect the interdependent world economy.

[11] Brink (2011), p. 313.

[12] Neither the SCM Agreement nor any other WTO Agreement includes a clear definition of "public body". Ahn (2021), p. 62. The EU (2018) recognized the need to clarify what constitutes a "public body": "Subsidies granted to SOEs are already captured by the SCM Agreement, in the same way as

The introduction of detailed norms for SOEs in the recent FTAs, most notably the Comprehensive and Progressive Agreement for Trans-Pacific Partnership ("CPTPP"),[13] has made the clear categorization of these related entities all the more important. As a matter fact, there is a strong commonality between the SOE chapter (Chapter 17) of the CPTPP and the subsidy norms in the SCM Agreement. The SOE chapter borrows the basic structure, though with different terminology, of the SCM Agreement. The similarity also appears in the relevant discussions of the EU's recent White Paper on Levelling the Playing Field as Regards Foreign Subsidies ("White Paper"), where many issues overlap with the new norms introduced in the CPTPP SOE chapter.[14]

It would then be critical to clarify the term "public body" in the SCM Agreement and to delineate the scope of the term vis-à-vis the scope of other related terms such as SOEs.[15] It would be fine for these related terms to overlap with one another. Nonetheless, the legal contours of these respective terms should be clear, so that contracting parties know in advance what specific commitments they assume when they join various trade agreements. As it currently stands, the terms "state-owned enterprises", "state enterprises", "state trading enterprise", and "public body", as

any other subsidy granted by the state. With regard to instances where SOEs themselves grant subsidies, the SCM Agreement captures them through the concept of a "public body". However, this has been interpreted in a rather narrow manner, which allows a considerable number of SOEs to escape the application of the SCM Agreement. The EU therefore should propose a clarification of what constitutes a public body, on the basis of a case-by-case analysis to determine whether a state-owned or a state-controlled enterprise performs a government function or furthers a government policy, as well as how to assess whether a member exercises meaningful control over the enterprise in question."

[13]Kawase recognizes Chapter 17 of the CPTPP as "the first comprehensive and detailed disciplines on SOEs". However, he notes that along with other problems of the chapter, the scope of application is narrow, with a large number of exceptions. See Kawase and Ambashi (2018); Kawase (2014).

[14]European Commission (2020), p. 41.

[15]Some note that the narrow interpretation of "public body" undermines the effectiveness of the SCM Agreement. "Article 1.1 clearly distinguishes the concept of 'government' from that of a 'public body.' This reflects the fact that subsidies may well be granted by entities connected to or influenced by government but that do not have the formal status of governmental agencies (such as state- owned or controlled financial institutions). Nevertheless, in the US-Countervailing Measures (China) and in the US-ad/CVD(China) cases, the AB held that the concept of public body should be understood in light of the general rules of customary international law on state responsibility as codified in the ILC Articles on State Responsibility. These rules determine whether conduct of a particular actor can be attributable to the state. Thus, the AB opined that state ownership or control are not in themselves sufficient to make a determination that an entity is a public body for purposes of Article 1.1; instead, the AB appeared to put considerable focus on whether the body was exercising regulatory authority (police power over other actors) in the granting of a subsidy-as opposed to merely following an industrial policy priority of the government that owns or controls it, for instance. The AB interpretation of 'public body' is wrong, in that it ignores the *lex specialis* character of the provision in question, clearly going beyond the rules of attribution in the ILC Articles of State Responsibility." Howse (2020), pp. 373–374 and 384–385.

they appear in various trade agreements, appear confusing and complex.[16] Respective definitions for these terms are provided, but how they should be understood in relation to other similar concepts in practice is anything but clear. In future subsidy norm discussions, this issue should merit immediate attention.

Another topic that should be discussed as soon as possible would be how to distinguish "good" subsidies from "bad" subsidies?[17] This question is to draw a dividing line between a legitimate national economy policy and illegitimate subsidization program. This task has been a difficult and elusive one since the inception of the SCM Agreement.[18] A vivid example can be found from various support measures adopted by many states in response to COVID-19.[19] What do we make of them—are they acceptable or legitimate under the current subsidy norms? While there would be strong consensus to support the practical need for such support measures, their consistency with the current subsidy norms under the SCM Agreement seems dubious. If anything, the SCM Agreement does not contain an exception clause to address these situations. This would be another evidence of showing the gap between norm and reality.

With governments around the world responding to various threats and emergencies, it would be critical now for new subsidy norms to draw a fine line between "good" subsidies and "bad" subsidies. The next question then is: what are "good" subsidies, and what do we do about them? Do we re-define "subsidy" so that necessary economic policies are not covered by the term in the first place? Or do we include some general exceptions in the new scheme in line with Article XX of the General Agreement on Tariffs and Trade 1994 ("GATT 1994"). Or do we consider inclusion of specific exceptions for bail out packages, a financial crisis, green subsidies, etc.? Future discussion of new subsidy norms should contemplate these issues.

Another issue that requires prompt attention is how to capture disguised subsidization, which seems to be a perennial task on the subsidy front.[20] From time to time, states have resorted to formulating and implementing disguised schemes for subsidization. They have fueled the frustration of other states. In future discussions, strong schemes to identify and deter these disguised measures should be strongly demanded.

Likewise, the permeation of the current SCM Agreement into other key areas is also important. The current subsidy norms are only applicable to the goods trade. Subsidization, however, can equally take place, in the services sector and investment

[16] For instance, the CPTPP attempts to clarify what an SOE is, and requires publication of "a list of a Party's state-owned enterprises". However, for anybody outside the Party, it is difficult to determine whether an entity meets the definition of SOE. Wolfe (2017), pp. 724–725. Also, see Ahn (2021), p. 62.

[17] Lester (2011), p. 347.

[18] Howse (2020), p. 378; Hoekman and Nelson (2020), p. 3111.

[19] Jozepa (2020), p. 3; Hoekman (2020), p. 68; Lee and Prabhakar (2021), p. 6.

[20] Matthes (2020), pp. 43–45; Bacchetta et al. (2021), p. 26.

area. The question then is how to extend the subsidy norms to these new areas. As services and investment sectors are distinct and different from the goods sector, some of the norms of the SCM Agreement would have to be changed or amended. Preparation of the new norms for these new sectors would require advance analyses of the similarities and differences between goods and services/investment.[21] Future subsidy norms should preferably deal with this issue as well.

4 Recent EU Initiative and Remaining Questions

The EU has made an important stride in initiating and spearheading the discussion on subsidies. The European Commission released its White Paper on 17 June 2020.[22] This project is an important development, not only for the EU, but also for the general discussion on subsidies, based upon the experience of the past 26 years and outstanding problems as illustrated above (Sect. 3). It is the right time to carefully consider how to deal with the question of subsidies in the new landscape of international trade and business transactions. All in all, the EU initiative is important and very timely for galvanizing the critical discussion on and regulation of subsidies.[23]

4.1 Main Contents of the White Paper

As explained above and as also elaborated in the "Gap Analysis" of the White Paper, current subsidy norms are not precise or detailed enough to identify and regulate foreign governments' subsidization schemes that distort the domestic market of another country and/or the global market.[24] Due to outdated texts and the restricted scope of treaty interpretation, the SCM Agreement has not been able to cope with the problem effectively. Concerns have been raised regarding how to ensure fair competition in the domestic and global markets. An amendment of the SCM Agreement is obviously one option, but getting one has turned out to be elusive so far in the larger context of the failure of the DDA. In the meantime, the level of frustration of states has been increasing. Against this backdrop, the recent initiative of the EU should be lauded for spearheading the crucial discussion at the right time. There have

[21] At the moment, the WTO SCM Agreement does not cover subsidies in the area of services or investment. At the moment, the SCM Agreement is limited to trade in goods, and the GATS do not yet have rules for subsidies in the area of trade in services, see European Commission (2020), p. 10. A patchwork of fragmented rules exists regarding investment and services over a number of investment treaties and FTAs. Kawase and Ambashi (2018), pp. 3–4.

[22] European Commission (2020), pp. 3–4; Meunier and Mickus (2020), p. 1079.

[23] Meunier and Mickus (2020), pp. 1079–1080; Wang and Li (2020), p. 368.

[24] See European Commission (2020), pp. 9–12.

been proposals and ideas to amend the SCM Agreement. They, however, did not come up with basic structures of future subsidy norms together with detailed explanations and rationales. The EU's White Paper is the first attempt to fill the gap; it offers the template for future norms and details background information and implementation schemes in a way that can evolve into the texts of future trade agreements. This attempt of the EU will contribute to the current discussion and debates over the subsidy regulations in the changed economic environment.

4.2 Some Remaining Questions

Indeed, the White Paper purports to provide a general framework for future subsidy rules. This is a significant development from previous discussions in this field. And yet, the White Paper still does not set forth specific provisions in detail. Accordingly, it appears to be somewhat premature to predict a future course of action and assess the contents at this stage. As one would say, problems may be able to be addressed one by one as details emerge to fill current gaps in the present document. Learning by doing should be equally permitted in this area as well.

That said, it would still be critical to check and confirm whether the framework itself may or may not pose a structural problem. Should there be structural problems, elaboration through experience and fine-tuning through practice may not be available. A structural problem, if any, would have to be identified and addressed early on, so that the proposed project could proceed in the right direction and achieve the intended objectives.

One example in this respect would be how to understand the scope of the very agreement in question—the SCM Agreement. Its scope is confined to trade in goods.[25] In short, regulation of subsidies under the current WTO regime is arguably limited to that trade. A similar agreement had been pursued in the trade in services, but it had not been consummated by the end of the UR negotiations.[26] The effect of a subsidy on foreign investment has not been discussed or contained in international investment agreements ("IIAs") either. To the extent that the White Paper aims to address services and investment as well as goods, a question may arise as to the

[25] See European Commission (2020), p. 41.

[26] Article XV of the GATS provides as follows: 1. Members recognize that, in certain circumstances, subsidies may have distortive effects on trade in services. Members shall enter into negotiations with a view to developing the necessary multilateral disciplines to avoid such trade-distortive effects. The negotiations shall also address the appropriateness of countervailing procedures. Such negotiations shall recognize the role of subsidies in relation to the development programmes of developing countries and take into account the needs of Members, particularly developing country Members, for flexibility in this area. For the purpose of such negotiations, Members shall exchange information concerning all subsidies related to trade in services that they provide to their domestic service suppliers. 2. Any Member which considers that it is adversely affected by a subsidy of another Member may request consultations with that Member on such matters. Such requests shall be accorded sympathetic consideration.

compatibility with the WTO Agreements or IIAs. As explained in Sect. 3 above, services and investment would have to be discussed in the context of subsidies at the end of the day. The need to address these issues in the future notwithstanding, the compatibility with the current WTO Agreements and IIAs may not necessarily be guaranteed as long as these agreements remain intact. Thus, the compatibility with the current agreements should be calibrated carefully.

In this regard, one way to view this phenomenon would be that because the WTO Agreements or IIAs are silent on such aspects (services/investment) of subsidies, a state should be free to introduce its own rules as it deems appropriate.[27] Another way to view this would be that new norms may violate the WTO Agreements or IIAs if they conflict with existing norms of these legal instruments. Future discussions based on the White Paper should preferably address this issue upfront in order to dispel any concern over this legal question.

As a matter of fact, the White Paper purports to expand the scope of subsidy norms to cover a wide range of market distortion. It sets forth "a broad material scope" that covers "all market situations" caused by foreign subsidies.[28] The White Paper goes on to propose three separate modules. Module 1 aims to cover market distortion caused by a subsidy provided to a foreign entity established in the EU. It thus covers all activities of a corporation established in the EU, which is under the control of a foreign parent company outside the EU. Module 2 covers situations where subsidies are provided to foreign entities to help them target and acquire EU companies. This situation would presumably also fall under Module 1. Apparently, the scenarios under Module 2 are more specific: i.e., they deal with mergers and acquisition attempts by foreign entities of EU companies where the transactions are financed by foreign governments' subsidy programs. Module 3, on the other hand, aims to cope with foreign subsidies provided to foreign companies operating in the EU to assist them in winning EU-commissioned government procurement contracts. Similar to Module 2, this module covers a specific situation of government procurement, which may also fall under the general market distortion situation contemplated under Module 1.

Generally speaking, no one would dispute the potentially harmful consequences stemming from subsidization of foreign governments in all situations described in Modules 1, 2 and 3. If anything, they all lead to market distortion and harmful consequences for the target country—the EU in this regard. These distortions and harmful consequences may also require and justify countermeasures of various sorts, such as those proposed in the White Paper. In the absence of applicable treaties or agreements, a countermeasure may thus be justified. In the case of WTO Agreements and IIAs, a countermeasure may be regulated or subject to the relevant provisions of these agreements.

By way of example, one may raise the question whether new schemes and rules contained in the three modules overstep the conventional reach of the SCM

[27] Absence of specific regulation in a treaty can be interpreted, according to the ordinary meaning principle of Article 31 of the Vienna Convention on the Law of Treaties, as permitting contracting parties to exercise discretion to fill the missing part.

[28] European Commission (2020), p. 14.

Agreement. In this respect, Article 32.1 of the SCM Agreement stipulates: "No specific action against a subsidy of another Member can be taken except in accordance with the provisions of GATT 1994, as interpreted by this Agreement."

The above provision effectively states that only those actions specified in the SCM Agreement and the GATT 1994 are permitted to the members of the WTO when it comes to subsidies. The above provision might arguably support the view that policy needs to counter foreign subsidies alone do not necessarily providc a legitimate basis to explore all avenues of countermeasures against those foreign subsidies. If anything, any measure to counter foreign subsidies should be in line with the SCM Agreement and the GATT 1994. In that line of argument, the proposed modules may be subject to legal challenges to the extent that they touch upon services trade and investment activities in the EU market. Again, if the WTO Agreements are amended or SCM Agreement is changed, there will not be a problem. Unless that happens, widening the scope of an anti-subsidy scheme may invite legal questions and possibly challenges.

In order to save the schemes of the modules, one would have to make an argument that Article 32.1 is only about trade in goods and does not concern services or investment. Consequently, it could be argued that the WTO norms are simply non-existent concerning services and investment, which are then left to the discretion of each WTO member as it sees appropriate. The answer to this question seems to be debatable: a country is free to adopt its own rules not covered by the WTO Agreements or IIAs, or it is not necessarily so, because the WTO Agreements and IIAs set forth an entire agreed-upon universe to regulate subsidy related measures. In this line of understanding a deviation from this agreed-upon universe may implicate the prior agreement. The answer to this question is anything but clear. One would expect a robust discussion on this question in elaborating and implementing the ideas contained in the White Paper going forward.

Regardless of the outcome of this inquiry into the meaning of the absence of norms, what is still important here is the possibility of the continuing application of the SCM Agreement to the three module scenarios. Such an application may take place when the modules' schemes 'affect' trade in goods one way or another. It is one thing to state "this is only for investment" or "this is only for services". It is quite another to say whether that particular measure for investment or service is somehow 'affecting' the trade of goods, in which case the SCM Agreement is implicated inevitably.[29] Oftentimes, goods, services, and investment are closely interrelated in business transactions, and affects one another.[30] It could be quite difficult to clinically isolate one from another, and take out only the goods, services, or investment part from a package of a governmental measure.[31] Accordingly, it

[29] There may be an overlap of the emerging norms and existing international instruments. See European Commission (2020), p. 40.

[30] For example, in the White Paper, 'foreign subsidy' is defined as "financial contribution benefitting directly or indirectly an undertaking in the EU, offering goods or services, or engaging in investments" (European Commission 2020, p. 47).

[31] Bernasconi-Osterwalder et al. (2020), pp. xii, 34–35; WTO (2020), pp. 35–36, 75–76, 91.

follows that the SCM Agreement stands ready to be applied to counter-subsidy measures in three respective modules even if they do not necessarily target trade in goods. This arguably offers another reason why a careful scrutiny of the three modules under Article 32.1 of the SCM Agreement is required.

Similarly, should application of modules affect foreign investment and investors, IIAs may come into play regardless of what the modules pronounce. IIAs have already become a hot potato issue globally,[32] and its reform has taken center stage recently. Implementation of the schemes under the modules may trigger application of IIAs to the extent that foreign investors and investment are concerned. As regards government procurement, the modules (in particular Module 3) may implicate the obligations under the Agreement on Government Procurement ("GPA").[33] The application of the GPA may differ from state to state as not all WTO members are parties to the GPA. How the new regulation in the White Paper would affect government procurement process in the EU, and the EU's application of the GPA is still an open question.

Ambiguities embedded in the key terms of the White Paper further complicate the inquiry in this regard. Consider, for example, the term "active in the EU market". Its meaning seems to be far from clear, to say the least. If a foreign company is "active in the EU market", then that company becomes subject to Module 1.[34] As a threshold element, this requirement is crucial, but its meaning is unclear. Consider also "positive impact within the EU"?[35] For one thing, the term "positive impact" does not appear in trade agreements, so it is not clear enough to provide reliable guidance to foreign corporations from a third country. Similarly, the term "entitlement to receive a subsidy" is also confusing. Note that it is *not* about "provision" or "receiving" of subsidies, but about "entitlement" to receive a subsidy.[36] This is

---

[32] See Bonnitcha (2017), pp. 6–7.

[33] As of April 2021, the Parties to the Agreement on Government Procurement are as follows: Armenia, Australia, Canada, European Union(with regard to its 27 member states: Austria, Belgium, Denmark, Finland, France, Germany, Greece, Ireland, Italy, Luxemburg, the Netherlands, Portugal, Spain and Sweden, Cyprus, Czech Republic, Estonia, Hungary, Latvia, Lithuania, Malta, Poland, Slovak Republic and Slovenia, Bulgaria and Romania, Croatia), Hong Kong, China, Iceland, Israel, Japan, Republic of Korea, Liechtenstein, Republic of Moldova, Montenegro, Netherlands with respect to Aruba, New Zealand, Norway, Singapore, Switzerland, Chinese Taipei, Ukraine, United Kingdom, United States. See https://www.wto.org/english/tratop_e/gproc_e/memobs_e.htm.

[34] European Commission (2020), p. 15: "Consideration should be given to the possibility of applying Module 1 not only to the undertakings established in the EU, but also, to certain undertakings that benefit from foreign subsidies and are otherwise active in the EU, such as when an undertaking established outside the EU seeks to acquire an EU target."

[35] European Commission (2020), p. 17: "Once it is established that a foreign subsidy is capable of distorting the internal market, and where there is evidence of a possible positive impact that the supported economic activity or investment might have within the EU or on public policy interests recognised by the EU, the distortion should be weighed up against such possible positive impact."

[36] European Commission (2020), p. 15: "A foreign subsidy would be considered to fall under Module 1 from the moment the beneficiary has an entitlement to receive the subsidy. The actual payment of the subsidy is not a necessary condition for bringing a subsidy within the scope of Module 1."

almost implying a *possibility* or *likelihood* of receiving a subsidy from a government, maybe in the future. Stated differently, it aims to regulate a subsidy that is not provided yet, but will likely be provided in the future. The term would leave the application of the provision unpredictable. Also, further consider the terms "structural measures" and "behavioral measures".[37] The meanings of those terms are also open to different views and opinions. Nor is a precedent found regarding the meanings of the terms. These core operative terms should be clarified, and fine-tuned, in order for the ideas laid out in the White Paper to be applied in a reliable manner.

Furthermore, what is not clear in the White Paper is how to accommodate legitimate governmental support measures when examining foreign subsidization. Although the SCM Agreement does not contain specific exceptions after its Part IV lapsed at the end of 1999, there is a strong consensus in resurrecting them when the agreement is amended in the future. In terms of exceptions, a strong argument could be made that general exceptions similar to Article XX of the GATT 1994 may be introduced to the SCM Agreement. Likewise, a strong argument can also be made that security exceptions may also apply, as an extension of Article XXI of the GATT 1994, to the SCM Agreement. Similarly, the GPA has its own exceptions in Article 3, comprising both general exceptions and security exceptions. Furthermore, recent IIAs also have security exceptions in place and prudential regulation exceptions to carve out legitimate governmental measures from the scope of investment agreements.

All these pieces of puzzles collectively indicate the growing importance of identifying and permitting legitimate government measures including subsidization measures. Diverse support measures adopted by many governments in the aftermath of COVID-19 provide a vivid example in this regard. Any subsidy rule discussion without accounting for this fast changing trend would sound hollow. It would be desirable for future discussions initiated by the White Paper to account for the issue of legitimate governmental support measures and allocate a sufficient amount of discussion on this topic.

In this regard, it should be noted that Module 1 illustrates an exception. According to the White Paper, "subsidies. . .to remedy a serious national or global disturbance of the economy" are not covered by Module 1.[38] While this is an important exception for a national economic crisis situation, it does not extend to other legitimate policy objectives such as environmental concern or health protection policies. Likewise, an exception to tax relief is also mentioned in the White Paper when they are "general measures."[39] This exception, however, does not apply to other legitimate governmental policies. The White Paper might want to include a more general clause to carve out various legitimate governmental programs as

[37] European Commission (2020), p. 19: "Redressive measures could be imposed to remedy the distortions caused by the foreign subsidy. . . . It may therefore be necessary to consider giving the competent supervisory authority a variety of alternative redressive measures. These could range from structural remedies and behavioural measures to redressive payments to the EU or the Member States."

[38] European Commission (2020), p. 16.

[39] European Commission (2020), p. 16.

exceptions or to list other specific descriptions of legitimate policies in order to accord states proper leeway in formulating and administering various essential support programs.

4.3 CPTPP: A Cautionary Tale?

The CPTPP contains a lot of interesting things to examine and digest in the context of the subsidy discussion. Chapter 17 of the CPTPP on SOEs seems to reflect the most recent discussion of many countries, including the United States, on the issue of subsidies and/or subsidy-related issues. Interestingly, in contrast to the SCM Agreement, Chapter 17 of the CPTPP contains a variety of exceptions. For instance, there are CPTPP-wide exceptions applicable to the SOE chapter[40] (Arts. 29.1, 29.2).

[40] Article 29.1 of the CPTPP provides: 1. For the purposes of Chapter 2 (National Treatment and Market Access for Goods), Chapter 3 (Rules of Origin and Origin Procedures), Chapter 4 (Textile and Apparel Goods), Chapter 5 (Customs Administration and Trade Facilitation), Chapter 7 (Sanitary and Phytosanitary Measures), Chapter 8 (Technical Barriers to Trade) and Chapter 17 (State-Owned Enterprises and Designated Monopolies), Article XX of GATT 1994 and its interpretative notes are incorporated into and made part of this Agreement, mutatis mutandis. [1] 2. The Parties understand that the measures referred to in Article XX(b) of GATT 1994 include environmental measures necessary to protect human, animal or plant life or health, and that Article XX (g) of GATT 1994 applies to measures relating to the conservation of living and non-living exhaustible natural resources. 3. For the purposes of Chapter 10 (Cross-Border Trade in Services), Chapter 12 (Temporary Entry for Business Persons), Chapter 13 (Telecommunications), Chapter 14 (Electronic Commerce) [2] and Chapter 17 (State-Owned Enterprises and Designated Monopolies), paragraphs (a), (b) and (c) of Article XIV of GATS are incorporated into and made part of this Agreement, mutatis mutandis. [3]The Parties understand that the measures referred to in Article XIV (b) of GATS include environmental measures necessary to protect human, animal or plant life or health. 4. Nothing in this Agreement shall be construed to prevent a Party from taking action, including maintaining or increasing a customs duty, that is authorised by the Dispute Settlement Body of the WTO or is taken as a result of a decision by a dispute settlement panel under a free trade agreement to which the Party taking action and the Party against which the action is taken are party. [1]For the purposes of Chapter 17 (State-Owned Enterprises and Designated Monopolies), Article XX of GATT 1994 and its interpretative notes are incorporated into and made part of this Agreement, mutatis mutandis, only with respect to measures of a Party (including the implementation of measures through the activities of a state-owned enterprise or designated monopoly) affecting the purchase, production or sale of goods, or affecting activities the end result of which is the production of goods. [2]This paragraph is without prejudice to whether a digital product should be classified as a good or service. [3]For the purposes of Chapter 17 (State-Owned Enterprises and Designated Monopolies), Article XIV of GATS (including its footnotes) is incorporated into and made part of this Agreement, mutatis mutandis, only with respect to measures of a Party (including the implementation of measures through the activities of a state-owned enterprise or designated monopoly) affecting the purchase or supply of services, or affecting activities the end result of which is the supply of services.

Moreover, there are SOE-chapter specific exceptions[41] For instance, the CPTPP-wide exceptions include general exceptions—interestingly, the SCM Agreement does not contain these.[42] And there are also security exceptions applicable to the SOE chapter—the SCM Agreement does not contain security exceptions either.[43] As regards the SOE chapter-specific exceptions, there are many carve-outs in the chapter, e.g., a *de minimis* exception, a global economic crisis exception, a bail-out exception, wealth-fund and pension-fund exception, government authority exception, etc.[44]

---

[41] Article 29.2 of the CPTPP provides: Nothing in this Agreement shall be construed to: (a) require a Party to furnish or allow access to any information the disclosure of which it determines to be contrary to its essential security interests; or (b) preclude a Party from applying measures that it considers necessary for the fulfilment of its obligations with respect to the maintenance or restoration of international peace or security, or the protection of its own essential security interests.

[42] Whether the GATT Article XX, the general exception clause, can be applied to the SCM Agreement has been a point of contention. See e.g. amicus brief in Canada-Renewable Energy Case (DS412), https://worldtradelaw.typepad.com/files/amicusds412.pdf. See also https://ielp.worldtradelaw.net/2012/05/gatt-article-xx-as-an-exception-to-the-scm-agreement.html.

[43] Again, it is unclear whether the general security exception clause, GATT Article XXI, can be applied to the SCM Agreement.

[44] Article 17.13 of the CPTPP provides: 1. Nothing in Article 17.4 (Non-discriminatory Treatment and Commercial Considerations) or Article 17.6 (Non-commercial Assistance) shall be construed to: (a) prevent the adoption or enforcement by any Party of measures to respond temporarily to a national or global economic emergency; or (b) apply to a state-owned enterprise with respect to which a Party has adopted or enforced measures on a temporary basis in response to a national or global economic emergency, for the duration of that emergency. 2. Article 17.4.1 (Non-discriminatory Treatment and Commercial Considerations) shall not apply with respect to the supply of financial services by a state-owned enterprise pursuant to a government mandate if that supply of financial services: (a) supports exports or imports, provided that these services are: (i) not intended to displace commercial financing; or (ii) offered on terms no more favourable than those that could be obtained for comparable financial services in the commercial market; (b) supports private investment outside the territory of the Party, provided that these services are: (i) not intended to displace commercial financing, or (ii) offered on terms no more favourable than those that could be obtained for comparable financial services in the commercial market; or (c) is offered on terms consistent with the Arrangement, provided the it falls within the scope of the Arrangement. 3. The supply of financial services by a state-owned enterprise pursuant to a government mandate shall be deemed not to give rise to adverse effects under Article 17.6.1(b) (Non-commercial Assistance) or Article 17.6.2(b), or under Article 17.6.1(c) or Article 17.6.2(c) where the Party in which the financial service is supplied requires a local presence in order to supply those services, if that supply of financial services. (a) supports exports and imports, provided that these services are: (i) not intended to displace commercial financing; or (ii) offered on terms no more favourable than those that could be obtained for comparable financial services in the commercial market; (b) supports private investment outside the territory of the Party, provided that these services are: (i) not intended to displace commercial financing; or (ii) offered on terms no more favourable than those that could be obtained for comparable financial services in the commercial market; or (c) is offered on terms consistent with the Arrangement, provided that it falls within the scope of the Arrangement. 4. Article 17.6 (Non-commercial Assistance) shall not apply with respect to an enterprise located outside the territory of a Party over which a state-owned enterprise of that Party has assumed temporary ownership as a consequence of foreclosure or a similar action in connection with defaulted debt, or payment of an insurance claim by the state-owned enterprise, associated with

The cumulative and overlapping exceptions clauses in the CPTPP may imply two things. First, if SOE norms demand these exceptions of various kinds, subsidy norms would similarly call for comparable exceptions. Again, the SOE chapter, in an effort to regulate governmental support for SOEs and ensuing market distortion, uses the template of the SCM Agreement. Secondly, the multiple exceptions would have to be organized, streamlined and coordinated, so that governments are apprised of guidelines for the permissible governmental support measures. The CPTPP experiments, therefore, will provide a useful benchmark and a rare testing ground for the future subsidy norms of trade agreements. At the end of the day, future subsidy norms would only have to include carefully selected and skillfully delineated exceptions, so that only good-faith (i.e., legitimate) government measures to achieve general economic policies or to respond to national emergencies can be carved out in future subsidy norms.

5 Concluding Thoughts

At present, the global community is exploring various ways to revive the sagging multilateralism. One of the main tasks in the process is to reform the current trade agreements. In particular, covered agreements annexed to the WTO Agreements need to be updated and upgraded to reflect the fast-changing circumstances of the global community and business reality. The SCM Agreement requires immediate attention in this regard as it regulates governmental support measures of various types. The dividing line between legitimate support measures and illegal subsidies has been murky and has become more so these days because of the pandemic and the digital economy. The amendment of the SCM Agreement, however, has been slow due to the competing interests of the WTO members.

In this respect, the recent endeavor of the EU is both important and timely.[45] The specific proposals contained in the White Paper of 2020 set forth a basic framework for future subsidy norms. They will offer a meaningful benchmark for future discussions on this topic. At the same time, there are several questions that may deserve careful attention in elaborating the proposals contained in the White Paper.

---

the supply of the financial services referred to in paragraphs 2 and 3, provided that any support the Party, a state enterprise or state-owned enterprise of the Party, provides to the enterprise during the period of temporary ownership is provided in order to recoup the state-owned enterprise's investment in accordance with a restructuring or liquidation plan that will result in the ultimate divestiture from the enterprise. 5. Article 17.4 (Non- discriminatory Treatment and Commercial Considerations), Article 17.6 (Non-commercial Assistance), Article 17.10 (Transparency) and Article 17.12 (Committee on State-Owned Enterprises and Designated Monopolies) shall not apply with respect to a state-owned enterprise or designated monopoly if in any one of the three previous consecutive fiscal years, the annual revenue derived from the commercial activities of the state-owned enterprise or designated monopoly was less than a threshold amount which shall be calculated in accordance with Annex 17-A.

[45] International Bar Association (2020); Jozepa (2020), p. 26; Meunier and Mickus (2020), p. 1089.

These questions concern structural issues in relation to the present WTO regime and the SCM Agreement. They also touch upon relationships with IIAs. Careful consideration of these structural issues may ensure that future endeavors to improve subsidy norms can proceed smoothly without triggering unnecessary legal challenges. Practical and workable subsidy norms will be able to provide predictable guidance to governments in formulating their national economic policies.

References

Ahn D (2021) Why reform is needed: WTO 'public body' Jurisprudence. Global Policy 12 (S3):61–70

Bacchetta M, Bekkers E, Piermartini R, Rubinova S, Stolzenburg V, Xu A (2021) COVID-19 and global value chains: a discussion of arguments on value chain organization and the role of WTO. WTO Staff Working Paper No. ERSD-2021-3, https://www.econstor.eu/bitstream/10419/229626/1/1745637702.pdf

Bernasconi-Osterwalder N, Leal Campos S, van der Ven C (2020) The Proposed Multilateral Framework on Investment Facilitation: An Analysis of its Relationship to International Trade and Investment Agreements, International Institute for Sustainable Development and CUTS International, https://www.iisd.org/index.php/system/files/2020-09/multilateral-framework-investment-facilitation-en.pdf

Bonnitcha J (2017) Assessing the Impacts of Investment Treaties: Overview of the evidence, IISD Report. https://www.iisd.org/system/files/publications/assessing-impacts-investment-treaties.pdf

Brink T (2011) What is a 'public body' for the purpose of determining a subsidy after the appellate body ruling in US – AD/CVD? Global Trade Cust J 6(6):313–315

Brown CP, Hillman JA (2019) WTO'ing a resolution to the China subsidy problem. J Int Econ Law 22(4):557–578

Capital Trade Incorporated (2009) An Assessment of China's Subsidies to Strategic and Heavyweight Industries. Submitted to the U.S.-China Economic and Security Review Commission. https://www.uscc.gov/research/assessment-chinas-subsidies-strategic-and-heavyweight-industries

EU (2018) WTO Modernization. Concert Paper. https://trade.ec.europa.eu/doclib/docs/2018/september/tradoc_157331.pdf

European Commission (2020) White Paper on Levelling the Playing Field as Regards Foreign Subsidies. COM(2020) 253 final of 17 June 2020

Hoekman B (2020) COVID-19 trade policy measures, G20 declarations and WTO reform. In: Evenett SJ, Baldwin R (eds) Revitalizing multilateralism: pragmatic ideas for the new WTO director-general. CEPR Press, London, pp 63–70

Hoekman B, Nelson D (2020) Rethinking international subsidy rules. World Econ 43(12):3104–3132

Howse R (2020) Making the WTO (Not So) great again: the case against responding to the Trump Trade Agenda through reform of WTO rules on subsidies and state enterprises. J Int Econ Law 23(2):371–389

International Bar Association (2020) The European Commission's White Paper on Levelling the Playing Field as Regards Foreign Subsidies. IBA Webinar. https://www.ibanet.org/European-Commission-White-Paper-Webinar.aspx

Jozepa I (2020) EU State Aid Rules and WTO Subsidies Agreement, House of Commons Library Briefing Paper Number SN06775, 16 September 2020

Kawase T (2014) Trans-Pacific Partnership Negotiations and Rulemaking to Regulate State-owned Enterprises. https://voxeu.org/article/trans-pacific-partnership-negotiations-and-rulemaking-regulate-state-owned-enterprises

Kawase T, Ambashi M (2018) Disciplines on State-Owned Enterprises under the Trans-Pacific Partnership Agreement: Overview and Assessment. ERIA Discussion Paper Series (February 2018), https://www.eria.org/ERIA-DP-2017-13.pdf

Lee H-G (2010) Specificity under art. 2 SCMA. Legal Stud Inst Chosun Univ 17(1):355–385 (in Korean)

Lee J, Yoo K-H (2011) The SCM agreement and the concept of "benefit". Korean J Int Econ Law 9(1):127–172. (in Korean)

Lee S, Prabhakar D (2021) COVID-19 Non-tariff measures: the good and the bad, through a sustainable development lens. UNCTAD Research Paper No. 60, UNCTAD/SER.RP/2021/3

Lester S (2011) The problem of subsidies as a means of protectionism: lessons from the WTO EC-aircraft case. Melbourne J Int Law 12(2):345–372

Matthes J (2020) China's market distortions and the impact of the Covid-19 Crisis. CESifo Forum 3/2020, 21:42–48

Meunier S, Mickus J (2020) Sizing up the competition: explaining reform of European Union competition policy in the COVID-19 Era. J Eur Integr 42(8):1077–1094

OECD (2009) Policy Responses to the Economic Crisis: Investing in Innovation for Long-Term Growth. https://www.oecd.org/sti/42983414.pdf

Wang L, Li Y (2020) The negotiation of EU-China comprehensive agreement on investment and its potential impact in the post-pandemic era. J Chin Econ Bus Stud 18(4):365–372

Wolfe R (2017) Sunshine over Shanghai: can the WTO illuminate the Murky World of Chinese SOEs? World Trade Rev 16(4):713–732

WTO (2020) Report on G20 Trade Measures (Mid-October 2019 to Mid-May 2020). https://www.wto.org/english/news_e/news20_e/report_trdev_jun20_e.pdf

“Levelling the Playing Field”

Achim Wambach

Contents

Abstract In only 20 years, China has risen to become the EU’s main trading partner. However, trade relations between Europe and China have come under stress, and political tensions have increased as well. China is not only perceived as a partner, but it has also become a “systemic rival”. Indeed, while Chinese firms have gained access to the European Single Market and its benefits, the same is not entirely true for European firms. In addition, European competition law does not take into account third-country state interference with the economy via state owned enterprises and subsidies although such state interference may distort competition in European markets. The European Commission has presented a proposal to deal with foreign state subsidies. Many open questions remain at this stage. However, whatever the final instrument will be, ensuring competition between companies on non-discriminatory terms, and thereby providing incentives for companies to engage in competition, is in the mutual interest of the EU and its external partners.

A. Wambach (✉)
ZEW – Leibniz-Centre for European Economic Research, Mannheim, Germany
e-mail: achim.wambach@zew.de

M. Chi et al. (eds.), *Asian Yearbook of International Economic Law 2022*,
Asian Yearbook of International Economic Law (2022) 2022: 181–192,
https://doi.org/10.1007/16517_2021_8, Published online: 9 February 2022

1 Introduction

Undistorted competition between companies without state intervention is the basic principle of the social market economy. In the European Single Market, this principle is safeguarded by two main instruments: competition policy and state aid control. The People's Republic of China (hereafter China), whose economy has experienced an impressive upswing in recent decades, pursues a different economic model with its "socialist market economy with Chinese characteristics". The Chinese state intervenes strongly in the economy in order to achieve its industrial policy goals, something which is not common practice in the European market.

This chapter addresses the question of whether and to what extent the social market economy must adapt in order to compete with a state capitalist system. It begins with an analysis of the rise of China as EU's main trading partner based on key economic developments and then contextualizes this development in the larger picture of long-term and recent trends in globalization. After debating why also due to these developments China is not just a partner, but has also become "a systemic rival", the text finalizes with the presentation of measures towards fair competition in international markets.

2 The Rise of China as the Main Trading Partner of the European Union

The economic rise of China to one of the largest economies in the world and the benefits this rise has brought to its people are impressive. In just 20 years, China's share in the global economy has increased from under 4% to over 18%.[1] With its accession to the World Trade Organization (WTO) in 2001, trade barriers between China and other WTO countries were reduced, which allowed China to take a leading position in global trade. In fact, China's share of worldwide exports (including Hong Kong) increased from about 6% in 2000 to about 15% in 2018 whereas the shares of the European Union (EU) and the United States (US) decreased over the same period (see Fig. 1).

As an economic partner in trade, China is of growing importance for Europe and vice versa. In 2020, China became the EU's main trading partner, followed by the USA; and the EU is China's second largest trading partner, with the ASEAN countries as the largest one. European trade (imports plus exports) in goods with China (including Hong Kong), which amounted to only EUR 130 billion in 2002, reached EUR 617 billion in 2020 (see Fig. 2). Of this total, EUR 226 billion were accounted for by EU exports to China and EUR 391 billion by imports from China to the EU.

[1] Statista (2020).

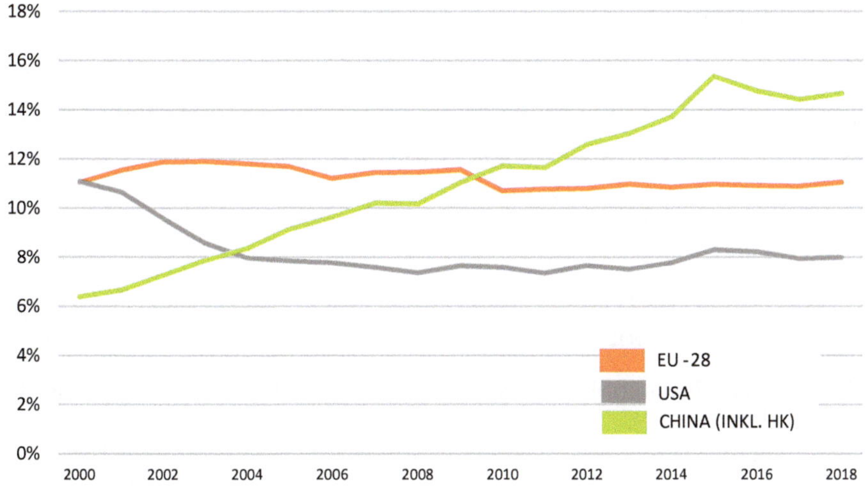

Fig. 1 Evolution of Shares of Worldwide Exports. Source: wits.worldbank.org—European Union Exports compare with countries Hong Kong, China, China, United States

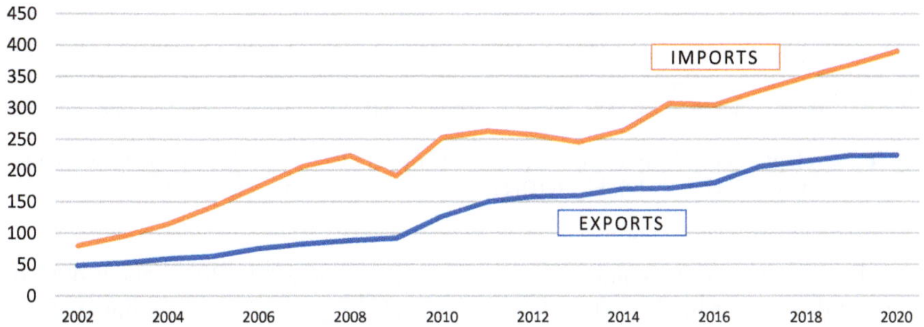

Fig. 2 Europe's International Trade in Goods with China in Bn. EUR. Source: Eurostat (ext_st_eu27_2020sitc)

In the services sector, China was in 2018 the EU's third strongest trading partner. The volume of trade in services between the EU and China more than doubled from 2010 to 2019 (see Fig. 3). In this context, the EU has a surplus vis-à-vis China. In 2019, EU exports to China accounted for approximately EUR 79 billion and EU imports from China (including Hong Kong) for approximately EUR 50 billion.

In addition to trade in goods and services, the volume of Chinese direct investment in the EU, particularly in the form of corporate investments and acquisitions,

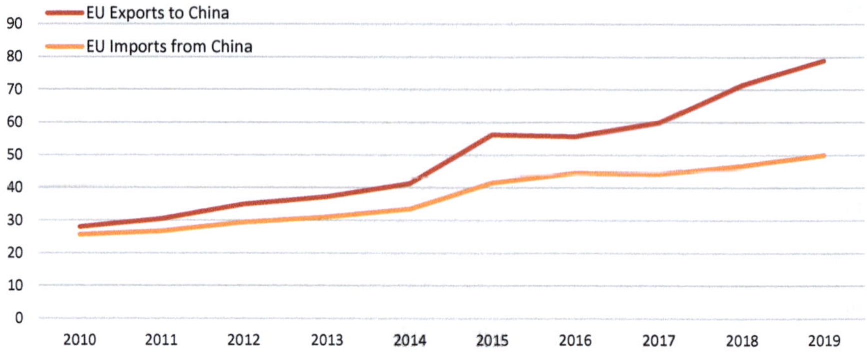

Fig. 3 Europe's International Trade in Services with China in Bn. EUR. Source: Eurostat (bop_its6_det)

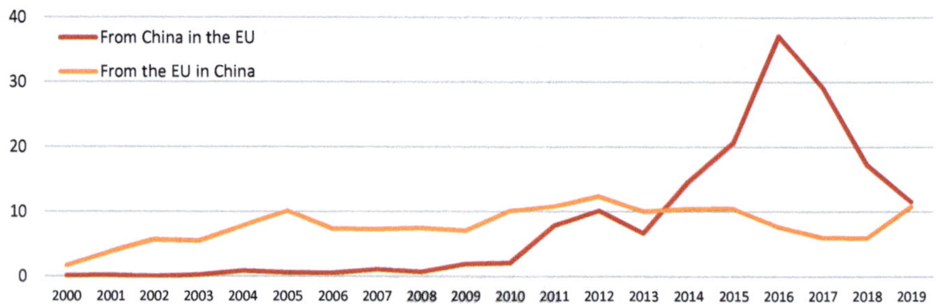

Fig. 4 Development of Yearly Direct Investments between EU-28 and China in Bn. EUR. Source: Monopolies Commission (2020), Fig. 6 (Data is based on Hanemann et al. 2019)

has also increased significantly over the past two decades.[2] In 2018, about 40% of Chinese direct investment was made in Europe, although it has been declining after a peak of about EUR 37.3 billion in 2016 (see Fig. 4). Despite the current decline, annual Chinese direct investment has significantly exceeded EU direct investment in China in recent years. The latter amounted to approximately EUR 10.9 billion in 2019.

3 Long-Term and Recent Development in World Trade

However, in recent years globalization in general, and specifically trade relations between Europe and China, have come under stress. Figure 5 shows WTO data concerning trends in world merchandise trade volume in the last two decades. The

[2]Data on the amount of Chinese direct investment varies depending on the source due to different calculation methods.

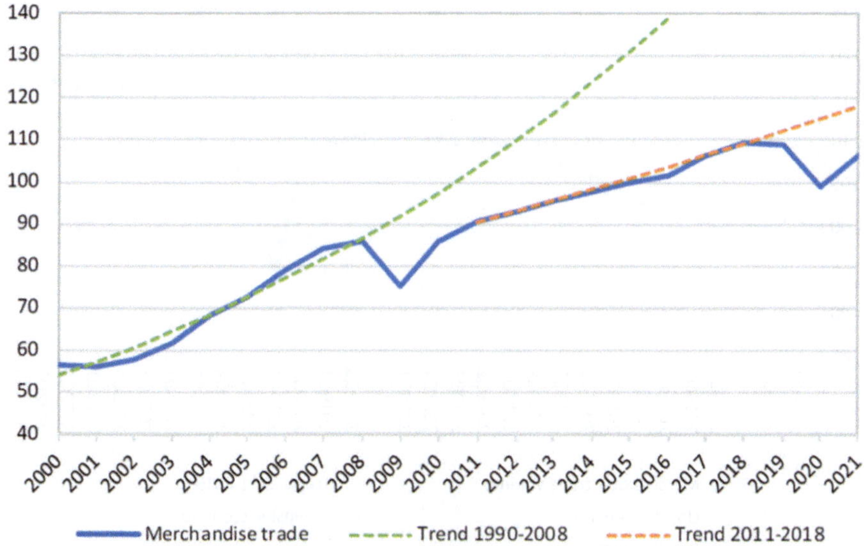

Fig. 5 World Merchandise Trade Volume, 2000–2021. Source: WTO Secretariat Estimates (October 2020) (Figures for 2020 and 2021 are projections)

blue line shows the increase in worldwide trade in goods, with a dent during the financial crisis and another one during the Covid 19 crisis. The green dotted line shows which trend would have been expected without the financial crisis. The financial crisis did not stop this trend completely, but globalization evolved afterwards at a much slower path, as shown by the orange dotted line. In addition to that, there are the effects of the ongoing Covid 19 crisis, for which different scenarios by the WTO are shown in Fig. 6. It is still unknown how strong the long-term effects of the ongoing crisis on world trade will be, but there are strong indications that the effects will be negative, as countries are contemplating how to bring back supply chains closer to their home countries.

4 A Partner Becomes Also a "Systemic Rival"[3]

Adding to this international stress in global trade relations political tensions have increased as well. This is reflected in numerous studies and reports on the relationship between China and the EU. The shift in perception becomes visible e.g. in a

[3] This term was used by the EU Commission in: European Commission (2019) p. 7; similar wording already before by the German industry association: BDI (2019).

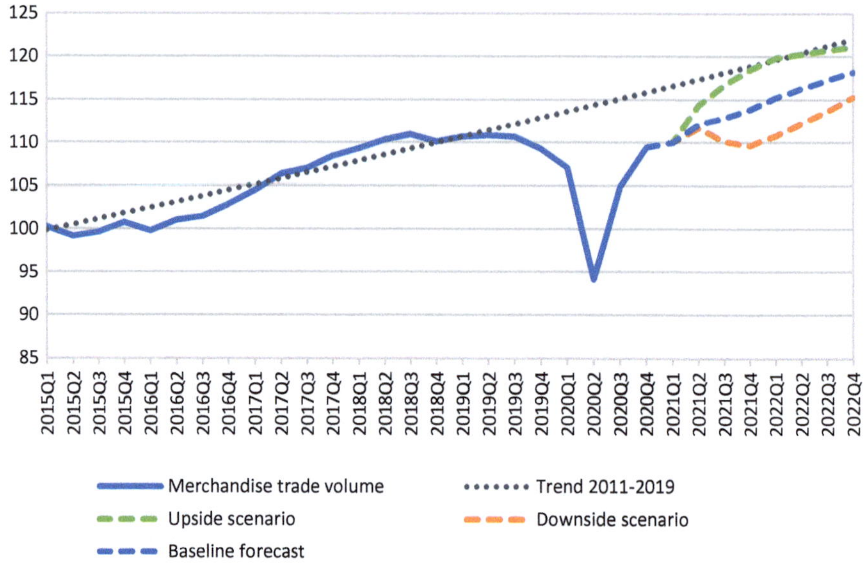

Fig. 6 World Merchandise Trade Volume, 2015Q1–2022Q4. Source: WTO and UNCTAD for trade volume data; WTO for forecasts (March 2021)

position paper published by the German industry association which identified China not only as a partner, but also as a systemic rival.[4] The German Federal Ministry for Economic Affairs and Energy employed similar wording in its "National Industrial Strategy 2030" published 2019.[5] Against this background, the EU Commission presented a proposal for an EU Regulation on foreign subsidies.[6]

The complaints raised by market participants relate to the competitive situation in Europe, international trade, and competition in China. It is not always clear whether the complaints are raised because of existing unfairness or because European market participants also feel the competitive threat of foreign market entrants from China and other countries. For example, regarding the situation in Europe, the German industry association complained of distortions in competition, noting that "the growing competition is not only the expression of dynamic entrepreneurship in China, but also largely due to targeted government support and guidance. [. . .] The technological competence growth of Chinese companies is financially supported and favored through various channels. Among other things, the Chinese government offers tax incentives [. . .] for high technology and new technology enterprises [. . .], special deductions for R&D operating expenses and tax exemptions for technology transfer. Also, favorable loans by state-owned banks, direct project-based financing via the state budget and state venture capital also promote the innovation efforts of

[4]BDI (2019).

[5]Federal Ministry for the Economy and Energy (2019).

[6]European Commission, (2021).

Chinese companies. The financial aid benefits Chinese companies not only in their own research and development projects, but also in the targeted acquisition of foreign technology through company takeovers abroad."[7]

Many complaints relating to the situation in China are in fact claims for reciprocally acceptable treatment. In this regard, the German industry association criticized the fact that "in several sectors, bans on investments, participation caps or the compulsion to enter into joint ventures [still exist]. In the service sector, which is also important for industrial companies to support their foreign business, the opening of the market since China's accession to the WTO has fallen far short of expectations. [. . .] Foreign companies are disadvantaged in public contracts. There remains a high asymmetry in market access between China and the EU."[8]

The discussion has some parallels to the discussion about Japanese companies entering the European markets 30 years ago. At that time, it was noted that the internationalization of trade resulted in imbalances and vulnerabilities.[9] The European economy was exposed to dominant Japanese supply in the area of microchip manufacture, and to strong competition in car manufacture. Hence, it was frequently claimed that Japanese success was mainly a product of industrial policy and subsidies. However various structural advantages inherent to the Japanese economy (e.g., existence of widely connected conglomerates, low barriers to financing, long-term oriented owners) contributed to the success of Japanese suppliers as well. The Monopolies Commission analysed the situation at that time and noted: "Given the size of world markets, it is to be expected that individual companies are in a position to significantly restrict international competition only in a few cases. The main dangers come from government measures and regulations aimed at influencing international market activity in favour of domestic companies".[10] However, in the 1990s, promotion of competition became part of the Japanese national agenda that structurally shifted the economic and political system toward market orientation leading to liberalisation and deregulation as well as the strengthening of competition law enforcement.[11]

Whereas the Chinese economic model is a hybrid model with elements of both state and market economy, the economic policy of the EU is conducted in accordance with the principle of an open market economy with undistorted competition. While the recent developments in trade enabled China to access the European Single Market and its benefits, the reverse has not been entirely true, as the Chinese state strongly interferes with the economy via state owned firms and subsidies. With the protagonist role China has assumed for the European economy, this has important implications, as the negative effects of state interventions on European companies tend to become more and more relevant.

---

[7]BDI (2019), p. 7 (own translation).

[8]BDI (2019), p. 3 (own translation).

[9]Monopolies Commission (1992), paras. 1010, 1083, 1084 et seqq., 1102 et seqq.

[10]Monopolies Commission (1992), para. 176 (own translation).

[11]Wakui (2018), pp. 33 et seqq.

5 Towards Fair Competition in International Markets

China's specific economic model gives rise to several problematic issues for European companies in the field of competition and globalization. Concerning the situation in Europe, the existing legal framework substantially protects the EU internal market from most of the possible power abuses. Instruments belonging to this framework are anti-dumping and anti-subsidy rules for cross-border trade and competition rules applicable to operations of companies from third countries. Anti-trust regulations and mechanisms to prevent abuse of market power complement these instruments and also take into account the strengthening of financial power due to subsidies. Besides, in the field of public procurement, European law allows for the use of non-tender criteria and the exclusion of abnormally low tenders in member states' procurement procedures. And in the field of mergers and investment, there are controls to safeguard public security.

Nevertheless, gaps exist in the current European legal framework. It is certainly a problem that European competition law does not take into account the support of companies through subsidies from third countries. In order to counteract possible distortions of competition, it makes sense to control subsidies and aid from third countries to companies in the European Single Market. This is not possible at the state level (since third countries are not members of the EU), but it is possible at the level of the companies that receive these subsidies.[12]

Addressing this problem in May 2021, the European Commission presented its proposal for an EU Regulation on foreign subsidies distorting the internal market, after having set out its initial ideas on the relevant issues in a White Paper in June 2020.[13] The Monopolies Commission had commented on the original ideas of the European Commission in its Biennial Report No. XXIII.[14] It shares the analysis of the problem and to a large extent the basic approach for solutions, but advocates modifications in individual questions. Notably, while the European Commission derives its concept of subsidies from foreign trade law, the Monopolies Commission's proposal is based on state aid law. The reason for the proposal by the Monopolies Commission is that it would put economic subsidies from third countries on an equal footing with those from European countries. The European Commission also proposes several sub-instruments ("*modules*") for cases where subsidized companies from third countries want to buy European companies or where they participate in public sector procurement processes. The Monopolies Commission, in contrast, proposes to integrate these sub-instruments into a general third-country aid control instrument, since the cause of the distortion of competition, the subsidy/aid by the third country, is the same in all cases.[15] The Regulation

[12] Wambach (2021).

[13] See European Commission, (2021) moreover, see European Commission, (2020).

[14] Monopolies Commission (2020), paras. 864 et seqq., esp. paras, 885 et seqq.

[15] Monopolies Commission (2020), paras. 864 et seqq., esp. paras, 885 et seqq.; Wambach (2021). For a more detailed overview see the contribution by Kühling, Weck and Reinhold in this volume.

proposed by the European Commission takes up several considerations brought forward by the Monopolies Commission. Most notably, it aligns its subsidy concept more to existing state aid law.[16]

However, whatever new instrument is installed and how it is designed, we have to also take into account that no full-fledged economic theory of harm has been worked out to date. With regard to the proposal by the European Commission, it needs to be clarified, whether the new instrument should apply to all deviations from the standards of undistorted market-economy competition or only apply where there is outright harm to the market structure (e.g., an acquisition of dominant market positions). Furthermore, it is unclear whether the remedies imposed should simply neutralize distortions of competition (e.g., through repayment/absorption of subsidies) or go beyond that, e.g., by allowing the authorities to prohibit acquisitions/investments or to impose market conduct requirements (e.g., licensing requirements). This is a problem of the European Commission's approach, which—unlike the Monopolies Commission—does not even proceed from "harm to competition" as a reason for intervention against third-country subsidies. Moreover, while it is true that state aid control in the EU exists, among others, for efficiency reasons, it should be noted that no direct efficiency argument applies in relation to foreign subsidies. This is to say, state aid helps to prevent "subsidy races" in the EU. However, if China subsidizes investment in Europe, this would be of less concern from a static European welfare point of view, as these subsidies are paid for by Chinese taxpayers.[17] It would only become problematic if these subsidies were used to establish lasting positions of market power.

In addition, we will have to reconcile (internal) competition policy, which is all about efficiency, and (external) international trade policy, which is about reciprocity and fairness. Reciprocity and fairness are not the same as efficiency, and are also less well defined. Taking this into account, it may be difficult to find harmonized criteria—integrating the internal and the external perspective—on how to distinguish "good" subsidies from "bad" subsidies.

In any case, whatever the instrument is, it should be applied with care. There should be a threshold for implementation of any new instrument, and a flexible enforcement approach should be used including balancing procedures, such as the EU interest test proposed by the European Commission, the justification grounds borrowed from state aid law (e.g., beneficial treatment of aid for R&D or for the achievement of important projects in the common interest), and the formal recognition of foreign subsidy-control systems. Moreover, while an argument can always be made for clear and simple rules, the new instruments should provide enough room

[16]European Commission, (2021), Art. 2.

[17]Monopolies Commission (2020), para. 891.

for learning on a case-by-case basis and for a later adaptation of the system, e.g., through an evaluation after 2–3 years.

6 Conclusion

It is in the joint interest of all market participants to establish a "level-playing-field" in international competition. Firms take part in this competition by competing on merits whereas countries compete on local business conditions. While selected interference in markets may in some cases be justified and beneficial, it needs to follow rules. Many questions can arise in this context: Is there a market failure? What is the relevant protected interest? Is the proposed intervention necessary and proportionate? The European Commission has presented a proposal to deal with interference in markets through the selected support of companies by state subsidies. The German Monopolies Commission shares the European Commission's analysis of the problem and to a large extent the basic approach for solutions, but it also advocates modifications in individual questions. Whatever the final instrument will be, ensuring competition between companies on non-discriminatory terms, and thereby providing incentives for companies to engage in competition, is in the mutual interest of the EU and its external partners.

References

BDI (2019) Grundsatzpapier China. Partner und systemischer Wettbewerber – Wie gehen wir mit Chinas staatlich gelenkter Volkswirtschaft um? January 2019

European Commission and High Representative of the Union for Foreign Affairs and Security Policy, Communication to the European Parliament, the European Council and the Council, EUChina – A strategic outlook, JOIN (2019) 5 final,12 March 2019

European Commission, Proposal for a Regulation of the European Parliament and of the Council on foreign subsidies distorting the internal market, COM(2021) 223 final, 5 May 2021

European Commission, White Paper on levelling the playing field as regards foreign subsidies, COM(2020) 253 final, 17 June 2020

Federal Ministry for the Economy and Energy, Nationale Industriestrategie 2030, Februar 2019

Hanemann T, Huotari M, Kratz A (2019) Chinese FDI in Europe: 2018 Trends and Impact of New Screening Policies, A report by Rhodium Group (RHG) and the Mercator Institute for China Studies (MERICS). https://merics.org/sites/default/files/2020-04/190311_MERICS-Rhodium%20Group_COFDI-Update_2019.pdf

Monopolies Commission (1992) Biennial Report IX, Wettbewerbspolitik oder Industriepolitik

Monopolies Commission (2020) Chinese state capitalism: A challenge for the European market economy (English translation of Chapter IV of the XXIII. Biennial Report).
Statista (2020) Anteil Chinas am globalen Bruttoinlandsprodukt (BIP) bis 2025, https://de.statista.com/statistik/daten/studie/167632/umfrage/anteil-chinas-am-globalen-bruttoinlandsprodukt-bip/#professional
Wakui M (2018) Antimonopoly law, competition law and policy in Japan, 2nd edn. Independently Published
Wambach A (2021) Im Wettbewerb mit China. In: Tietmeyer A, Solaro P (eds) Neue Herausforderungen der Sozialen Marktwirtschaft. Wiesbaden, pp 153–172

Prof. Achim Wambach Ph.D., is President of ZEW—Leibniz-Centre for European Economic Research, as well as former Chair and current Member of the Monopolies Commission.

State Capitalism in ASEAN: The State-Owned Enterprises Under the ASEAN Regional Competition Policy

Alexandr Svetlicinii

Contents

Abstract The role of the state-owned enterprises (SOEs) as market players from the perspective of competition law and policy is gaining importance in the times of global economic recession. The countries around the globe re-examine their approaches to competitive neutrality and level playing field when it comes to both domestic and foreign SOEs. The Association of Southeast Asian Nations (ASEAN) is comprised of ten countries (Brunei Darussalam, Cambodia, Indonesia, Lao PDR, Malaysia, Myanmar, Philippines, Singapore, Thailand and Vietnam) in the South-East Asian region that pursue a certain degree of regional economic integration. The ASEAN Economic Community is a regional economic integration project that pursues a level-playing field for all types of companies through the implementation of an effective competition policy. Currently, the ASEAN member states differ substantially in relation to the role of SOEs in their national economies, as well as application of the competition rules to the commercial practices of the SOEs. These economic and regulatory differences, as well as priorities of the economic recovery

---

A. Svetlicinii (✉)
University of Macau, Faculty of Law, Macao SAR, China
e-mail: AlexandrS@um.edu.mo

M. Chi et al. (eds.), *Asian Yearbook of International Economic Law 2022*,
Asian Yearbook of International Economic Law (2022) 2022: 193–204,
https://doi.org/10.1007/16517_2021_7, Published online: 9 December 2021

will have an impact on the process of regional harmonization both in terms of competition legislation and its enforcement.

This presentation focuses on the treatment of SOEs under the ASEAN regional competition policy, which will highlight the regulatory approach of the ASEAN member states towards SOEs in particular and towards state intervention in the economy in general.

1 State-Owned Enterprises and Economic Policies

The role of the SOEs as market players is hardly a novel topic in the field of competition law and policy,[1] but it gains on importance in the times of global economic recession partly caused by COVID-19 pandemic.[2]

The economic activities of SOEs, their investments, and trading practices have raised a number of questions on whether competition law is adequately equipped to deal with these entities and with their market conduct that can have potential anti-competitive effects.[3] SOEs and their operations are often guided by the national industrial policies, being "national champions"[4] in certain industries, protected and promoted by their respective states, within their borders but also on the international markets. In order to counteract the market-distorting effects that can be caused by foreign SOEs, countries around the world have been adopting various regulatory checks and barriers that will be applicable to the trading and investment activities of SOEs thus supplementing competition law enforcement and merger control.[5] Among the most prominent and recent examples is the FDI screening framework in the European Union—the FDI Screening Regulation.[6] When determining whether a foreign investment is likely to affect security and public order, the EU Member States are advised to consider among others "whether the foreign investor is directly or indirectly controlled by the government, including state bodies or armed forces, of a third country, including through ownership structure or significant funding".[7] In order to remedy possible market-distorting effects stemming from the foreign subsidies, of which the SOEs are frequent recipients, the EU proposed to introduce

[1] See e.g. Sappington and Sidak (2003); Sokol (2009).

[2] See Abate et al. (2020).

[3] See e.g. Slot (2015); Lallemand-Kirche et al. (2017); Kovacic (2017).

[4] See OECD (2009).

[5] See Fox and Healey (2014).

[6] Regulation (EU) 2019/452 of the European Parliament and of the Council of 19 March 2019 establishing a framework for the screening of foreign direct investments into the Union, OJ L 79I, 21 March 2019, p. 1.

[7] Regulation (EU) 2019/452, Article 4(2)(a).

additional screening mechanism that would target various forms of financial support granted by foreign states to the companies operating or investing in the EU.[8]

The author's previous research on how the EU merger control was dealing with acquisitions notified by the Chinese SOEs highlighted a number of challenging questions that had to be addressed by the European Commission.[9] These are related to applying traditional merger control standards to the SOEs, such as calculating the aggregate turnover under the applicable notification thresholds, treating different SOEs as parts of the same economic entity or different economic entities, and trying to forecast the (anti)competitive conduct of the SOEs on the market post-merger.[10] The latter exercise is complicated by the fact that the market conducts of the SOEs can be motivated not only by profit-generating objectives, but also by certain strategic considerations such as implementation of the national industrial policies. These challenging questions have prompted numerous proposals to reform the existing merger control rules in the EU.[11]

Another important point to mention in relation to the SOEs is that the COVID-19 disruptions and the expected economic recovery will bring the SOEs back into the spotlight because they would appear as primary candidates for state support and would also be expected to continue carrying out certain public-interest functions,[12] which will reinforce the concerns about the competitive neutrality and the level-playing field.[13]

2 State-Owned Enterprises and Competition Law

In the majority of the jurisdictions around the world competition law is ownership-neutral and is applied without discrimination to private and state-owned undertakings alike, following the principle of competitive neutrality.[14]

---

[8] European Commission, Proposal for a Regulation on foreign subsidies distorting the internal market, COM(2021) 223 final, 5 May 2021. See also Soltesz (2020).

[9] See Svetlicinii (2020).

[10] See e.g. Svetlicinii (2017a); Svetlicinii (2018).

[11] See e.g. A Franco-German Manifesto for a European Industrial Policy Fit for the twenty-first Century (19 February 2019), https://www.bmwi.de/Redaktion/DE/Downloads/F/franco-german-manifesto-for-a-european-industrial-policy.pdf%3F__blob%3DpublicationFile%26v%3D2; Federal Ministry for Economic Affairs and Energy, National Industrial Strategy 2030: Strategic Guidelines for a German and European Industrial Policy (5 February 2019), https://www.bmwi.de/Redaktion/EN/Publikationen/Industry/national-industry-strategy-2030.html; Federal Ministry for Economic Affairs and Energy, Modernising EU Competition Policy (4 July 2019), https://www.bmwi.de/Redaktion/DE/Downloads/M-O/modernising-eu competition-policy.html; Dutch Permanent Representation to the EU, Non-Paper Strengthening the Level Playing Field on the Internal Market (9 December 2019), https://www.permanentrepresentations.nl/documents/publications/2019/12/09/non-paper-on-level-playing-field

[12] See European Commission (2021).

[13] See Svetlicinii (2021).

[14] See OECD (2012).

At the same time, the application of competition rules to commercial activities of SOEs has been conditioned by a number of factors. One issue concerns numerous exemptions and carve-outs for SOEs and other entities that perform certain public functions or offer services of general economic interest.[15] Another issue is related to the level-playing field because SOEs are frequent recipients of state aid or other forms of state support, which can then boost their market power and allow cross-subsidization of loss-making activities that may foreclose more efficient competitors from the affected markets.[16] Finally, the SOEs are frequently operating in highly regulated markets where sectoral legislation enforced by the regulatory authorities can take prevalence over competition law. The said sectoral legislation may have other policy objectives, distinct or inconsistent with maintaining competition on the regulated markets.[17]

3 ASEAN Economic Community: Regional Economic Integration Model

The ASEAN Economic Community (AEC) is an example of a regional economic integration project that bears both differences and similarities with the EU model.[18] It also provides blueprints for better economic integration of the South-East Asian economies, making them more competitive at the global level.[19]

The ASEAN Economic Community Blueprint,[20] among its objectives, provides for a level-playing field for all types of companies through the implementation of an effective competition policy. Before discussing whether and how this objective can be achieved, one should note that in many areas the ASEAN member states adopt a so-called "ASEAN way" of cooperation, which is essentially a consensus-based decision-making and voluntary commitments in the absence of supra-national rules or enforcement authorities which would ensure an effective monitoring and enforcement of such commitments.[21]

---

[15] See Willemyns (2016); Matsushita and Lim (2020).

[16] See Wu (2019).

[17] See e.g. Wisuttisak and Fong (2018).

[18] See Drexl (2018); Valockova (2015).

[19] See Thanadsillapakul (2014).

[20] ASEAN Economic Community Blueprint, adopted on 20 November 2007 in Singapore, https://asean.org/wp-content/uploads/archive/5187-10.pdf. It was succeeded by ASEAN Economic Community Blueprint 2025, adopted on 22 November 2015 in Kuala Lumpur, https://www.asean.org/storage/2016/03/AECBP_2025r_FINAL.pdf.

[21] See e.g. Luu (2012); Lee and Fukunaga (2014).

4 ASEAN Competition Law and Policy

The AEC Blueprint provides for adoption of competition legislation in *all* ASEAN member states, i.e., something that one would find very common in the EU but for the ASEAN community, competition legislation was far from being the norm until relatively recently.

Besides the adoption of competition legislation, the AEC Blueprint calls for harmonization of competition policies, competition laws and their enforcement, the strengthening of the capacities of the national competition authorities (NCAs) and, in this way, aims at creating a level-playing field by fostering an effective enforcement of competition legislation in all ASEAN member states.[22]

In order to ensure a certain degree of harmonization of the existing competition rules and drafting of new legislation, the ASEAN Experts Group on Competition[23] issued its Regional Guidelines on Competition Policy in 2010.[24] It should be noted that they are non-binding, i.e., this is just a recommendation for the ASEAN member states to consider when they draft or amend their competition legislation.[25] The Guidelines provide that the principle of competitive neutrality should be upheld and SOEs should be equally covered by the members' competition laws.[26] Exemptions should not be allowed for the SOEs as such, but for certain public policy reasons only.[27]

5 Competition Laws in ASEAN Countries

The application of the competitive neutrality principle varies across the ASEAN member states. Some member states, like Indonesia,[28] Singapore,[29] Thailand,[30] and Vietnam[31] have adopted their competition legislation prior to the issuance of the 2010 guidelines. At the same time, half of the ASEAN member states have adopted

[22] See ASEAN Secretariat (2018), pp. 3–4.

[23] ASEAN Experts Group on Competition, https://asean-competition.org/aegc.

[24] ASEAN Secretariat (2010).

[25] See e.g. Svetlicinii (2017b).

[26] ASEAN Secretariat (2010), para 3.1.2: "Competition policy should be an instrument of general application, i.e., applying to all economic sectors and to all businesses engaged in commercial economic activities (production and supply of goods and services), including State-owned enterprises, having effect within the AMSs' territory, unless exempted by law."

[27] ASEAN Secretariat (2010), para 3.5.1: "The key rationale for granting exemptions or exclusions from competition law provisions to specific industries or activities includes strategic and national interest, security, public, economic and/or social considerations."

[28] See Juwana (2002).

[29] ASEAN Secretariat (2018), p. 52. See also Ong (2006).

[30] ASEAN Secretariat (2018), p. 65. See also Thanitcul (2002); Williams (2004).

[31] ASEAN Secretariat (2018), p. 72. See also Furse (2010).

Table 1 Competition law systems of the ASEAN member states (as of May 2021)

ASEAN member state	Competition legislation (year of adoption)	National competition authority
Brunei Darussalam	Competition Order 2015	Competition Commission of Brunei Darussalam (CCBD) (http://www.ccbd.gov.bn/)
Cambodia	–	–
Indonesia	Law on Prohibition of Monopolistic Practices and Unfair Business Competition 1999	Commission for the Supervision of Business Competition (KPPU) (http://eng.kppu.go.id/)
Lao PDR	Law on Business Competition 2015	Lao Competition Commission (Ministry of Industry and Commerce) (http://www.moic.gov.la/)
Malaysia	Competition Act 2010	Malaysia Competition Commission (MyCC) (https://www.mycc.gov.my/)
Myanmar	Competition Law 2015	Myanmar Competition Commission (Ministry of Commerce) (https://mmcc.gov.mm)
Philippines	Philippine Competition Act 2015	Philippine Competition Commission (https://www.phcc.gov.ph)
Singapore	Competition Act 2004	Competition and Consumer Commission of Singapore (CCCS) (https://www.cccs.gov.sg/)
Thailand	Trade Competition Act 1999[a] (2017)[b]	Office of Trade Competition Commission (https://otcc.or.th/)
Vietnam	Competition Law 2004 (2018)[c]	Vietnam Competition Authority (http://vcca.gov.vn/)

[a]Trade Competition Act B.E. 2542 (1999)
[b]Trade Competition Act B.E. 2560 (2017) in force since 5 October 2017
[c]New Competition Law came into force on 1 July 2019

their competition legislation after 2010.[32] As a result, within the latter group we can see a larger degree of harmonization[33] as some member states used the Regional Guidelines as a benchmark or point of reference.

When it comes to the NCAs, we observe that in terms of their powers (investigative and sanctioning) and their independence, they differ substantially among the ASEAN member states. In some countries, the competition authority is an independent administrative agency while in others, these agencies are part of the executive, so it is likely that their decisions are also affected by executive policies. This creates a diverse background on the subject of the competition rules, institutions and, as a result—the enforcement mechanisms and patterns in ASEAN.[34]

See more information on the competition law systems of the ASEAN member states in Table 1.

[32]See e.g. Porananond and Aung (2019).
[33]See Maximiano et al. (2019).
[34]See Siadari and Arai (2018).

6 State-Owned Enterprises in ASEAN Member States

When it comes to the way how the ASEAN member states have covered SOEs in their competition legislation, we should compare the economic sectors where the respective SOEs are active and the sectoral exemptions included in the respective competition laws. In certain sectors, often those dominated by SOEs, the sectoral legislation has prevalence over general competition law.[35] Supervision is also entrusted to sectoral regulators, which often pursue different objectives, rather than solely market competition. As a result, some sectors are basically exempt from the application of the competition rules.[36]

The role and importance of SOEs for the national economy differs across ASEAN member states. As a result, we observe stark differences in the market shares of the SOEs and the amount of support they receive from their respective governments. Due to the specifics of the state-economy relationship, some countries like Laos, Vietnam, or Myanmar have a very strong SOE sector, which fulfills a number of public policy functions. But even these governments are implementing a gradual SOE reform.[37] The primary objective of these reforms is to make the SOEs more efficient, less resource-consuming, and more competitive on the global markets. The pace of these reforms also differs from country to country. As a result, not all of them are ready to expose their SOEs to active competition enforcement or competition from the domestic private sector or foreign investors.[38]

Finally, even in those ASEAN member states where SOEs are formally covered by the competition rules, or when they do not operate in the sectors which are explicitly exempted, we observe a very diverse enforcement practice.[39] It is often due to the degree of independence (or lack thereof) of the NCAs. In other situations, this is due to the scope of the investigative and sanctioning powers that the competition authorities can effectively exercise in practice. Some ASEAN competition authorities have successfully applied competition rules to sanction the anti-competitive behavior of the SOEs.[40] Others have no such record—which can be interpreted as an implicit policy of exempting the SOEs from competition enforcement.

To summarize, first, there are sectoral exemptions and priority of sectoral regulations, which exempt certain sectors—very often those where SOEs are operating—from the application of competition rules or from their actual enforcement. Second, despite the general recognition of the principle of competitive neutrality as an objective of AEC, it appears that it is not uniformly applied by the ASEAN member

[35]This is the case in Malaysia. See Wisuttisak and Fong (2018), pp. 120–124.

[36]This is the case in Thailand. See Valockova (2015), p. 12.

[37]See e.g. Futaba (2009); Songvilay et al. (2017); Mai (2017).

[38]See e.g. Tang Van (2016).

[39]See OECD (2018) covers following ASEAN member states: Brunei, Indonesia, Malaysia, Myanmar, Philippines, Singapore, Thailand, Vietnam.

[40]See e.g. Siswanto and Hutajulu (2019).

states as they continue to accord various forms of support to their SOEs, which also affects application of competition rules in the respective sectors. Third, in several ASEAN member states, SOEs are very important economic actors and major drivers of state economic policies. Given their importance, it is very unlikely that state support and reliance would end anytime soon. Fourth common feature is the ongoing SOE reform. The SOEs are being gradually transformed into more efficient market players. This process has progressed at different speeds in various ASEAN member states, so there is no uniformity in that regard. Finally, there is a varying degree of antitrust enforcement. Even in those countries where competition law formally applies to SOEs, the case record often shows absent or little enforcement.

7 State-Owned Enterprises and ASEAN Regional Economic Integration: Ways Forward

Building on the previous experience of "ASEAN way" of regional cooperation, it is highly unlikely that the ASEAN countries will opt for any binding supranational rules related to competition. It should be expected that they will continue the path of gradual harmonization of their national competition laws.[41] And as their NCAs become more experienced and accumulate a more solid enforcement record, we could see certain harmonization of investigative and sanctioning practices. With the growth of regional integration among the ASEAN member states, especially in terms of investment, if there would be more instances or cases of cross-border economic activity involving SOEs, we could expect some form of regional cooperation agreements, or principles on SOE operations and practices overseas.[42]

Of course, all these expectations or forecasts would have to be adjusted taking into account the very unpredictable development of the COVID-19 pandemic in the region and the ways how the ASEAN member states will approach the challenge of economic recovery.[43] Many of the developments observed above might be reversed, or their progress might be slowed down due to the increased importance that the states attribute to their SOEs, and generally their domestic companies, during the process of economic rebound.[44]

From this brief overview of the role of competition policy in ASEAN, the approach of the ASEAN member states towards SOEs and state involvement in

[41] See e.g. Ahamat and Rahman (2014).

[42] See e.g. OECD, SOEs Operating Abroad: An Application of the OECD Guidelines on Corporate Governance of State-Owned Enterprises to the Cross-Border Operations of SOEs, http://www.oecd.org/corporate/ca/corporategovernanceofstate-ownedenterprises/44215438.pdf. See also Cho and Kurtz (2018); Ahamat (2020), pp. 1–21.

[43] See Zulkhibri and Sinay (2020).

[44] See Economic impact of COVID-19 outbreak on ASEAN, ASEAN Policy Brief, April 2020, https://asean.org/storage/2020/04/ASEAN-Policy-Brief-April-2020_FINAL.pdf.

the operation of the markets, one can observe a very diverse region with different approaches to SOEs and their role in the economy. It will certainly create challenges for the EU and other actors that attempt to build an international consensus on the issue of subsidies, an issue that has been addressed in the Monopolies Commission report.[45]

References

Abate C, Elgouacem A, Kozluk T, Stráský J, Vitale C (2020) State ownership will gain importance as a result of COVID-19. https://voxeu.org/article/state-ownership-will-gain-importance-result-covid-19

Ahamat H (2020) The role of competition law in the investment policy in ASEAN. In: Chaisse J, Choukroune L, Jusoh S (eds) Handbook of international investment law and policy, Springer International Publishing, pp 1–21

Ahamat H, Rahman NA (2014) Delimiting the social boundaries of competition law in ASEAN: a Commmon approach? IIUM Law J 22(2):165–196

ASEAN Secretariat (2010) ASEAN Regional Guidelines on Competition Policy. https://asean-competition.org/read-publication-asean-regional-guidelines-on-competition-policy

ASEAN Secretariat (2018) Handbook on Competition Policy and Law in ASEAN for Business 2017. https://asean.org/storage/2016/12/Handbook-on-Competition-Policy-and-Law-in-ASEAN-for-Business-2017_Full.pdf

Cho S, Kurtz J (2018) Legalizing the ASEAN way: adapting and reimagining the ASEAN investment regime. Am J Comp Law 66(2):233–266

Drexl J (2018) The transplantability of the EU's competition law framework into the ASEAN region. In: Ong B (ed) The regionalisation of competition law and policy within the ASEAN economic community. Cambridge University Press, pp 210–235

European Commission (2021) Temporary Framework for State Aid Measures to Support the Economy in the Current COVID-19 Outbreak (consolidated version), https://ec.europa.eu/competition/state_aid/what_is_new/TF_informal_consolidated_version_as_amended_28_january_2021_en.pdf

Fox EM, Healey D (2014) When the state harms competition - the role for competition law. Antitrust Law J 79(3):769–820

Furse M (2010) Competition law in Vietnam: a critique. World Compet Law Econ Rev 33(1):163–176

Futaba I (2009) Vietnamese Local State-Owned Enterprises (SOEs) at Crossroads: Implications of SOE Restructuring at the Local Level. Institute of Developing Economies. Discussion Paper 193, http://hdl.handle.net/2344/835

Juwana H (2002) An overview of Indonesia's antimonopoly law. Wash Univ Glob Stud Law Rev 1(1):185–199

Kovacic WE (2017) Competition policy and state-owned enterprises in China. World Trade Rev 16(4):693–711

Lallemand-Kirche G, Tixier C, Piffaut H (2017) The treatment of state-owned enterprises in EU competition law: new developments and future challenges. J Eur Compet Law Pract 8(5):295–308

Lee C, Fukunaga Y (2014) ASEAN regional cooperation on competition policy. J Asian Econ 35: 77–91

[45] See Monopolies Commission (2020).

Luu HL (2012) Regional harmonization of competition law and policy: an ASEAN approach. Asian J Int Law 2(2):291–321

Mai F (2017) Vietnamese State-owned Enterprises under International Economic Integration. RIETI Discussion Paper Series 17-E-121, https://www.rieti.go.jp/jp/publications/dp/17e121.pdf

Matsushita M, Lim CL (2020) Taming leviathan as merchant: lingering questions about the practical application of trans-Pacific partenrship's state-owned enterprises rules. World Trade Rev 19:402–423

Maximiano R, Burgess R, Meester W (2019) Promoting convergence in ASEAN competition laws and practice. In: Burnier da Silveira P, Kovacic WE (eds) Global competition enforcement: new players, new challenges. Wolters Kluwer, pp 233–262

Monopolies Commission (2020) Chinese State Capitalism: A Challenge for the European Market Economy (English translation of Chapter I of the XXIII. Biennial Report), https://www.monopolkommission.de/images/HG23/Main_Report_XXIII_Chinese_state_capitalism.pdf

OECD (2009) Competition Policy, Industrial Policy and National Champions. https://www.oecd.org/daf/competition/44548025.pdf

OECD (2012) Competitive Neutrality: Maintaining a level playing field between public and private businesses, https://www.oecd.org/daf/ca/competitiveneutralitymaintainingalevelplayingfieldbetweenpublicandprivatebusiness.htm

OECD (2018) Competition Law in Asia-Pacific: A Guide to Selected Jurisdictions

Ong B (2006) The origins, objectives and structure of competition law in Singapore. World Compet Law Econ Rev 29(2):269–284

Poranandond P, Aung PM (2019) Emerging trend in competition law in Southeast Asia: perspectives from Myanmar and Thailand. World Compet Law Econ Rev 42(4):577–602

Sappington DEM, Sidak JG (2003) Competition law for state-owned enterprises. Antitrust Law J 71:479–523

Siadari DLY, Arai K (2018) International enforcement of ASEAN competition law. J Eur Compet Law Pract 9(5):328–335

Siswanto A, Hutajulu MJ (2019) State-owned enterpirses (SOEs) in Indonesia's competition law and practice. Yustisia 8(1):93–108

Slot PJ (2015) The application of the EU merger control rules to state owned enterprises. Eur Compet Law Rev 36(11):484–492

Sokol DD (2009) Competition policy and comparative corporate governance of state-owned enterprises. Brigham Young Univ Law Rev 6:1713–1812

Soltesz U (2020) Commission dreams of hybrid creatures: new tools under the white paper on foreign subsidies. Eur Compet Law Rev 41(12):609–614

Songvilay L, Insisienmay S, Turner M (2017) Trial and error in state-owned Enterprise reform in Laos. Asian Perspect 42:239–262

Svetlicinii A (2017a) The acquisitions of the Chinese state-owned enterprises under the EU merger control regime: time for reflection? Revue Lamy de la concurrence 67:30–36

Svetlicinii A (2017b) Building regional competition policy in ASEAN: lessons from the European competition network. Asia Europe J 15(3):341–357

Svetlicinii A (2018) The acquisitions of the Chinese state-owned enterprises under the National Merger Control Regimes of the EU member states: searching for a coherent approach. Mark Compet Law Rev 2(1):99–120

Svetlicinii A (2020) Chinese state owned enterprises and EU merger control. Routledge, London

Svetlicinii A (2021) Economic nationalism during COVID-19: is the EU merger control ready? Eur Compet Law Rev 42(2):69–74

Tang Van N (2016) Competition Neutrality: Challenges of Application for Vietnam, World Trade Institute Working Paper No. 19/2016, https://www.wti.org/research/publications/1035/competitive-neutrality-challenges-of-application-for-vietnam/

Thanadsillapakul L (2014) The harmonisation of ASEAN competition laws and policy and economic integration. Uniform Law Rev 9(3):479–500

Thanitcul S (2002) Competition law in Thailand: a preliminary analysis. Wash Univ Global Stud Law Rev 1(1):171–184

Valockova B (2015) EU competition law: a roadmap for ASEAN?, EU Centre in Singapore. Working Paper No. 25 (November 2015), http://aei.pitt.edu/97414/1/WP25-EU-Competition-Law.pdf

Willemyns I (2016) Disciplines on state-owned enterprises in international economic law: are we moving in the right direction? J Int Econ Law 19:657–680

Williams M (2004) Competition law in Thailand: seeds of success or fated to fail? World Compet Law Econ Rev 27(3):459–494

Wisuttisak P, Fong CM (2018) Competition law, state-owned enterprises and regional market integration in ASEAN. In: Ong B (ed) The regionalisation of competition law and policy within the ASEAN economic community. Cambridge University Press, pp 94–139

Wu Y (2019) Reforming WTO rules on state-owned enterprises: SOEs and financial advantages. Northwest J Int Law Bus 39(3):275–308

Zulkhibri M, Sinay JB (2020) Assessing ASEAN Economic Policy Responses in a Pandemic. ASEAN Policy Brief No. 02, https://asean.org/storage/2020/06/ASEAN-Policy-Brief-02_31-May-2020.pdf

Part IV
Book Review

Gregory Shaffer, Emerging Powers and the World Trading System: The Past and Future of International Economic Law

Cambridge University Press, 2021, ISBN 9781108817127

Weihuan Zhou

The rise of emerging powers in global affairs has been widely documented and yet is attracting growing attention in policymaking and academic studies. While the scope of emerging powers has been evolving, there is no doubt that China, India and Brazil are the most prominent ones in the current international economic legal order. Professor Shaffer's book offers a thorough analysis of the development of trade law capacity in the three emerging powers (based on years of fieldwork), and it does so through an innovative theoretical framework of "transnational legal ordering and orders". This framework is powerful as it "places international and national institutional development within a single analytic frame", enabling an analysis of "the recursive interaction of lawmaking, interpretation, implementation, and practice at the international, national, and local levels" (pp. 23 and 29). Through this framework, this book goes significantly beyond documenting legal capacity-building in the emerging powers to provide an insightful discussion of how the multilateral trading system, established under the auspices of the World Trade Organization (WTO), has spurred legal capacity-building in these countries, and simultaneously how these countries have utilized and mobilized such capacity to influence international rulemaking and create new norms and standards. As Professor Shaffer summarized eloquently and succinctly, "Legal capacity is a critical part of the larger story because it is the medium through which structural economic change becomes expressed in institutional terms" (p. 299). "The engagement of Brazil, India, and China with the WTO led to significant changes not only in their laws, but also in their institutions, professions, the relation of the bureaucracy to the private sector, and their norms and practices" (p. 305). The outcome of contests within these states, in

W. Zhou (✉)
Herbert Smith Freehills CIBEL Centre, Faculty of Law and Justice, UNSW Sydney, Sydney, NSW, Australia
e-mail: weihuan.zhou@unsw.edu.au

M. Chi et al. (eds.), *Asian Yearbook of International Economic Law 2022*,
Asian Yearbook of International Economic Law (2022) 2022: 207–212,
https://doi.org/10.1007/16517_2021_9, Published online: 10 December 2021

turn, has impacted domestic constituencies and provoked policy changes in established economic powers, particularly the United States (US) (p. 306).

Given my areas of expertise, I shall focus on China in this book review. "Because of China's centrality for the trade legal order's future" (p. 21), this book dedicates two chapters (instead of one for each of the other two emerging powers) to discussing China's trade law capacity-building and growing influence in the WTO (chapter 6) and its new initiatives, particularly the Belt and Road Initiative (BRI), which have the potential to reshape the international economic legal order from outside the WTO (chapter 7).

Compared to India, Brazil and many other developing economies, China is a latecomer to the world trading system and joined the WTO only in 2001 after fifteen years of accession negotiations. Nevertheless, China was able to build strong capacities in WTO law in a relatively short period of time, predominantly through a top-down approach, with the central government playing a critical role. This book explores China's legal capacity-building through government-led initiatives and activities that incentivized other major stakeholders, including educational institutions, think tanks, law firms, industry associations and businesses, to proactively build and use trade law expertise in pursuit of their own institutional goals. Legal capacity was essential when China needed to implement a wide range of commitments in the years immediately after its entry into the WTO. Over time, such capacity has become even more important for China to pursue and defend its interests in the organization. In preparation for China's WTO accession, the central government rolled out a series of initiatives leading to "the development of a team of professionals well versed in WTO rules", substantial restructuring of internal organs (particularly within the Ministry of Commerce), and robust action plans at the local level, including the establishment of WTO Centers to advise governments and companies on WTO/trade-related matters (pp. 182–185). In response to the government policies and initiatives, other stakeholders also endeavored to build capacities in WTO law, resulting in a remarkable development of educational and research expertise (i.e. academia), capabilities to assist the government in WTO negotiations and dispute settlement (i.e. law firms), and in-house expertise to deal with trade barriers and actions overseas (i.e. companies), including through privately-sponsored industry associations (pp. 186–199). Thus, the international trade regime has prompted massive structural changes and the creation of a strong and expansive trade law community in China contributing to its unprecedented economic transformation.

With its growing legal capacity, China ratcheted up its engagement in WTO affairs and acquired increasing influence in the system. This trend has involved a wide spectrum of activities and events over years including, for instance, China's involvement in the negotiation agendas put forward by major developing countries and in the 'small/elite negotiating groups' that played a decisive role in the Doha Round (p. 199) and, more recently, its more proactive role in negotiations on emerging issues such as digital trade (p. 202). Furthermore, China learned to use fundamental WTO principles, particularly 'special and differential treatment' for developing countries and reciprocity, to defend its interests and retain policy space in negotiations (pp. 199–202). These principles will remain crucial for China in future trade negotiations at bilateral, plurilateral and multilateral levels. In WTO's dispute settlement mechanism (DSM), China's engagement trajectory has presented a remarkable shift from a 'rule taker' (2001–2005) to a 'rule shaker' (2006–2009), and then a 'rule maker' (since 2010) (p. 203). Following the US and the European Union (EU), China is now one of the most active and sophisticated users of the DSM. On the one hand, legal capacity has been one of the key considerations in China's decisions on whether and how to deal with a potential trade dispute. On the other hand, China has built such capacity by joining disputes as a complainant, respondent or third party (pp. 204–207). More importantly, through this capacity building, China has not only influenced the development of WTO jurisprudence but also learned how to implement adverse WTO rulings in ways that deliver adequate compliance without jeopardizing its economic goals and interests[1] (pp. 204–216). In addition, as China faces numerous anti-dumping and countervailing actions taken by its major trading partners, it has also become adept at deploying its trade law capacity in taking similar actions for a variety of purposes including retaliation[2] (pp. 216–219). Overall, China's ambitious approaches to building trade law capacity have been exceptionally successful, enabling it to become a formidable player in the global trading system. While China has been a staunch defender of the system, it has also exploited the system's weaknesses to pursue its own interests in negotiations and dispute settlement, just like the other existing powers. For China, any commitments to multilateral cooperation, trade liberalization and market-oriented reforms must not compromise its political stability, which is fundamentally based on its state-led model of economic development (p. 220).

China's deployment of trade law capacity extends beyond the WTO. In analyzing China's engagement in bilateral and plurilateral trade and investment agreements, particularly its efforts to develop the BRI, this book identifies and expounds China's "vision of placing itself at the center of the transnational legal ordering of trade, finance, and investment in Asia and beyond" (p. 222). Unlike typical trade or investment treaties, the BRI is primarily based on non-binding memoranda of understanding between China and partner governments or institutions and countless project-based contracts. Through this "soft law" approach, China seeks to create a framework for broader and deeper economic cooperation in infrastructure connectivity, trade and investment facilitation, financial integration, and policy and people-to-people exchanges. This framework arguably advances a different model of international economic order, one designed to maximize flexibility and the possibility for cooperation. This book characterizes China's BRI as a revisionist model and provides a detailed discussion of how this model is leading to "a decentralized Sino-centric order that complements, competes with, and reorients the existing international economic law order" (pp. 228–229). In particular, China has managed to develop an expansive network of "strategic partnership" to promote trade and

[1] See also Zhou (2019).

[2] See also Zhou and Zhang (2017).

investment, export Chinese standards (e.g. through BRI contracts), and drive "an ongoing shift toward Asia as a center for transnational dispute settlement" (pp. 230–239). The BRI is further complemented by a China-led financial institution—the Asian Infrastructure Investment Bank (which now has over 100 members, including all major developed countries other than the US and Japan)—whose main function is to provide finance for BRI projects (pp. 239–242). In addition, China has been expanding its normal trade and investment agreements to gain preferential access to foreign markets and pursue certain political and strategic goals (e.g. seeking recognition as a market economy and acquiring advanced technologies), while maintaining "a paradigm that is more sensitive to national sovereignty . . . leaving more room for policy space" compared to US agreements (pp. 242–249). Finally, as technological advancement and innovation is central to its development strategies and industrial policies, China has taken considerable effort to strengthen its domestic regime for the protection of intellectual property rights. China's rapid rise as a global competitor and potential leader in the technology space, facilitated by its state capitalism, has elicited defensive reactions from advanced economies, particularly the US (pp. 349–362). As the US-China rivalry continues to intensify, China is most likely to further develop and promote its model of economic governance domestically, regionally and globally, thereby driving an ongoing shift from "a centralized legal order to a decentralized ecology of coexisting and competing transnational institutions" (p. 268).

Faced with China's rise, the US has reacted through a series of strategies and actions, with the major ones discussed in chapter 8 of this book. At the multilateral level, for example, the US has been partnering with the EU and Japan to push for more rigorous rules on (Chinese) state-owned enterprises (SOEs) and industrial subsidies. At the regional level, the US "aimed to build coalitions of countries to set new rules through megaregional agreements" and under the Obama administration, led the negotiation of the Trans-Pacific Partnership which was regarded as a critical approach to "pivot to Asia" and contain China (p. 282). The Trump administration withdrew from the TPP (viewing it as being ineffective to shape Chinese behavior) and resorted to unilateral action that subsequently dragged China into a two-year-long trade war, eventually compelling China to agree to a bilateral deal with predominantly one-sided obligations[3] (pp. 283–284). Neither the US's unilateral action, nor the conclusion of the bilateral deal, however, have been effective in de-escalating the US-China strategic competition which goes beyond trade to involve growing concerns about social welfare, economic distribution, geoeconomic rivalry and national security (pp. 286–290). At the core of these concerns is China's rise, fostered by a unique system of state capitalism. Thus, the key challenge is managing the US-China relationship by developing a framework with "governing principles that accommodate different economic systems" (p. 294). Professor Shaffer argues:

[3] See also Zhou and Gao (2020).

> There is no one development model, and a plurality of models will make for a more resilient global economy ... What is needed is a multilateral framework that accommodates a diversity of models, with variation in response to domestic preferences, development contexts, and experimental strategies. Such an order should prohibit beggar-thy-neighbor policies while permitting countries to protect their social framework from the externalities of other countries' policies (p. 291).

This book leaves us with abundant food for thought. Let me conclude this review with three observations. First, compared to the US and the EU, China's legal capacity and expertise in international economic affairs remains under-developed. There is, therefore, currently a wave of policies and activities in China aimed at further developing such capacity and expertise by educating and training a pool of talent specializing in transnational legal and commercial matters. This time, China's legal capacity-building may no longer focus on WTO/trade law but on international investment law, private international law and laws in foreign jurisdictions that are essential for further developing the BRI. Nevertheless, through "transnational legal ordering", such capacity-building will remain transferrable and impactful leading to a more influential China in international institutions and at least indirectly, in the domestic policymaking of its trading partners. Second, despite the considerable external pressure, particularly from the US, China continues to strengthen its state capitalism and the leadership of the Communist Party. It remains firmly committed to a new growth model based on technological advancement and independence, innovation and global competitiveness. These, in turn, are supported by ambitious and expansive industrial policies. While China's development model will remain a major concern of its trading partners, it would be unwise to believe any external pressure can push China to sacrifice its development goals and political stability. Thus, as Professor Shaffer has argued in this book, the fundamental challenge is how to reform the existing multilateral trading system, or create a new framework, to accommodate different economic systems and facilitate cooperation. This brings me to my final point, which is about what this book has left for us to fill. In my view, a major outstanding question lies precisely in what exactly is needed or can be done in future trade negotiations to accommodate not only the competing interests of the US and China but also the diverse range of interests of other major players in the system, such as the EU and India. Professor Shaffer concludes in this book: "The challenge for states will be how to maintain and adapt the international trade legal order to changing political and economic contexts" (p. 316). This is a formidable task, especially when it comes to negotiations of sensitive issues such as SOEs, industrial subsidies, and security-related matters. These and other similarly significant and controversial issues are at the heart of any trade negotiations that involve the US and China, and will be decisive of whether international cooperation can be reinvigorated. It falls upon us, who believe in the utility of the multilateral trading system, to carry on the difficult and unfinished task of (re-)constructing an architecture for international trade regulation.

References

Zhou W (2019) China's implementation of the rulings of the World Trade Organization. Hart Publishing, Oxford

Zhou W, Gao H (2020) US-China Phase One Deal: A Brief Account. Regulating for Globalization Blog of 22 January 2020, http://regulatingforglobalization.com/2020/01/22/us-china-phase-one-deal-a-brief-account/

Zhou W, Zhang S (2017) Anti-dumping and China's implementation of WTO rulings. China Q, 230:512–527

MIX
Papier aus verantwortungsvollen Quellen
Paper from responsible sources
FSC® C105338

If you have any concerns about our products,
you can contact us on
ProductSafety@springernature.com

In case Publisher is established outside the EU,
the EU authorized representative is:
Springer Nature Customer Service Center GmbH
Europaplatz 3, 69115 Heidelberg, Germany

Printed by Libri Plureos GmbH
in Hamburg, Germany